RICH WORLD, POOR WORLD

by
GEOFFREY LEAN

Foreword by
BARBARA WARD

London
GEORGE ALLEN & UNWIN
Boston Sydney

First published in Great Britain 1978

ISBN 0 04 309010 9

British Library Cataloguing in Publication Data

Lean, Geoffrey
Rich world, poor world.
1. Economic history – 1945 – 2. Underdeveloped areas – Economic conditions
3. International economic relations
I. Title
330.9′172′2 HC59

ISBN 0-04-309010-9
0-04-30912-5 Pbk

Typeset in 11 on 12 point Baskerville by
Trade Linotype Limited
and printed in Great Britain
by Biddles Limited, Guildford, Surrey

Contents

Foreword

BY BARBARA WARD

We are in the midst of a general but confused debate about the world economy within which, whether they want to or not, all the nations have to live and work. After a quarter of a century of very rapid material growth, the industrialised powers find themselves in an unaccustomed and obdurate combination of inflation and unemployment. The poorest nations, containing a billion people, are caught between rising population, rising world prices and rising debt. Nevertheless, they support the relatively and absolutely prosperous oil producers in their pressure on the 'old rich' to create a new economic order. And so far no group of nations or types of consultation or official or unofficial conferences have been able to disentangle the fears and interests of the various groups and construct a planetary system acceptable to at least the majority.

Mr Geoffrey Lean's book helps to explain this impasse. He not only describes very clearly the debate about the 'new economic order' but he shows how uncertainties about future supplies of food, contradictory projections of population growth, unreadiness of local elites to consider basic human needs and above all the vast uncertainties of energy supplies under the shadow of the plutonium economy introduce so many contradictory facts and forecasts that even if all the developed nations showed the highest measure of understanding and good will, they might still be uncertain about what should or should not be included in any effective form of global bargaining.

However, while the complexity of the issues is made abundantly clear, the message of Mr Lean's guidance through the maze is that all the powers, rich and poor alike, have to help each other out of it or risk blowing themselves and the maze up together. And since all the material means of effective navigation—research, trained manpower, capital resources, commercial experience—lie in overwhelming superiority on the side of the wealthy, it is to them that the plea is chiefly addressed. They must let their moral energy equal their material resources and repeat for the 20th century's 'two planets'—the planet of the rich and the planet of the poor—the policies which enlightened self interest introduced a century ago into Disraeli's Britain with its 'two nations' of wealth and poverty. Debate must give way to decision and to the beginnings of a more generous, just and cooperative economic order. It is no longer rhetoric to say that survival literally depends upon the choice.

July 1977

Author's Acknowledgements

It is impossible to thank all of those who have helped me turn a vague conception that there was a need for a work like this into a finished book. Virtually everyone I have spoken to in the last four years has had a hand in it, some by providing information or ideas, others, less directly, through the stimulus of their conversation and their knowledge of the world.

I would, however, like to thank Barbara Ward for the interest she took in the book and for writing the foreword, and to express my gratitude particularly to those who undertook the task of working through the manuscript in draft. David Runnals and David Satterthwaite both read through the entire script and made penetrating and knowledgeable comments on its content. Kim C. Beazley, Dr Michael Flood, Dr David Gosling, A. R. K. Mackenzie, Walter C. Patterson, Dr Paul Rogers and Professor Alan Williams did the same for chapters within their fields of expertise. My father, Garth Lean, worked through the manuscript several times, helping me to improve its style, while George Brock gave valuable stylistic comments on an early draft. John Austin helped me a great deal with the original conception and with advice on early versions.

The finished work bears the mark of all these people, and has benefited from it, but naturally the responsibility for the book, the opinions expressed in it, and the choice of facts is entirely my own. And, needless to say, any mistakes are the result not of their expertise, but of my lack of it.

I also want to thank my publishers. The book was conceived jointly with them and it would be a very much poorer volume but for their close attention to it. I am also grateful to Jon Tinker and Earthscan for sending me to Brazil for two weeks in 1976, an experience which particularly helped me with chapters 15 and 16. Special thanks too to John Edwards, Editor of the *Yorkshire Post*, and Gordon Linacre, Managing Director of Yorkshire Post Newspapers, both for their personal encouragement and for assenting to my having three months leave of absence to complete the first draft; and above all to my wife, Judy, who cheerfully put up with two and a half years without holidays or weekend breaks, with the constant clattering of my typewriter and piles of papers all over the house, and who constantly encouraged me and helped me to think through ideas. The book is as much hers as mine.

RICH WORLD, POOR WORLD

Note

Except where inappropriate, sums of money are expressed in US dollars. Conversions have been made on the exchange rates of early 1977.

Throughout the text the word 'billion' denotes one thousand million, and 'trillion' one million million.

Chapter 1

Introduction

I entered journalism in 1969 at about the same time that 'environment' was becoming a regularly used word. The *Yorkshire Post* was looking for someone who would learn about it, I was a new face in the office with no particular responsibilities, and so I was asked to take it on.

I knew very little. Pollution meant little more to me than the problem of litter. Population growth was an over-publicised bore. Hunger and poverty in the developing countries were tragic and depressing, but they would surely disappear in the general nature of economic growth, helped by charity from the rich world. I had not yet heard of a world-wide energy crisis, or thought hard about nuclear proliferation, let alone nuclear terrorism.

So I needed to do a great deal of homework, but as I did it I became convinced that what happened in these fields was central to the future of the world. The next stage was doubt about whether the world had a future at all, the 'doom' stage. Further research, however, has led me to a new conviction, much more exciting and full of hope.

Working on this book has been a crucial part of the process. I set out originally, in 1974, to collect together the basic facts behind a bewildering complex of crises. Since then I have attended conference after conference, travelled some 26,000 miles, read hundreds of books, papers and reports, and a stack of articles eighteen feet high. I have been able to discuss the issues with scores of people intimately concerned, from the heads of United Nations agencies to slum-dwellers in Rio de Janeiro, and from academics to politicians. Of course, all the subjects covered in this book have been developing rapidly as I have worked, and as new evidence has arisen my views have been changing too. Indeed I have often felt as if I have been trying to hit ten moving targets simultaneously while perched on a moving platform. (I have striven in these circumstances to make the coverage of all the issues up to date at least to the summer of 1977.)

At any rate, my hopes grew and my conceptions expanded with the research. So this is now a book concerned as much with discussing solutions as with explaining crises. It aims to report new thinking and practical answers, as well as the facts behind the human predicament as we approach a new millennium.

The word, millennium, can mean a golden age. In practice, Western civilisation has approached each one full of doubts about the future. As the year AD 1000 loomed up there was a widespread feeling that the world was going to end, not unlike that engendered by predictions of doom today. This time, however, the new millennium could begin to live up to the promise in the word. For the first time in history, we have the ability and the means to ensure that everyone has enough food and resources on which to live a positive life. The necessary strategies are being worked out, and we could probably achieve the task in a generation: but fundamental changes in our policies will be required.

The most obvious symptom of the failure of our present world system is hunger, the subject of the first chapter. The ways in which hunger and starvation can be ended lead on naturally to the need for a new international economic order and for new priorities in poor countries themselves. But will the population explosion destroy any hope of development, or will it in fact be defused by the new development strategies?

Meanwhile, if no serious attempt is made to meet the needs of the poor, the rich are also certain to suffer. One consequence would be increasing conflict and instability; to which the proliferation of nuclear weapons to small nations and terrorist groups could add a particularly frightening dimension.

At the heart of the proliferation problem is, of course, the spread of nuclear power—one of the many means proposed for resolving the energy crisis facing the rich world and the poor world alike, and the centre of widespread debate. Energy is *the* vital resource; if we have plentiful energy, from whatever sources, we need have little fear of other shortages; but lack of it would cause our economies to fail. The other possible limit to growth is pollution.

Meanwhile, the growth of the cities is so rapid that, by the beginning of the next century, Man is likely to be a predominantly urban species for the first time in his existence. Most of the interlocking crises discussed in this book are concentrated in the cities, and it is here that they will have to be solved. In the end, however, no lasting solutions are possible without a revolution in attitudes.

There are two main dangers facing us—that we will fail to meet the basic needs of poor people, and that we will place too heavy a demand on the resources of the planet. But there are such enormous possibilities for providing everyone with a decent standard of life without exceeding the world's limits, and at remarkably little cost to the rich world, that we would have only ourselves to blame if events led to catastrophe. Catastrophe will only result from a failure of our wills and our imaginations, and only if we are so blinded by our preconceptions that we fail to see the prospect of the millennium.

So why, as the American comic strip character, Pogo, said, do we stand here confronted by insurmountable opportunities?

Chapter 2

The Growing Imbalance

Every year Man produces enough grain to build a causeway around the world fifty-four feet wide and six feet high. Every year that causeway is demolished and consumed, and every year it is built anew. Enough food is produced, in fact, adequately to feed everyone on earth; yet by the United Nations Food and Agriculture Organisation's most conservative estimate well over 460 million people are suffering chronic malnutrition.* By other calculations a billion people—a quarter of the population of the world—may suffer severe hunger or malnutrition, at least during part of the year. More than 60 million people are actually dying of starvation.

As the population of the world increases, and as affluence swells the appetites of the already well fed, we have to build another causeway alongside the first. It has to be the same width, the size of a dual carriageway, and the same height, the stature of a man. Every year this second causeway has to be six hundred miles longer; and every year we have to start again from scratch.

We can achieve this extra task as well. It will be perfectly practical to feed the doubled population that is projected for around the year 2015, not only averting disaster, but putting an end to widespread hunger altogether. The technical and financial outlay required is surprisingly small. The question is whether we will have the moral and political will to do it.

Dr Norman Borlaug, who won a Nobel Peace Prize for developing new high-yielding crops, is no pessimist. But he says that the

*This FAO estimate is not only 'conservative'. It is based on data gathered in 1969 and 1971—in other words, before the 'world food crisis' that began developing from 1972. The numbers will undoubtedly be greater now.

situation is becoming so serious that 'It is no longer a question of tens of thousands dying, no longer of millions, but maybe of tens of millions or hundreds of millions.' This would be the greatest catastrophe in the history of the world, and it would be totally unnecessary.

The development of the food crisis is rooted in the polarisation of our planet into two worlds, the rich north and the poor south. In the world as a whole, food production kept well ahead of population growth in the 1950s and 1960s. This was a magnificent achievement, and complacency about world food grew with it, a complacency only punctured by occasional years of bad harvests. But all the time the unseen crisis was developing.

In the 1950s and 1960s developing countries expanded their food production as fast as did the rich world. But their needs grew much faster. The achievement of individual poor countries varies widely, but in thirty-four of them output slipped behind population growth between 1952 and 1972. Meanwhile in the rich world, where population growth has been relatively slow, food production soared ahead of need. Though much of it was absorbed in over-consumption, the problem worrying the major food producers of the rich world was their own over-production and its effect on prices. In the 1960s and early 1970s the United States held about a seventh of its cropland out of production, and the other main exporting countries also reduced their acreages. Surplus grain was distributed as food aid; yet chronic malnutrition was still deepening and spreading as the position of the poor world grew worse.

In the early 1970s this imbalance sharpened into a 'crisis' which came to a head at the time of the UN World Food Conference in November 1974. The immediate cause was the bad harvests of 1972 and 1974 when, for the first time in twenty years, the world crop declined; but the real reason lay in the long-term trends and recent erosions of our margins of safety. World grain stocks held mainly in the U.S.A.—which had served for decades as our insurance against disaster—had been allowed to plunge steeply down to beneath the danger level. When the World Food Conference met there were only twenty-six days' supply left—around the minimum that the US liked to keep for its own security alone.

This was partly due to massive, and secret, grain purchases made by the Russians, who showed a flair for somewhat unscrupulous capitalism; but it was made worse by the failure to build up stocks during 1973, a good year for crops in which the main exporting countries still kept land out of production. The situation was aggravated by the boom of the early 1970s, greater appetites and increased feeding of grain to livestock. There was also much speculation in food.

Scarcity and demand caused cereal prices to quadruple in the two years to February 1974. Poor people and nations could not afford to buy the grain even if it was there. As the need for urgent help grew, food aid from the rich world declined. In the eighteen months before the World Food Conference it was at half its average level of the previous ten years.

The same problems affected fertiliser. One million tons of fertiliser used in the developing world can provide an extra 10 million tons of grain, or a year's food for fifty million Asians or Africans. By 1974 the world faced a 1·5m. to 2m. tons shortage of fertiliser, partly because manufacturers had held back from expansion after the glut of the 1960s, and partly because both America and Japan placed a *de facto* embargo on fertiliser exports. Prices jumped by 300 or 400 per cent between 1971 and 1974, as the increased cost of oil and the soaring prices charged by both Morocco and the United States for phosphates magnified the effects of shortage and growing demand. The price of oil itself severely hit mechanised agriculture in the poor world, and simultaneously mopped up foreign exchange which poor countries could have used to buy food and fertiliser.

As it happened the world just scraped through the 1974 crisis—if you can call 'scraping through' a process during which hundreds of millions of already hungry people have to eat even less food, and death-rates increase in at least a dozen countries. But the short-term crisis was only an intensification of the basic situation. The chronic state of imbalance, often called a problem of 'distribution', continues.

The word 'distribution' conjures up vast technical problems; where the food is grown, how it is transported, marketed, stored and shipped, and where it ends up. It boils down, however, to a situation where hundreds of millions of people eat far too little and other hundreds of millions eat far too much. Over-nutrition helps kill more people in rich countries than anything else, particularly through its contribution to heart disease and cancer. Under-nutrition is the major factor in deaths in poor ones. It is a situation that benefits nobody but the undertaker.

At the beginning of the 1970s the people of Western Europe, Australasia and Japan were consuming 23 per cent more calories than they needed. The people of North America were ahead of them at 26 per cent. But the people of the Soviet Union and Eastern Europe won the prize at 27 per cent. At the same time three-fifths of all developing countries did not get enough food to give each person a minimum subsistence diet.* As always, talking in averages conceals the plight of the poorest. Inequality is not a matter of geography, and greed knows no boundaries. In countries as widely dispersed as India and Brazil the richest 10 per cent of the population consume more than twice as many calories per head as the poorest 20 per cent. In India 224 million people, more than a third of her population, get less than three-quarters of the calories they need.

In the poor world as a whole a quarter, even 30 per cent, of the children die before they are five years old. Half of these deaths, more than 15 million a year, are at least partly caused by malnutrition. It is easy enough in the rich world to forget the tragedy in the statistics. As Bernard Clavel, the French artist and writer, has said: 'We must constantly remind ourselves that a thousand dead children are a thousand times the agony of a child, a thousand times the child we once were ourselves, a thousand times the child we have held in our arms, a thousand times "*our*" child.' Of those who survive somewhere between one-half and two-thirds of the world's small children are malnourished. Oxfam posters have been accused of overkill, of making people less sensitive to tragedy, but it is worth remembering just how many children the shape on the poster represents.

Some 300 million have grossly retarded physical growth because of malnutrition. In the Far East alone some 100,000 children lose their sight every year through lack of vitamin A—blindness that

*Needs vary with size, race, climate and the activity by which a man earns his living, and the figures take this into account. Without this weighting the figures are even more stark. North America gets enough to give each citizen 3,320 calories a day. The poorest countries get enough for less than 1,750 calories each.

could be prevented at a cost of one penny per child per year. And this is only the beginning of the toll taken by hunger.

While the delegates to the 1974 World Food Conference met in clamorous session in the main hall of the Palazzo dei Congressi, Henry Labouisse, the thoughtful American who is executive director of the United Nations Children's Fund (UNICEF), told me the results of research on one of the more subtle and devastating effects of malnutrition. A child's mental development, it seems clear, depends on how he or she is fed from the very start of life. If he does not get enough nourishment in his first two years the brain will not develop properly. Yet it would cost less than £10 a year to enable each child to get the extra food it needs.

Malnourished children are all the more easily picked off by sickness. Not only the malnourished, but some two billion people —half the world's population—do not get enough of the right food for protection against disease.

All this is the 'normal' condition of the world. We have grown to accept it, and only occasionally does a particularly poignant image grasp our imagination—the families reduced to picking the last withered leaves from trees around a waterhole for the last meal they can foresee; the Bangladeshis who sold their land for a few meals, after which the food ran out; the woman in West Bengal, so maddened by hunger that she burnt her only child and began to eat it; and perhaps most pathetic of all, the people who die within sight of full food stalls—unable to buy even the meagre ration, at subsidised prices, of 1 lb. of rice or wheat a head per week.

This last picture is a haunting miniature of the whole world food situation. The immediate problem is not production, it is that hundreds of millions of people cannot afford to buy the food that is produced.

Each citizen in the rich world consumes up to about a ton of grain every year—the equivalent of more than six loaves of bread each a day. Of course we do not literally eat that much bread. What happens is that we buy up to 90 per cent of our grain at the butchers and the dairy, for most of it is fed to livestock to produce meat, milk, cheese and eggs. When an animal grazes on otherwise unproductive grassland it is efficiently using its digestive system to turn a resource that man cannot use into food that he can eat.

But when the animal is fed on grain it will take several pounds of grain to produce one pound of meat or dairy produce. A ratio often quoted for beef is ten to one. Other animal products are less wasteful, but whatever the ratio, the world's food supply is being used up at a frightening pace.

Intensive feeding of livestock on factory farms has increased rapidly in recent years. It has had its uses from a narrow economic standpoint. It has provided a means of using the 'surplus' of grain production in the rich world and of protecting farmers by keeping up the price. But it has also used up grain that hungry people desperately need, and it has been a major force in pushing the prices of grain beyond their reach—particularly during the crisis of the early 1970s.

The result is that people in the countries with the richest diets* consume five times as much grain as those in poor countries—for the average citizen of a poor country gets only 400 lb. of grain a year. In fact animals in the rich world eat more grain— about a third of the world's crop—than the people of India and China put together. Half the world's fish catch goes to animal feed or to fertilisers. By the time it ends up as food on somebody's plate it has lost three-quarters of its nutritional value. Almost all the world production of soya beans goes to feed animals. Groundnuts go the same way.

More serious still, a good deal of some of these products are imported from poor countries, many of whose people need the food themselves. For example, it was calculated some years ago that if fishmeal exported from Chile and Peru for animal feed had been used at home all the people of Latin America could have eaten as well as Southern Europeans.† In Brazil production of soya beans for export to feed animals has been sharply increased, replacing crops of the traditional beans that make up the staple diet of lower-income families. Poor people do not have the money and the buying power to compete, and their governments need the foreign exchange. It is a case of export *and* die.

*The amount of grain consumed varies widely in rich countries from about a ton per head per year in Canada, Russia and America, to about half a ton in Britain and other EEC countries. This turns the standard jibe about sacred cows back on the rich world.

†Some point out that the meal is largely made of anchovies which people cannot eat in bulk. But anchoveta were dried and distributed as food throughout the Inca empire.

The trend is likely to continue, for, understandably enough, people seem to choose to eat meat as soon as they can afford it. In 1950 the people of America ate 50 lb. of beef a head. By 1973 it had jumped to 119 lb. each. Much of the recent disruption of grain stocks can be laid at the door of a meat-eating drive in the Soviet Union. The massive grain imports of 1972 went to feed not people but cattle, chicken and pigs, so that the Russian standard of eating should not decline. Perhaps it was a wise precaution. After all, in December 1970 the Polish regime was brought down by riots over the price of meat, and when the resulting price freeze ended in the summer of 1976 workers went on strike and ripped up railway lines. The rises had to be withdrawn again. Extra meat production has been promised, and is being planned in other parts of Eastern Europe as well.

Meat consumption in Japan leapt up by almost 60 per cent between 1969 and 1972. And in Teheran, where much of Iran's new wealth is concentrated, the amount of meat eaten doubled in twelve months in 1974–5.

Meat eating is not the only way in which we indirectly consume grain. Professor Jean Mayer, the nutritionist, says that 40–50 million people could be fed on the grain that goes into the beer and spirits drunk in America each year. He says: 'The same amount of food that is feeding 210 million Americans would feed 1·5 billion Chinese on the average Chinese diet.' Britain's 56 million people use enough grain to feed 246 million. Even pets do better than poor people. A medium-sized dog in Britain gets through as much grain in a year as the average citizen in a poor country—and in a more nutritious form. It therefore eats very much better than a *poor* man in a poor country.

The gap between the food available to rich and poor will widen in the next ten years, if present trends continue. The FAO's assessment, prepared for the World Food Conference in 1974, concluded that, although there is no foreseeable prospect of the world producing less than enough for all, the 'distribution' problem will grow worse. The report, which was accepted by most of the nations that took part in the preparatory committee work, predicted that by 1985 the developing countries, despite meeting 90 per cent of their own demand, would have an annual deficit of 85 million tons, three times the recent level. With bad harvests the gap could rise to 120m. tons or more.* Its estimate that rich countries could produce surpluses that would far outweigh the deficit is little consolation, because the poor countries could not afford to pay for that much food. Even if they are able to import the grain, the poorest people will still not get enough to eat; so, by the FAO's most conservative estimate, the number of malnourished will have risen by 1985 from 460m to 750m people. That figure, of course, does not include the tens of millions who will die in the meantime. If such an appalling imbalance is allowed to continue great power will be placed in the hands of the rich countries that produce surpluses.

'The real power of the future', says Ismail Sabri Abdullah, the eminent Egyptian economist, 'will not be nuclear or even energy, but will belong to whoever possesses the source of food.' As almost all other parts of the world have changed from being food-selling to food-buying areas, over the last thirty years North America, particularly the United States, has come virtually to monopolise grain exports. Already there have been signs that such power might be misused. The Ford administration made clear its readiness to use food as a 'weapon'.

Indeed in 1974, the year of the food 'crisis', more than half U.S. food aid went to Vietnam, Cambodia, Laos, Israel, Jordan and Malta—countries where the U.S. had an obvious political interest—rather than to those most in need. The United States Congress has tried to limit the use of food aid for other than humanitarian purposes, but a secret CIA research report said baldly that a worsening grain imbalance 'could give the US a measure of power it had never had before and possibly an economic and political dominance greater than that of the immediate post World War II years'. In years of bad harvests, says the report, even 'the major powers' could be at least partially dependent on United States food.

Although her grain belt and the hard work of her farmers may indeed give America a formidable weapon, she would be unwise to be complacent. Exercising that power could do much more

*Other estimates produce similar pictures of imbalance. The World Bank predicts a Third World deficit of 77 million tons in 1985, while the International Food Policy Research Institute in Washington puts it at between 100m and 200m tons.

damage to her international standing than did her involvement in the Vietnam war, while the sight of millions of children starving on television could have an even more traumatic effect on public opinion at home. Furthermore poor nations, and perhaps embittered men too, will soon have access to nuclear weapons. If, in a situation where millions of people were starving, a country rich in grain were refusing to supply food for reasons of power politics who could be certain that these would not be used?

The precarious food situation is being given a particularly unsettling twist, for it seems that the climate is changing. It has often changed in the past. Between the fifteenth and nineteenth centuries, for example, the Northern Hemisphere was much colder than it is now. The Thames froze over eight times in the seventeenth century alone, and during the American Revolution the British army could trundle its artillery across the ice from Manhattan to Staten Island. Before this there had been a much warmer period; wine was made from local vineyards as far north as York. Research into the natural records left by the weather—in tree-rings, in great columns of ice from Greenland, in pollen laid down deep in the earth, in mud at the bottom of lakes, and in fossils and shells that settled beneath the ocean—is revealing earlier links in the long chain of climatic change. It seems that important changes can happen quite quickly. It appears too that even quite small changes in temperature can seriously affect the growing seasons of crops. More important these can be accompanied by disturbances in the pattern of rainfall.

The first half of the present century was, on average, exceptionally warm in the Northern Hemisphere. Indeed, the years between 1930 and 1960 may have been the most abnormal in the last millennium. This is important because during these thirty years the world's population increased by a billion, cities swelled at a hectic rate, agriculture expanded to take in more and more of the planet's available land, and prairie-style farming grew apace. These trends continue, and make us all the more vulnerable to any unfavourable change in climate.

From the 1940s until about 1970 the Northern Hemisphere cooled. Then in the early 1970s the trend seemed to halt. What will happen next? Nobody can make any firm predictions; we have far too little knowledge of how the climate works for that. But, if anything, the balance of scholarly debate seems to be shifting in favour of those who think that we are in for a further cooling.

Professor Hubert Lamb, Director of the Climatic Research Unit at East Anglia University, and a pioneer in the field, has written that the cooling and resulting changes in rainfall patterns 'must on balance adversely affect the total production of food grains in the great grain-growing areas in middle latitudes'. He points out that the English growing season has already been cut by two weeks since the 1939–45 war; and that the season for North American maize seems to have shortened by at least three weeks. Yet a cooling might also result in higher crop yields further south through producing a more temperate climate there. Whether or not the overall climatic change was detrimental to crop growth, shifts in the seasons could be unsettling to the present pattern of agriculture.

The greater variability in the weather, particularly in rainfall, that might accompany a general cooling would present a far bigger threat to food production than a falling thermometer. At a time of general cooling weather systems tend to be bigger and move more slowly. There is more likely to be a climate of extremes in which long periods of one sort of weather may be followed by a long spell of the opposite. As Professor Lamb said in 1975, 'It will be more hot, more cold, more wet and more dry'. The summer of 1976, which brought an unprecedented heat-wave and drought to Britain and prolonged torrential rains to Eastern Europe at least partially bears him out, as do the record rains which came to Britain that autumn, the great freeze that gripped much of America in the following winter, the drought that succeeded it and the June snows that stopped English cricket matches the year before.

Even the optimistic experts conclude that such change makes major crops failures likely within a decade. One of the most pessimistic, Professor Reid Bryson of the University of Wisconsin, believes that the United States may be heading for a 200-year drought! Very few climatologists are as gloomy, however. The changes they foresee, serious as they are, may make food supplies more precarious—but we could counteract them if we took the prospects of change seriously and made the right preparations in time. The most important single step we could take is to return to keeping major stocks of grain. We could also assess the potential impact of changes on crops, and consider ways of breeding new strains and growing old ones that will make our food less dependent on the climate.

So much food is wasted, and there is so great a potential for growing more in the world, that unless there is a total disaster the climate need not be the determining factor in whether or not we are able to feed the world. Appalling—and ominous—though the present food crisis and its projected development may be, there is no doubt that it can be solved. The likelihood of a changing climate makes it all the more urgent that we set out to implement the solutions.

Stockpiling food is an obvious insurance against bad harvests; as Joseph saw when he used seven good years to build up enough reserves to last for seven bad ones. It is particularly vital during a time of unstable weather. It stabilises prices and ensures supplies.

During the years of plenty grain reserves, and the land held out of production in the United States, together provided an unplanned, but effective, system of security which averted several serious famines in the 1960s. Throughout the decade these provided a buffer of between two and three months' supply for the world. By the World Food Conference of 1974 there remained less than a month's supply. Though Dr Kissinger then proposed that reserves should be urgently increased by 60 million tons, they remained at around that dangerous level for two more years while the world failed to agree on what system of stocks to set up and on who should pay for them. The good harvests of 1976 and 1977 made it possible for the world to begin to work its way back to security.

Stocks did indeed increase, but to no more than what they were in 1972 when they had been able to fall beneath the danger level almost overnight. And ironically the good harvests brought fresh anxiety about world food security. For as the 'surpluses' grew, the price of wheat plummeted. In August 1977, in response to pressure from farmers, President Carter proposed that the United States' wheat acreage should be cut by a fifth. Although he also proposed setting up an emergency reserve of six million tons to provide aid for developing countries in case of bad harvests, there was concern, even within his administration, that taking this land out of production could help cause another food crisis like the one of the early 1970s. For no international system of stocks had yet been set up.

It is obviously not right that America should once again finance the world's food insurance almost single-handed, though one reason that other nations did not take prompt action after the 1974 conference was the hope that she would do so. Stockpiles are very expensive. The best, and probably cheapest, system would be for stocks to be financed and controlled internationally. Failing this there must be effective national control. Leaving stocks in private hands is of little benefit unless there is legislation to ensure government regulation; for since private firms are presumably in business to make as much profit as possible, they are unlikely to want to stabilise prices and maintain a steady supply in the way that the world needs. The Ford administration did not seem to acknowledge this, and, indeed, appeared to lose interest in the idea of international stocking altogether. However, by the summer of 1977 falling prices had dampened the enthusiasm of U.S. farmers and grain companies for the free market and there was a new administration, less reluctant to intervene in it. President Carter's government accordingly called for a network of nationally controlled stocks, internationally co-ordinated and financed; and rich and poor nations alike were able to agree in principle that there should be some such system. But the details were left for further negotiation, and most U.S. experts thought that the size of the reserve proposed by their government, 30 million tons, was far too small for effective security. Indeed such as stock seemed liable to be wiped out by the first big emergency.

Effective security also depends on greater responsibility from the Soviet Union. Massive and unpredictable Russian grain purchases first helped destroy the old stockpiles and then helped prevent new ones being built. Finally, in 1975, the United States forced the Soviet Union to sign a five-year agreement to help steady the market, but Russia was still refusing to give demand projections and doing little to co-operate with the world community. A permanent improvement in Russia's agriculture would also help. Under Mr Brezhnev's leadership investment has rapidly increased, but the country's agriculture is still ruled by a bureaucracy that offers neither material or moral incentives. The story of the agriculturist Ivan Khudenko is illuminating. His new ideas were aimed at lessening bureaucracy and achieving payment by results. Output went up 300 per cent on one farm where he applied them. The farm was closed. Before long Khudenko was arraigned before a court on a trumped-up charge and was imprisoned; in 1974, according to underground sources, he died in jail. The generally poor Soviet performance has certain political advantages for the West, but in world food terms it erodes security and tends to put up prices for the poorest.

Waste should lie heavily on the consciences of rich countries, communist and non-communist alike. Sir Charles Pereira announced when chief scientist at the U.K. Ministry of Agriculture that a quarter of all Britain's food supplies are wasted. Even before it comes ashore, one sixth of the world's fish catch is wasted at sea. And in Russia, when fruit, vegetables and grain rotted in the fields in 1973, Mr Brezhnev complained, 'Nobody—neither the planning nor the other authorities—could estimate the sum total of the losses'. American experts had a try, however, and calculated the losses at 36 million tons.

A marginal change in our eating habits could make an enormous difference to the world food supply. 'If Americans would decrease the meat they eat by 10 per cent', says Jean Mayer, 'it would release enough grain to feed 60 million people.' Others have estimated that if Americans did without one hamburger a week it would free enough grain to feed 25 million people in poor countries.

Indeed, far greater reductions in our consumption may be good for us. The American Heart Association recommends a one-third cut in meat consumption in order to reduce the incidence of coronaries. Meat from grass-fed beasts is not only much cheaper to produce, it seems to be better for health than meat grown by protein feeding in factory farms.

Alarmed both by the rise in heart disease and the world food situation, the Norwegian Government is adjusting its system of food subsidies to steer people away from grain-fed meat towards cereals, and has embarked on a campaign of public education.

Calls to reduce meat consumption have met an enthusiastic response from churches, universities and other groups; but they have also been attacked for naivety. When Senator Hubert Humphrey suggested at the time of the World Food Conference that Americans cut back by one hamburger a week he was attacked by Earl Butz, the Agriculture Secretary, as 'a fuzzy thinking do-gooder'. Hard on Mr Butz's heels came Britain's Agriculture Minister, Fred Peart, who told a rather bemused press conference, 'I believe a lot of people in Britain are not eating enough meat. I do not want malnutrition to appear in Britain.' And other Ministers joined in.

Early in 1976 a War on Want report was jubilantly publicised by a carnivorous press as exposing the futility of eating less meat, even though it concluded: 'The impact of a drastic reduction in the demand for feed grain can have a profound impact on the availability of cereals for the poor throughout the world. We suggest that governments actively seek to promote the substitution of cereal-based for meat-based produce.'

The truth is, of course, that it is naïve to think that eating less meat will solve the world food problem, but it is also naïve to pretend that it will have no effect. Certainly a continuing escalation of meat eating will keep grain from hungry people. And in stringent conditions cutting back on meat eating may help the poor considerably.

The acute short-term crisis of 1974 was eased significantly when, as a result of the world recession, the peoples of the affluent countries ate less meat. Mr Richard Bell, one of Earl Butz's chief aides at the Food Conference and the U.S. Department of Agriculture official in charge of foreign assistance, said in early 1975: 'The demand for grain for livestock feeding is 29 million tons down on 1974. Americans are cutting back on their meat in a way we ourselves never anticipated.' This was a major force in toppling the prices of wheat from \$5·08 a bushel at the time of the conference to around \$3·78 four months later, even though wheat stocks were low. This not only enabled poor countries to buy more food, but also increased the amount of aid given by rich countries—for the quantities of food aid are usually established in sums of money rather than in bushels of wheat.

Of course *by itself* eating less meat achieves little, and it may even be counter-productive. It can merely make grain available. It does not necessarily ensure that the grain lands in the bowls of starving people. It will do no good unless the extra grain is bought by the poor, or by governments for food aid or stocks—and bought at the right price. For if farmers cannot get a good price, and are not encouraged by some other means to keep up production, they are likely to sow less grain in future.

Aid is the traditional way of transferring food from rich to poor. Between 1965 and 1972 the U.S.A. provided 84 per cent of all food aid to developing countries. Canada provided most of the rest. Aid has begun to recover from the disastrously low levels of 1973–74—though it has still to reach even the inadequate level agreed by the World Food Conference. The United States, Australia and Canada—though not the EEC—have become more generous since then, though, in honesty, generosity has not been the sole motive for giving aid in the past. Quite apart from its use for political influence, U.S. food aid has been widely used as a loss leader to wean countries onto American grain and thus promote exports.

Food aid, necessary though it will be for some time to come, is clearly not the long-term answer. A country which receives food aid may use it as an excuse to neglect its own agriculture and rural development. This happened during the 1960s. If rich country surpluses are dumped cheaply on poor nations local farmers may be seriously damaged—and then when the dumping stops the situation is even worse than it was before. Continual food aid is a humiliation to the receiver, and places the donor in a dangerous position of power. Nations such as India have been extremely reluctant, rightly or wrongly, to ask for food aid when they need it, and even less keen to submit to humiliating conditions. These effects could be ameliorated by controlling aid more sensitively than in the past and using it to stimulate a country's own production and make up its deficiency. We should also concentrate as much as possible on multilateral rather than bilateral systems. Leaving food aid overwhelmingly in the hands of America is fair neither to the U.S.A. nor to the rest of the world. Most other countries may not be able to export grain but can give money that can be used to purchase American food for overseas relief. This can best be done through an international agency.

But the only real long-term answer is more radical. We have to create a new pattern of food production and distribution in the world to ensure that developing countries will be able to grow enough for their needs—and that their people can afford to buy the food that is produced.

Chapter 3

The Patchwork Revolution

The potential for increasing food production in the poor world is enormous. Production can be raised either by bringing more land into service or by producing more food from the land that is already under cultivation. India, for example, could produce at least 230 million tons of grain a year in place of her present 105 million tons. Even Bangladesh, the international symbol of a hungry country, should be able to double her food production with established techniques—and treble it with new ones.*

Rather less than 11 per cent of the world's total land surface is cultivated. Since, however, vast areas are taken up by desert, mountain, tundra and other terrains which defy cultivation, only about 24 per cent of the world's ice-free land—or 7·86 billion acres—is potentially arable. This still leaves more than double the amount of land used at present, however; more than enough to take care of population growth. Unfortunately, the uncultivated land is not spread evenly about the globe. In Africa only 22 per cent of the potential arable land is being farmed. In Asia, where the problem of hunger is most acute, 83 per cent of it is already in use. Naturally, the land that already is being cultivated is by and large the best and most accessible. New land will usually need more capital, more energy and more fertiliser than was needed to

*David Hopper, President of the Canadian International Development Research Centre, reckons that the 100 million acres of rich alluvial plain in the Indus–Ganges–Brahmaputra basin could produce 80 per cent of the present world output of grain, while the largely uncultivated South Sudan could yield as much food as we now produce from the entire globe. But could grandiose schemes for developing these areas ever be practicable?

bring existing land under the plough. It will also need more care, because the soil will generally be more fragile. Indeed, lack of care, on long-cultivated lands as well as virgin ones, is causing us to lose ground when we should be gaining it.

Bad agricultural practice and short-sighted exploitation destroy millions upon millions of acres of productive land each year. The problem is nearly as old as agriculture itself. The sterile, acid Yorkshire Moors seem to have become this way because stone age man burned down the forests that once covered them through indiscriminate clearance. The virtual destruction of the biblical cedars of Lebanon was only part of a pattern of tree-felling and overgrazing that over centuries created huge tracts of desert between the Mediterranean and Afghanistan. North Africa, now largely barren, was once the bread-basket of the Roman Empire, the equivalent of the American grainlands today. Changing climate contributes to the increase of deserts around the world; but the process is overwhelmingly man's own fault. He exhausts the soil by working it too hard without refreshment; he subjects his land to overgrazing from domestic animals; he cuts down forests which not only provide protection against erosion but also help to increase rainfall and to retain the water which does fall. Deforestation of the foothills of the Himalayas is one reason for the increase in both the frequency and severity of flooding in the Indian sub-continent. By one estimate annual soil loss through erosion is running at more than half a ton of earth for every man, woman and child on the planet.

If the present situation is allowed to continue, the world will lose one third of its arable land to the deserts by the end of the century. If this is added to what is expected to be eaten up by the spread of cities, there will be less than half as much cultivated land per person in the year 2000 as there is now—even if, in the meantime, some 750 million acres of new ground can be pressed into service. Clearly man has to go on the offensive to make sure that his cropland expands rather than shrinks. And indeed, if proper care is taken, the creeping deserts can not only be halted but be quickly turned back, as work in the Sudan, Mauritania, Tunisia and many other countries has shown.

Some land will never be suitable for crops, and in these areas it is animals eating the existing vegetation that will create food most efficiently. But care must be taken over grazing land, just as over land put under the plough.

The FAO reckons that a campaign to eliminate tsetse fly in Africa would release an area larger than the total agricultural area of the United States for cattle, and make possible the production of 1·5 million tons of meat per annum. This projection gives some idea of the potential—yet it needs to be balanced with caution. The FAO propose that most of the job be done by spraying the area with pesticide from the air—a process which, past history shows, may not control the pest in the long run, and may lead to the poisoning of people. Nor, if the area is cleared, will it necessarily be suitable for ranching cattle. The grazing cow—a colonial import—has proved one of the most effective creators of desert in Africa; whereas the wild animals which are native to the area can produce six times as much meat per acre and conserve the land* as well. Generally resistant to the tsetse fly, they already provide food for local people who could not possibly buy the beef that is planned in their place. Even the people of the cities, who could afford the beef, seem to prefer the taste of game, when they can get it. So it would seem much more sensible to encourage and conserve such animals, cropping them for meat while preserving wildlife through proper management, than to go in for grandiose plans for cattle.

New areas can, and must, be brought into production, but a balanced and thought-out approach is needed, based on what the land can support. Exactly the same kind of approach is needed at sea. Even a fairly pessimistic assessment reckons that, given proper management, conservation and pollution control, we could increase our fish catch from the recent maximum of 70 million tons a year to 100 million tons. The FAO estimates it could be at least 110 million tons, and exploiting less conventional resources, particularly the prawn-like Antarctic krill, could increase the marine harvest very much more.

*While cows first eat the best grass, finish it, and then move onto eliminating the other grasses in order, the thirty or so native species on savannah land each specialise in one particular type of vegetation—from the dik-dik eating the shortest grass to the giraffes browsing off the tops of trees. Thus a constant supply and cycle is assured. And the benefits of wild animals are not confined to Africa—there are now suggestions that it would be more sensible and profitable to farm red deer than sheep in the Scottish Highlands.

On the other hand stocks of heavily exploited species—from herrings to anchovies, from whales to sardines—have already plummetted down because of overfishing. After a steady and rapid expansion of 5 per cent a year since 1950, the amount of fish harvested from the sea has been declining recently, while fleets have grown bigger and equipment has improved. Other species of fish and other seas remain unexploited as yet, but they too are capable of being overfished. The choice is between settling for a steady sustainable income of a catch well above our present level or of grabbing too hard, trying to expand too fast without proper controls and destroying a large part of our capital.

A sensible strategy on fishing could be particularly beneficial to poor countries. The most promising oceans for increased catches are bordered by poor countries. Furthermore, much of the overfishing was carried out to provide more animal feed; and there a reduction in protein feeding could do nothing but good.

Fish-farming opens up other possibilities. Certain fish, like carp, which will feed on vegetation and wastes, can achieve good yields—as the monks who built European fish ponds knew, and as increasing numbers of Asian and African villagers are discovering. There also appears to be potential for raising fish on sewage effluent, so long as it is free of toxic pollutants. In all, the FAO reckons, the developing world could double its production of fish by 1985.

The production of a pound of grain requires from 60 to 225 gallons of water, while a pound of meat may take anything from 2,500 to 6,000 gallons or more. Although 70 per cent of the world's surface is covered by ocean, less than 3 per cent of the world's water is fresh, and three-quarters of that is frozen, mainly at the poles.* Almost all of what is left is underground, and the available water is, of course, distributed extremely unevenly both around the world and within nations.

In some parts of the world land must be irrigated before it can produce at all. In others irrigation will greatly boost yields per acre and increase the number of harvests in a year. But it too needs to

*Desalination of sea-water, on present technology at least, takes a great deal of energy and is uneconomic in almost every part of the world.

be managed with more care. Irrigation has been practised successfully since the days of the early Egyptian, Indian and Chinese civilisations, but used wrongly it can waterlog the soil and make it salty and sterile. The decline and fall of other ancient civilisations can be traced to just such a progress, and today the world loses as much land every year by this means as it gains through new irrigation schemes. However, work in Pakistan, where nearly three-quarters of the irrigated land is affected, has shown that the land can be reclaimed; while Israel provides a modern model of efficient water use.

However, many of the river systems most suitable for irrigation are already fully used, and big dams are proving a mixed blessing. The Aswan High Dam in Egypt was better thought out than some of those built at the same period. It has provided a valuable source of energy for the country, and made it possible to double- and treble-crop more land. But it also traps behind its wall the 125 million tons of rich silt that annually washed down the Nile and settled on the land of the ancient valley and delta, keeping it fertile for thousands of intensely cultivated years; and among other side-effects it has severely damaged the sardine fisheries in the eastern end of the Mediterranean.

Jon Tinker, Director of the international environment information unit, Earthscan, writes: 'There are hardly any large scale dams, hydroelectric or irrigation schemes in the world, and certainly none in the tropics and subtropics, which have not caused substantial and usually avoidable environmental damage.' Filling big dams has even caused earthquakes.

The bigger the area of water in storage and in irrigation canals, the greater may be the risk of waterborne diseases. The further the distance is from the storage to the fields the more water will be lost in evaporation, and the more expensive it may be to transport the rest. For all these reasons, more and more attention is now being paid to irrigation on a much smaller scale, and particularly to what can be done from simple wells scattered in village after village. In some places groundwater resources may be drying up; but most of the potential seems still to be under developed. There is as much water stored in the top half of the earth's crust as there would be in 130 years' flow of all the world's rivers. Tube wells can be quickly and cheaply installed and can recover their costs in about two years, and small pumps can lift water directly from rivers to where it is needed.

By the same token renovating old irrigation schemes, many of which are operating only half as efficiently as they should, is probably much more important than installing grandiose new ones. This one measure alone could increase the poor world's output of grain by about 20 per cent. In theory, at least, it could enable India to be fed from one-third of its land. Proper water management is therefore one of the most important factors in increasing yields.

Most of the recent growth in the world's harvest has come about through more intensive cultivation of the land under production than through expanding such land. World Bank officials say that tropical farms could easily multiply their yields between six and sixteen times over with the aid of the best of modern science. The problem, of course, is that the best of science, like so much else, is rarely available to the poor. Money, fertilisers, pesticides, energy and research are overwhelmingly concentrated in rich countries, though both the need for food and the potential for increasing yields is at its greatest in poor ones.

Money, of course, is the key to almost any attempt to improve or extend agriculture, and the difference between the cash available to rich and poor nations is obvious enough. The FAO proposed at the time of the World Food Conference that rich countries should give and lend five billion dollars a year (at 1972 prices) to help the poor countries to feed themselves, a sum exactly equivalent to the turnover of Britain's gambling industry, or one tenth of the nation's spending on alcohol. Ten cents a week from each person in the rich world would not seem an exorbitant request, but we are still far from providing what is needed despite the creation of a new international fund.

Often a little money could effectively produce a great deal of food. For example, in India and in Africa up to 30 per cent of the harvest is lost in storage through rats, pests and diseases—enough to make up the difference between plenty and want several times over. Often considerable ingenuity is used by the farmers in constructing stores to resist pests and disease, but these can be improved enormously at little cost, and thus reduce the losses after harvest. On the same reckoning a greater use of fertilisers, pesticides and good quality seeds could quickly increase average yields per acre by 50 per cent in a great many developing countries, and very much more could be done in the longer term. Yet the rich countries, with a quarter of the world's population, use 85 per cent of its fertilisers and 93 per cent of its pesticides.*

Fertiliser can generally produce much more food in developing countries than in rich ones. Artificial fertiliser has an addictive effect, and under the law of diminishing returns more and more is needed to get the same results. Thus a ton of fertiliser can produce twice as much food in India as from the jaded soils of Europe, America or Japan. So the pattern of fertiliser use, let alone the Japanese and American action in stopping exports when supplies grew scarce, makes little sense for world food production. Despite narrow national interests, it would seem wisest to use more fertiliser where it will do most good.

The situation appears absurd when the amount of fertiliser used for relatively frivolous purposes is considered. By some estimates 3 million tons a year are used in the U.S.A. on lawns, cemeteries, gardens and golf-courses. That is more than is used by all the farmers in India, and about double the amount that the poor world desperately needed in 1974. This shortfall has since eased but the prospects a few years hence are far from encouraging. The UN has forecast a world shortage of 19 million tons in 1980–1, three-quarters of it in the poor world. Clearly there is a desperate need to build more fertiliser plants, particularly in developing countries. Help from the rich world will be needed, but this is an area that offers especial scope for co-operation between developing countries. The natural gas now flared off at oil wells in OPEC countries could enable them to produce five times as much nitrogenous fertiliser as the expected consumption of all the poor countries put together in 1980–1. Indonesia now meets all her needs from her own gas supply. Regional co-operation could, it is said, make Asia and the Pacific countries self-sufficient in fertiliser within ten years. Greater use of manure and compost would help

*The FAO definition includes weeds, fungi and viruses as pests as well as insects, and thus the term 'pesticide' also covers herbicides, fungicides and the like.

too, even though it could not provide for all needs. There is seven times the nutrients in the available wastes of developing countries than in all the artificial fertiliser they use.

The imbalance in pesticide use is even greater. At least one third of the potential harvest of poor countries is lost to pests every year. Meanwhile, about 20 per cent of the world's supply of pestkiller is used on U.S. golf-courses, parks and lawns, along with all that fertiliser. High levels of pesticide application to crops there, as in other developed countries, causes deep concern about pollution, and often leads to increased losses of food as the pests become immune. The United States has multiplied its use of pesticide a dozen times over in the last 30 years, only to see a doubling in the proportion of crops lost.

Energy is just as unevenly distributed. In 1975 alone India may have lost a million tons of wheat, enough to feed five million people, simply for lack of fuel to run irrigation pumps. Meanwhile, Western agriculture—and particularly food processing, packaging and distribution—is saturated with fuel; feeding each person in Britain and the United States now takes the equivalent of 16cwt of oil a year, more than three times the per capita use of energy for all purposes in the poor world. Of course, however much some poor country governments may try, it is just not possible for them to duplicate either this energy intensive system or even the Western levels of fertiliser and pesticide application. At present, at least, there are not enough raw materials. But importing the fuel-glutted technology—or the weakened and poisoned soils—of developed countries would not be desirable anyway. What is needed is the smaller amounts of these vital resources necessary to bring the *best* of modern science, and greatly increased crop yields, to poor people.

Research can boost yields dramatically at little cost by developing better strains of crops and better ways of growing them, but almost all the food crops of the developing world have been neglected by science. At least eleven times as much money is spent on agricultural research in rich countries as in poor ones. Developing countries are themselves to blame, as well as global inequality. Agriculture is usually unfashionable in poor countries, adequate funds are not made available, and many trained agronomists never practise their profession.

Most of the agricultural research in developing countries is directed at improving cash crops for export rather than the harvests of food for the local people. Cash crops may go to feed cattle for meat production, they may be speciality foods like pineapples, strawberries and asparagus, or, like jute, cotton and carnations, may not be food at all. Cash crops benefit not only from most of the research but also from the bulk of the fertiliser, pesticides and energy used in poor country agriculture. They take up much of the best land. This pattern was established forcibly in colonial days—after all cash crops were one of the main reasons for having colonies. It has been continued by independent governments who need the foreign exchange, and this has been encouraged by multinational firms and foreign aid. Cash crops can reveal some glaring examples of misplaced priorities—during years of famine in the late 1960s and early 1970s, for example, the production of export crops in Mali actually increased, while food for domestic consumption fell to a quarter of its former level.

Developing countries certainly need to concentrate much more attention and resources on producing food for their own people, and rich countries need to help them to do so. But that in itself is not the full answer. Remarkable increases in production have been achieved when research, fertiliser and other resources have been made available, but the problem of hunger has still remained unsolved.

'Whoever could make two ears of corn or two blades of grass to grow upon a spot of ground where only one grew before', the King of Brobdingnag told Gulliver, 'would deserve more of mankind than the whole race of politicians put together.' That, more or less, was what the fathers of the Green Revolution did.

Dr Norman Borlaug in Mexico pioneered the development of new strains of wheat and maize that would mature more quickly than traditional varieties and could use three times as much fertiliser productively. At the same time similar strains of rice were developed at the International Rice Research Institute in the Philippines. Sowings of the new seeds spread from 41,000 acres in 1966 to over 80 million acres in 1973. India doubled her wheat crop within seven years, Colombia doubled her rice harvest in ten.

As long as they are used properly and receive enough fertiliser, water and pesticide, the new varieties are two or three times more productive than the old ones. Unfortunately, they are totally dependent on these resources, and without any one of them they can actually produce less than traditional strains. This makes the harvests particularly reliant on the rich world. Indeed, when supplies grew scarce in the early 1970s the Green Revolution could continue no more.

But even when the fertiliser and pesticides were sufficient, the new seeds failed to beat hunger. India came to the brink of self-sufficiency in cereals. She was able to provide massive food aid to the newly independent Bangladesh, and for a short while came second only to the United States as an aid giver. But malnutrition was still widespread, and the poor were as hungry as ever. It was the same in Mexico. The new seeds enabled her to export a tenth of her crop for as long as five years, but, according to one UN report, they did little to increase the per capita consumption of food.

This shows the food problem in its true light. It results more from a lack of consumption than a failure of production. While efforts in the past have usually been concentrated on increasing the world's harvest, poor people have not been able to afford to buy the food that is produced.

As a result the Green Revolution in some ways made the food problem worse. Most of the benefit of the new seeds went to the farmers who were already relatively wealthy. It was they who could best afford to buy the seeds and the extra fertilisers, pesticides and other aids on which the higher yields depended. Usually the small farmer could not even afford to borrow the money, and only at exorbitant rates of interest. All too often it led to the big farmers increasing their land, turning off tenants and taking over smallholdings. Machinery was often needed to make the most of the Revolution's potential, but its introduction can cut agricultural employment, giving yet another twist to the plight of the poor man. Where poverty continues, let alone deepens, the food crisis cannot be solved. Tackling poverty, concentrating on consumption as well as production, has to be part of any successful strategy.

Fortunately, the most productive way of growing food does almost automatically increase the prosperity of the bulk of the people. For yields can be greatly increased and poverty beaten back simultaneously by concentrating development on the world's most neglected resource, the *small* farmer.

Both the World Bank and the FAO have found that, beyond any shadow of doubt, small farms produce much more food per acre than big ones. The small farmer cultivates his plot more intensively. It is more manageable, and he works harder. He is not so interested in maximising profits as in getting as much as possible out of the land, for while a prosperous farmer will balance the amount of investment and work put in against the return, the small one desperately needs all the food he can produce. In India and Thailand small farmers get about half as much again out of every acre. In Latin America, where land-holdings are particularly unequal, the difference in production is spectacular. The smallest farms in Brazil and Argentina are eight times as productive as the biggest ones, and in Colombia they produce *fourteen* times as much per acre. Of course, big farms usually get higher productivity *per man*, but poor countries need to get as much food as possible out of every *acre*. Labour is no problem, for there is massive under-employment, most of it in the countryside and much of it among the small farmers and their families. What is more, small farmers could greatly increase their yields given a chance to do so. All this means that the sensible strategy is not to concentrate help on the rich and big farmers but on the poor and small ones. Rather than repeat the mistakes of the Green Revolution, we need to launch a Patchwork Revolution.

Most poor countries produce less food from each acre than most rich ones, which is scarcely surprising in view of the imbalance in the use of fertiliser and other resources. But in Taiwan and Egypt, where the average farm is only about two or three acres the yields are many times higher, well out-distancing even almost all the developed nations. Obviously differences in soil and climate will account for part of this high productivity but, significantly, both countries carried out many of the measures thought necessary to realise the remarkable potential of the small farmer. So, in her own way, did China, which has achieved the remarkable feat of feeding more than a fifth of the world's population.

Politically diverse as they are, all three countries brought in genuine land reform. In Egypt, incidentally, it was carried out by Sayed Marei, now the President of the World Food Council, who started with himself—'giving away 800 acres of the best soil in Egypt'. Japan and South Korea can also trace their high productivity back to land reform.

In most developing countries some 80 per cent of the land is held by about 3 per cent of the landowners. The bulk of the people have very little, and in many countries a third of the 'active agricultural population' has no land. Tenants make up more than a quarter of the farmers of India, more than a third of Indonesian farmers, more than half the farmers of the Philippines. Their land tenure tends to be insecure. Often they have to give as much as half their produce to the landlord. During the Green Revolution in the Punjab rents went up from 50 per cent of the crop to 70 per cent. There is little incentive for the tenant, and such rents keep him constantly in poverty, or worse. Without land reform he can hardly advance at all. And even the small farmers who own their land usually have far too little to enable them to feed their families properly. Even such an orthodox institution as the World Bank now says that land reform is essential as a first step.

But land reform is no answer by itself. The small farmer, productive though he may be, is a poor man. Almost all the 80 million smallholders of the world who farm less than five acres live below the poverty line. If he is given no support there is little he can do to improve his land; he may even have to sell it back to the big landowner.

Providing credit is probably the most important form of support. The small man must have some way of buying fertiliser, water, new seeds and simple machinery. He needs short-term credit to avoid having to sell his crop immediately at the end of the harvest —the season of lowest prices—and long-term credit to improve his land.

Moises Diaz Bonilla, a 26-year-old father of two, barely ekes out a subsistence living on a patch of ground in Honduras. He worries about drought, which can come as often as every year. Yet his land sits on ample water lying only a hundred feet below ground. The cost of drilling a well and installing a pump is only a hundred dollars. But it might as well cost a million dollars, because he cannot raise the money to pay for it. Similarly he could get much better prices for his produce if he could take it to the nearest urban market, but that would cost fifteen dollars a harvest—another capital charge beyond his means. He has therefore to sell it at much lower prices to a middleman. His is a typical predicament, for almost no small farmers receive proper credit. Instead they are dependent on local money lenders whose rates are usually extremely high, often 40 per cent a year.

There are successful credit schemes for small farmers in various countries, and they can be particularly helpful when they are linked with co-operatives. Co-operatives, when they succeed and have honest officials, can make it easier to negotiate credit and buy necessities, as well as to provide such facilities as storage, irrigation, machinery and technical advice of use to the whole community. They can negotiate to sell harvests in bulk and become independent of middlemen. But, like credit, they have to be part of a package of change, based on land reform, if they are to be really effective. Taiwan and Egypt, writes Edgar Owens, the agricultural economist, instituted 'land reform, protection of tenant farmers, co-operatives that work, high taxes to finance the cost of rural public investment, integrity in public administration and the accounting of farmers' funds'.*

When thinking of how to help poor farmers, we in the West are inclined to send out a tractor or some sophisticated piece of machinery, sometimes with great individual generosity. But when it arrives it can put people out of work, forty men per tractor in Kerala, three hundred men per combine harvester in the Punjab. And although we see it red and shiny as it leaves our shores, we do not see it later, rusting by the roadside for lack of parts or service, or crippled by the cost of fuel.

The Chinese, Egyptian and Taiwan alternative—which is gaining acceptance in many more states—has been 'intermediate technology'. This means using tools and machinery to supplement rather than replace human effort. It involves using the technology appropriate to the conditions. Sometimes small tractors may be exactly what are needed; at other times they may do great damage. No blueprint can be laid down, just the general principle that technology must fit in with local needs; but often the appropriate

*It should be noted, however, that the Egyptian reforms which helped to bring about the country's high productivity took place many years ago. Lately the government has been paying much less attention to small farmers, and the growth of agricultural output has suffered.

technology will be relatively simple, representing an easily manageable improvement on the traditional means the farmers know.

A similar blend of the best of science and the farmers' traditional wisdom can bring great improvements in crops. For in this Patchwork Revolution the new high-yielding varieties can come into their own. The trouble with the Green Revolution was that it was usually applied with scientific tunnel vision, the dogged belief that technological breakthrough will solve a crisis regardless of social conditions. When these conditions change the new seeds could indeed help put an end to hunger.

The 'miracle seeds' are still available, and there will certainly be more of them. Already there have been promising developments with triticale, a cross between wheat and rye which produces high yields and is particularly tolerant of poor soil and high altitudes. There are hopes of producing a strain of rice that will thrive in salty conditions, and this should be a boon to the farmers whose land is often flooded by the sea. There are hopes, too, of producing high yields from another strain which responds to floods by growing taller and taller, so that the farmers can go out and harvest it by boat! Even more promising is the development of varieties of maize and rice which will fix their own nitrogen like beans, and so have their own built-in fertiliser. There are hopes of enormous increases in the yields of hitherto neglected crops like sorghum, millet and cassava, scarcely known to the rich consumers for whom most research is carried out, but the staple diet of some 400 million people in the poor world. Even some of the much-touted 'new foods', like algae grown on waste, could have great potential in a Patchwork Revolution; but without these social changes, of course, they can play no more part in ending hunger than did the original Green Revolution.

New varieties, however, should not be imposed upon the small farmer but integrated with the best of his traditional practices. He has evolved his agriculture over centuries, during which a single mistake could mean ruin. That does not mean that he has always been right; for example, small subsistence farms wringing too much from the land have been responsible for some of the expansion of the deserts. But he will surely be wise when he insists, as he is likely to, on growing several crops on his patch rather than relying on just one crop like the big farmers who took up the

Green Revolution. Such mixed farming will be more secure from the vagaries of weather, disease, pests and the fertiliser market, and it should improve the soil rather than impoverish it. Indeed, proof of the potential of mixed farming has come from the International Rice Research Institute itself. Its studies have found that all the intercropping systems of small farmers produce at least 30 per cent more food than monocultures, and that one way of intercropping corn and rice on small lots is 80 per cent more productive than growing them separately. Indeed, 'scientific man' might himself learn from the small farmer's caution—for we have been becoming more and more dependent on a handful of basic crops while killing off other species which might provide us with food if our present crops should fail.

The intensive care that small farmers can give their land opens up particular potential for multicropping, the practice of growing two or three harvests a year on the same ground. Where enough water is available this can increase yields between four and eight times over. Research and past experience have shown that the small farmer is not needlessly reactionary, that he is quick to adapt to new techniques if he sees that they can pay and if he has the credit and other facilities needed to enable him to use them.

The World Bank, and independent authorities, believe that all these measures could raise food production by 5 per cent a year —way ahead of population growth, and faster even than the rate of increase in the total harvest brought by the Green Revolution. The cost of bringing about this increase is about eighty dollars a head over a ten-year period, and so the total expenditure of such a programme would range between 60 billion and 100 billion dollars depending on whether it was restricted to just the poorest people or included all small farmers.

The beauty of the Patchwork Revolution is that it not only increases food production but tackles poverty, for it is the small farmers and the country people of the developing world who make up the vast bulk of the poor and the hungry. Because they need the food, and because they are poor, small farmers will need little encouragement to grow more. Raising their prosperity can lead to the development of the whole countryside, which seems the best strategy for developing the economies of poor nations. It makes sense. It is cheap, when the cost of not solving the food and poverty problem is considered. Whether it will be implemented is another matter, for it will involve an enormous change of attitude in both rich and poor countries.

The central question is still not whether we can produce enough food, but whether people can afford to buy it or grow it. Solving the food crisis boils down to achieving development. For that there has to be a change in the relationship not only between rich and poor nations but also between the rich and poor within developing countries.

Chapter 4

Rich World, Poor World

In the summer of 1975 the World Health Organisation uncovered an extensive new international traffic—in human blood. Western companies, it reported, were making immense profits by buying blood from poor people in Africa, Asia and Latin America and selling it for ten times the price in rich countries. One Filipino woman, the mother of eleven children, took to giving blood, sometimes several times a week, just to keep her family alive. Finally she died, bled to death—a miserable illustration of the risk faced by the poor and undernourished donors who needed the money, but who could not afford to part with what they had to sell.

The trade could also endanger the health of the people who received such poor quality blood drawn from sick and hungry people. The WHO feared that the traffic could upset their efforts to encourage really beneficial and efficient blood services.

This story may seem a squalid aberration of an orderly system of trade between nations, but to millions of people in the poor world, to leaders of the United Nations and to some prominent Western economists it could be almost a parable, illustrating their assessment of the present world economic order. As they see it, the system is draining the poor of their lifeblood. In their desperation to get foreign exchange and to earn money to buy necessities from abroad, the poor nations find themselves forced to sell their most basic commodities at low prices for somebody else's profit. Their poverty deepens. Meanwhile, so the argument runs, the system is not even working well for the rich. Because it is based on perpetual and intensifying poverty in the world as a whole, it is making even wealthy economies anaemic. So there has to be a new and efficient system which benefits everyone.

'Nonsense,' comes the traditionalist retort. 'At the market-place, everyone is equal. It is a crude and elementary economic error to suppose that the poor are forced by poverty to trade and get a bad bargain.' And, the argument goes on, it is the duty of the rich to get richer, for by putting their own needs and demands first they cannot help but spread prosperity to the poor. It is perhaps natural that this argument is heard overwhelmingly from the rich themselves.

The debate is not always as polarised as this, and it is not always carried on as bluntly; but it has been at the heart of the dialogue between rich and poor countries.

The developing countries are deeply disillusioned with the international economic system which seems designed to perpetuate their poverty. Backed by OPEC's power, they have been demanding a 'new international economic order'. A growing weight of expert opinion has been shifting to a conviction that a new order is indeed needed. While not envisaging the collapse of the world economy and the creation of a totally new system, this would entail fundamental reforms to give poor countries a chance to develop.

For long the rich countries rejected the demands of the poor outright, but since 1975 they have been talking them over with poor countries. Both sides seemed to accept, before they sat down together, that international prosperity—and even world peace—hangs upon agreement.*

*Of course there are enormous differences among the nations that make up each group. The 'rich' or 'developed' countries include both the market economy, 'free', OECD countries (The First World) and the Russian Communist countries (The Second World). They include countries as diverse in per capita income as the United States and Spain, nations as rich in natural resources as Australia or Canada, and nations as dependent on world trade as Japan or Britain.

The Third World (also referred to in this book as the 'poor' or 'developing' countries) is equally diverse. It includes a few countries that are now absolutely rich—the handful of low-population oil-exporting states like Saudi Arabia, Kuwait and Qatar. Then there are the less poor; more populous oil exporters like Venezuela or Nigeria, plus some fifteen countries (including Argentina, Brazil, Singapore, Mexico and Zambia) which account for nine-tenths of the Third World's manufactured exports and for most of its acceleration of growth in the last decades. Three-quarters of the people of developing countries live outside these relatively better-off nations. And some 29 countries, with a population of 240 million, are classified by the United Nations as 'least developed'; they are the poorest of all. China is in a class by herself; a country of 800 million people which is among the poor yet which, as far as we know, provides all her people with enough. She is excluded from many United Nations statistics.

One quarter of the world's people control 80 per cent of its income, 90 per cent of its gold reserves, and consume 80 per cent of its protein. Just as important, 98 per cent of all scientific research and development is directed primarily at improving the lives of this wealthy quarter rather than those of the other three-quarters of mankind.

At least a thousand million people in Africa, Asia, the Middle East and the West Pacific seem to have no health services at all. More than 800 million people in the world are illiterate. Even in ten years' time less than half of Africa's children and only two-thirds of the children of Asia are expected to have the chance of primary education.

At least 460 million people receive far too little to eat. Some 300 million people in the non-communist developing world—about 40 per cent of the workforce—do not have enough work to provide themselves and their families with a living income.

In the summer of 1975, as a special sacrifice during recession, the British trade union movement agreed to limit pay increases for the next year to an extra £6 a week. A few weeks later the World Bank produced its annual report, which showed that 650 million people in the world had less than £6 to live on for every three months.* Hundreds of millions more are little better off. Despite twenty years of unprecedented global economic growth and institutionalised aid-giving, despite the liberation of almost all the colonies and nearly two complete United Nations special 'Development Decades', there are more poor, hungry, sick and shelterless people than there have ever been.

The gap between rich and poor nations will go on growing so long as our present economic system continues. It was estimated in 1975 that, at best, the billion people of the poorest countries of the world would increase their annual incomes by only three dollars over the present decade, while people in the West, on average, increased their by nine hundred; and, as it turned out, the poorest

*Of course, the purchasing power of money is greater in poorer countries. If adjustment is made for this, trying to live on this income is like trying to make do with less than $250 or about £145 a year in Western Europe. In all, 1200 million people in the non-communist developing countries—two-thirds of the people—have to try to live on the equivalent of an annual European income of less than $500 (or £290).

countries have suffered disproportionately from the world recession.

There is indeed a world of people almost unimaginably poor to Western minds, in terms of money, in terms of facilities like health and education, above all in terms of the absence of any prospects for a better future. The cliché of a 'poor world' is really the only way to convey the extraordinary polarisation of wealth and opportunity that we take so much for granted, a polarisation shown, for example, by the fact that American women spend more money on cosmetics than there is in the combined budgets of all newly independent African states. It is as if we were talking about two planets instead of one.

In fact, 40 per cent of the people on the globe are so poor that they hardly enter the world economy as purchasers at all. A system which has failed to give them the money to become consumers is not only unfair; it is also inefficient. It has failed in the fundamental job of stimulating demand. And so, keeping the poor world at an 'artificially low standard of living' as a British Minister for Overseas Development once told me, 'makes absolute bloody nonsense'.

Thus Barbara Ward argues that the failure to enfranchise the poor in economic terms has been a factor in bringing on the world recession. The International Monetary Fund has warned that the position of the developing countries may delay emergence from it. And the leaders of the seven main industrialised powers brought themselves to declare after their economic summit of May 1977: 'The world economy can only grow on a sustained and equitable basis if developing countries share in that growth.' A new economic order which properly develops the poor world lies in the best interests of the rich world as well.

The present system is, of course, a market one; no bad thing, for it is difficult—and frightening—to imagine the kind of bureaucracy that could control all the interactions of supply and demand in a centrally planned world economy. But, despite the traditionalists, a completely free market will not cure poverty. An uncontrolled market allocates scarce resources to those who can pay for them, denying them to those who need them most.

Although they constantly talk about the free international market, the rich Western countries do not allow an uncontrolled interplay of market forces in their own domestic affairs. Instead we have seen the growth of taxation and of welfare states which has distributed wealth far more widely than could have happened automatically. But there is no such international system to effect a fairer distribution *between* nations. Aid at a fraction of 1 per cent of the gross national product of rich countries can hardly be called a tax, let alone a redistributive one. In addition, the so-called international free market system, though it is certainly free of any effective mechanism for sharing wealth more evenly, is heavily loaded towards the interests of the rich.

The facts of history—among them the industrial revolution in the West and the use of the colonies to provide raw materials—have created an international division of labour. Poor countries have only 7 per cent of the world's industry between them; only a few have been able to industrialise to any extent, and then only in exceptional circumstances.* Their role is still providing raw materials for factories in the rich world. Indeed, a surprising number of them are dependent on the export of just one commodity. Jute or sisal, rubber or sugar, coffee, tea or cocoa, copper, tin or bauxite, among others, go out from their ports. They import processed foods, clothes, machinery and consumer goods from the rich world. This is the pattern of trade, and that is what counts most in development because poor countries earn ten times more convertible currency by trading with rich ones than they receive from them in aid.

The rich countries have a near-monopoly of the production of manufactured goods, and can therefore set the price† of the fertilisers, ploughs, buses and lorries, medicines, machine-tools, turbines for electrical power stations, books, pots and pans, and all the other things which the poor countries need. Prices have gone steadily up and up. Inflation in the rich world is passed on—and with a vengeance. The great oil price rises, for example, fed back an increase of between 30 and 40 per cent in the cost of the manufactures imported by poor countries.

*Over half the industrial output of the poor countries comes from five countries. The whole of black Africa contributes about one two-hundredth of world industry.

†This need not be a matter of conspiracy or of formal price fixing agreements—companies are usually in competition—but just the result of the way the economic system operates.

The position is made worse by the way in which the rich countries can also, in effect, usually determine the price of what poor countries try to sell them in return. Often they effectively own these goods anyway, for they have been mined or grown by a multinational company based in the rich world. Almost always the size of the demand for the raw materials is in the hands of the rich, for they own the factories which will process them, and their people will buy most of the finished products. Furthermore, poor countries rarely have a near-monopoly of a product—they supply only one fifth of the world's raw materials—and, in addition, industries in rich countries produce synthetic substances to compete with several of the most crucial raw materials like rubber, sugar, jute and sisal.* Prices of raw materials have not followed the orderly upward path of manufactured goods. Instead they have zigzagged up and down, as dictated largely by the state of the rich economies. As a result poor economies are thrown into havoc, and rational planning becomes impossible. In a single year a country's foreign exchange earnings can drop by a third, a half, or even more. How can Zambia, 95 per cent dependent on copper for its exports, plan its economy when prices swing between £400, £1,400 and £550 a ton within three years? President Nyerere of Tanzania comments: 'When we were preparing our First Five Year Development Plan, the price of sisal was £148 per ton. We felt that this price was not likely to continue so we planned on the basis that it might average £95 a ton. It dropped to less than £70.'

Because they swung so much it is harder to pick a trend for commodity prices than for those of manufactured goods. Comparisons depend heavily on the years chosen. Some estimates reckon that in the twenty years leading up to the early 1970s the value of commodities fell by 17 per cent or so when compared with the cost of manufactured goods, while studies by both the World Bank and UNCTAD put this decline at a third.† Certainly some

*The rich world is now spending over £500 million a year on researching into new synthetics, and a U.S. Congressional committee has reported that artificial tea, coffee and cocoa may soon be joining the plastics, synthetic fibres and cottons in competition with poor country exports.

†This is the orthodox U.N. view, conceded, incidentally, by President Giscard d'Estaing among others. But another UNCTAD investigation which took different years for comparison concluded that the long-term trend of raw material prices generally kept pace with manufactures despite big short-term

commodities did even worse than this—twenty-five tons of rubber would buy six tractors in 1960, but only two in 1975. In all, the developing countries who were not members of OPEC increased the volume of their exports by a third between 1955 and 1975, but saw their revenues rise by only 4 per cent.

Producers from poor countries may get very little even when the price of the product is high. The commodity may change hands many times before it reaches the factory, increasing the price at every stage. Once it has been through the factory the price escalates far more. The poor primary producer misses all the value that is added to his material when it is processed and manufactured.

Mahbub El Haq, a World Bank economist, has studied the twelve major commodities, excluding oil, which make up about 80 per cent of the export earnings of developing countries. He found that when they had been processed or made into industrial goods they were worth $200 billion. But the primary producers were paid only $30 billion for them.

Obviously, if the poor countries were able to industrialise they themselves would benefit from the value added by processing and manufacture. This would also break the industrial monopoly of the rich and diversify poor economies, making them less dependent on raw material prices. In fact, the poor countries want to boost their share of the world's industry from around 7 per cent to 25 per cent by the end of the century. Unfortunately, the present economic order prevents them doing so. The very pattern of its trade militates against industrialisation: for example, when export revenues swing about from year to year and the cost of capital equipment from the rich world continues to climb, it is hard to find the necessary resources. And there are many other obstacles, too.

---

fluctuations. It was regarded as freak and never published. But it illustrates the difficulty. The waters are particularly muddied by an unprecedented boom in commodity prices in 1973 and 1974. But the prices of manufactures kept pace with the boom, and went on rising when raw material prices slumped right back in 1975. But even if we accept the view of the unpublished UNCTAD report, the poor countries still did badly. For they needed *rising* prices to get terms of trade that would really cover development. And there is no dispute over the damage caused by short-term fluctuations.

Imagine for a moment that you are a citizen of a poor country trying to set up an industry. You are faced with many of the normal problems of businessmen elsewhere, but they will be enormously intensified. It may be hard to find capital or trained men and women. It may also be difficult to get hold of technical knowledge, because this is often protected by patents which effectively confine its use to rich world companies.

However, let us assume that you have overcome these problems, and consider where you are going to sell your products. In the long term, the best thing for you and for your country is to build up a big home market; but because of the distribution of wealth in the world this, generally speaking, is small or non-existent. So to begin with, at any rate, you will have to sell as much as possible to the rich world.

There will be the advantages of cheaper labour and locally available raw materials for some industries. But you will also be competing against rivals who have markets and connections already set up across the world, the best technology and research scientists, long production runs and mass-production techniques.

Even if the market for exporting processed and manufactured goods were free, life would not be easy for you. But poor country exporters have generally to leap over a whole series of barriers before they can reach the well protected markets of the rich.

The barriers include tariffs, which grow higher with the degree of processing that the material has undergone. This is to generalise, for the tariffs and rates vary, but if you look at the average full rates applied by the rich countries a pattern emerges. Raw materials like raw cotton and rubber, metal ores and wood, face penalties of under 5 per cent; for semi-manufactured goods, like metal, they are at least double; and for finished goods, whether wood, cotton, jute or clothing, they are up to twice as high again. Food processing is an industry which suits developing countries, but it comes up against the same discrimination. Raw cocoa is allowed free into Japan, for example, but if it is made into cocoa powder the tariff is 30 per cent, and if it is turned into chocolate it is 35 per cent. Meanwhile non-tariff barriers, like quotas, import ceilings, and other, more sophisticated devices are even more effective in restricting poor country exports. They also grow more severe with the degree of manufacturing that the goods have undergone.

It is a far cry from the pious official pronouncements about free trade. There could hardly be a clearer message to poor countries—'It is not worth your while to industrialise'. Rich countries argue the need to protect their own industries, but this gets little response from the poor whose raw materials have long been exploited. Their cynicism deepens when they see that quotas and other non-tariff barriers discriminate against them and that the tariffs they face are on average about 50 per cent higher than those erected by rich countries against other developed nations. There are, of course, exceptions—and some systems for giving preference to developing countries. Nevertheless the poor can hardly be blamed for feeling that the rich, who let out such howls of protest when OPEC showed its power, have long operated a much greater, more damaging and pervasive cartel—over manufacturing industry itself.

It is natural that workers from the poor world should migrate to the rich. John Cole calls this 'a measure of our failure to achieve a rational economic system'. For example, before British rule there was a healthy textile industry in India. The colonial government tried to destroy it with a complex system of tariffs because they feared it would compete with the business of Lancashire. Today there are quotas to protect the Lancashire mills. But those mills are full of Indians, who might have done the same jobs more happily and beneficially at home if our system of trade had made it possible for them to do so.

The migration of skilled men to seek work on the other side of the tariff barriers does more damage to the economies of the poor countries. It cannot be repaid by the remittance that immigrants send back to their families. And the 'brain drain' of highly skilled and professional people to the U.S.A. from the developing world benefits that country by hundreds of millions more dollars than she provides in foreign aid.

Surely, though, the rich share their wealth by giving generous aid? Certainly there are people who insist that rich countries are too generous, not realising, perhaps, that generosity is often not the motive at all. Sometimes it is merely aimed at providing business expansion at home, while there is plenty of evidence that both monetary and food aid are used as instruments of foreign policy, even of blackmail. 'The international distribution of aid', concluded one report, 'is at present determined largely by political, commercial and military considerations.'

Anyway, although the money provided has been increasing, inflation has meant that aid has really declined over the last decade or so, while the number of people in need has grown. Between the mid 1960s and 1974 the amount of aid provided per head of population in the poor world declined in real terms from about \$3·70 a year to about \$2·95.

In 1960 the rich 'Western' OECD countries provided an average of about 0·5 per cent of their GNP to official aid.* Ten years later the United Nations called for this to be increased to 0·7 per cent. But the call seems to have fallen on blocked ears. In 1975 it was only 0·35 per cent. Of all the Western nations only Sweden and the Netherlands hit the target. Britain could spare only 0·38 per cent of her GNP, and the United States only 0·26 per cent. During those fifteen years the economies of the rich countries had grown by more than 67 per cent. Over the last ten years, as the countries themselves admit, they devoted none of their increased wealth to aid. Had they been willing to divert only half a per cent of it, they would have reached the UN target.

The U.S.S.R. and Eastern Europe have a much worse record still. From 1955 to 1975 the communist world offered less than did the Western world in 1974 alone.† Both worlds, however, are put to shame by the oil exporters. The OPEC countries provided 2·7 per cent of their GNP in 1975—more than seven times the proportion supplied by the Western countries. Yet this may underestimate their contribution, for they committed much more than they handed over. New aid donors do not have experience in

*My definition of aid follows the Pearson Commission Report's recommendation that only public assistance to poor countries should be counted. There is also investment on commercial terms in Third World countries by private companies and rich countries often include this in their accounts of aid provided. But the object of these companies is almost always merely to make profits, rather than to aid poor countries. This kind of investment is not counted as aid when companies extend their businesses in other rich countries, so it seems illogical to classify it as such when it is invested in poor countries—particularly when the operations of multinational companies often have a far from beneficial effect.

†China is, of course, a poor nation herself—so her aid is an economic sacrifice, if an ideological weapon.

setting up programmes, and so what is actually provided can lag behind what is promised.

While it is true that OPEC's assets are more liquid (in more senses than one!), the OPEC nations are generally very much poorer than developed countries. As they spend more on their own development, the proportion they give in aid is likely to decline. Indeed, there are already signs that this is happening. They cannot make up for a major decline in Western aid.

This decline hit the neediest countries hardest. The UN reports that they are getting 'dismally small amounts' compared with wealthier developing countries. Meanwhile the terms on which Western aid is provided have also been getting worse. Contrary to popular belief, a good deal of aid is not gifts of money but loans on concessional terms. At the beginning of the 1960s more than three-quarters of aid was given rather than lent; by the end of the decade the proportion of gifts had fallen to less than half. This —and the general decline of aid at a time of rising need, which drove poor countries to raise more capital on the commercial market—helped plunge the Third World heavily into debt. At the last count developing countries owed the Western world more than $174 billion. The amount of money that has to be paid back every year to service such debts comes to about half the money provided in aid. In 1971 a tenth of all poor countries' export earnings went to pay off debts. Indeed, about one third of India's export earnings each year flow straight out of the country again for this reason. She has to repay the U.S.S.R. five times as much each year as she receives from the superpower in aid, Russia being a much tougher usurer than the capitalist countries. OPEC provides aid on harder terms than the west, according to the rival OECD.

Aid is further devalued in other ways. Most of it is 'tied'. The receiving nation has to use it to buy goods and services from its benefactors. In practice this means that it has to pay an average of at least 20 per cent more than if the choice of imports were free—indeed sometimes it may be charged several times the price of equivalent goods on the open market. Ninety-three per cent of American aid is tied and more than 80 per cent of West Germany's; for Britain the proportion is rather less.

Dr Kenneth King, an Assistant Director General of the Food

and Agriculture Organisation, reckons that even the aid which escapes being repaid as interest in loans generally goes straight back to the giver. By the time overheads in rich countries have been paid, he says, their equipment has been bought and their field workers' salaries have been paid and partly banked at home, about 70 per cent of the money given has actually gone back to the rich. He adds: 'Aid creates more jobs and leads to the expansion and creation of more industries in the developed than in the developing countries.'

So whether by aid or trade, the United Nations' First Development Decade did virtually nothing to shift the balance of wealth in the world. During the 1960s the world's gross international product increased by a thousand billion dollars. Eighty per cent of this increase went to rich countries, with per capita incomes of over a thousand dollars a year. Only 6 per cent went to the half of humanity who live in countries where average income is less than two hundred dollars a year.

If this is what the old international order has to offer it is not surprising that poor countries want a new one. Much of their sense of grievance is not about a lack of money; it is about a lack of dignity and independence. They see themselves trapped in an economic system which allows them little more power over their own fate than did the colonial system.

I. G. Patel, Deputy Administrator of the United Nations Development Programme, puts it like this:

> Most of the developing countries have such bitter memories of colonial exploitation or racial and other forms of discrimination that deep underneath the desire for economic progress lies the psychological need to put the hurt and humiliation behind them once and for all. What the developing countries really want on a psychological plane is to regain their sense of dignity and self-respect which they enjoyed for long centuries and which they lost only during the brief period of Western domination.

This is the kind of feeling that makes poor countries demand a new economic order not as a favour or an act of charity but as a matter of right; and the rich countries do not yet seem to have realised the depth of determination and emotional commitment involved. President Nyerere speaks for many poor country leaders on this: 'My own view is that every human being on this planet has a right to the world. He has the right to food, he has the right to clothing, to education, to good health, to housing and, if we do not have a world government, at least we have a kind of international ethic. We could, if we wanted, establish conventions which would transfer resources from the rich to the poor as a matter of right, not a system of begging.'

Dr Patel, who is in a good position to know, argues that the developing countries are not, however, after equality with the rich:

> What all of them without exception want is a basic minimum for all their people so as to achieve a measure of security against internal strife and a minimum of national resilience or strength to withstand natural and other disasters without subservience to other nations. And it does not require a very high level of per capita income—of say more than $400 to $500 per head per annum.

That esimate may well be too modest. What is more, aspirations will surely rise as progress is made, and demands will certainly escalate if it is not. But the poor countries' wish for redistribution is not a desire for levelling. Their language may sometimes be of the far left, but the proposals are usually of the centre.

A new economic order would not require people in the West to give up anything they already have, except the view that it is their right to grow richer and richer at a faster pace every year, while the mass of humanity is left to suffer. They would not even have to accept zero growth. By one authoritative estimate, the gap in average incomes between rich and poor nations could be cut in half by the turn of the century, with the rich still more than doubling their standard of living. Another estimate says that in forty years the disparity between the poorest 10 per cent of nations and the richest 10 per cent could be cut to no more than that at present existing between the least developed and the wealthiest EEC countries—and again the rich would double their income.

So very great sacrifices are not being called for. Indeed, there is growing disenchantment within rich countries at the failure of a total preoccupation with growth to bring a satisfying life. 'Developed countries', comments Barbara Ward, with characteristic pungency, 'no longer represent a fully workable or desirable model even to themselves.'

I do not believe, as some do, that our evils can be laid at the door of economic growth. What has been destructive is our attitude to it. For the single-minded pursuit of economic growth is enshrined as the overriding goal of rich countries, even as the answer to all their problems. And this unbalanced concentration upon it has meant that, far from solving problems, we have neglected many and allowed others to emerge. The answer is not to stop growth but to see it in a new perspective; to be free enough from our preoccupation with it to be able to contemplate changes in our economic system.

Growth has brought great benefits. No one should underestimate, for example, the importance of the drive in most rich countries to eliminate poverty and provide more employment, to distribute wealth more fairly and build a compassionate welfare system. All of these have been made possible by economic growth.

And yet, despite twenty-five years of unprecedented boom, none of these goals has been fully achieved. That is a result not of lack of wealth but of our priorities. We have concentrated more on growth for its own sake than on properly distributing its benefits. While an abrupt end to growth is no answer—it would sharply increase poverty and unemployment—it must now be clear that growth is no panacea.

Similarly, greater prosperity has relieved the mass hopelessness that characterised, say, Hogarthian London. But has not a lopsided preoccupation with material growth brought a new meaninglessness to our society, one which displays many of the same symptoms? The United Nations Centre for Social Development and Humanitarian Affairs reports that delinquency, criminality, violence and drug abuse in rich countries are side effects of our determination to concentrate overwhelmingly on material development.

Other bodies take this argument further. One symposium of eminent economists, administrators and health experts concluded that over-consumption of goods was as unhealthy as over-eating.

'Man has a limited capacity to absorb material goods,' they reported. 'It does not help us to produce and consume more if the result is an ever increasing need for tranquillisers and mental hospitals.' When half the hospital beds in Europe and North America are taken by the mentally ill, it is worth pondering their view. The prevailing philosophy is that happiness and quality of life come from growth. We are many times richer than our grandfathers, but can we fairly say that we are many times happier?*

Is there also a penalty for those who produce for our overconsumption? The demand for more and more cheap consumer goods has led to the need for more and more mass production and mechanisation. This has meant that the *creative* part of the work, the making of the article, has been handed over to the machine, while man's job has been to serve and service the mechanical creator. Dr E. F. Schumacher, the economist and author of *Small is Beautiful*, called this 'soulless, meaningless, mechanical, monotonous, moronic work . . . an insult to human nature which must necessarily produce either escapism or aggression'. What are the social, mental and economic costs of this development? Is one cause of inflation the demand to receive in the wage packet the satisfaction that is lost at work?

Studies in Sweden suggest that the advances in human welfare associated with economic growth, such as longer expectation of life, came to a halt in the mid-1960s, while alienation and boredom at work, mental illness, social tension, suicides, alcoholism and loneliness kept increasing. Life expectancy of American men peaked in the early 1960s, and actually began to fall at the end of the decade as stress-induced diseases claimed more and more lives. Meanwhile alcoholism is the fourth most prevalent disease in America, a phenomenal problem in the U.S.S.R., and has increased by 60 per cent in Britain over the past decade.

Mother Theresa of Calcutta recently visited London. She has spent her life caring for the most destitute people of a city which has become the world's symbol of poverty and squalor. Many of those people are beyond all human hope. All she can do for them

*In the poor and ravaged West Germany of the early 1950s 25 per cent of the population considered itself 'happy'. By the prosperous early 1970s, despite the intervening 'economic miracle', the 'happy' Germans had risen only to 26 per cent of the people!

is to see that they die, as she puts it, 'within sight of a loving face'.

Instead of expressing envy of London's wealth and a longing for the same sort of prosperity and relative social security for the poorest citizens of Calcutta, she commented: 'Here you have a different kind of poverty. A poverty of loneliness and being unwanted, a poverty of spirit, and that is the worst disease of the world today.'

An unbalanced preoccupation with growth for its own sake is also at the root of the crises of pollution and the depletion of resources. Pollution has ravaged the quality of life and brought disease and death, not least to the workers in the factories that are supposed to churn out the artefacts of the good life.* Indeed the orthodox plans for increasing our use of energy to provide maximum growth pose unparallelled threats to our societies.† Meanwhile waste and overconsumption—encouraged, incidentally, by the low prices paid for poor country products—are largely to blame for the crisis in resources. The world is not immediately threatened by a sudden depletion of energy and minerals; but it is equally clear that the rich world cannot go on *increasing* its use of resources (of which energy is by far the most important and most under the strain) at the present rate.§ This in itself should force us to alter our conceptions of growth and to redirect our economies through planning for change rather than wait for change to be forced upon us.

Of course, controlling growth in the rich world would necessitate changes in society. More jobs would have to be directed to improving the quality of life rather than to production for its own sake. There would also have to be a real determination to eliminate

*See Chapters 13 and 14.

†See Chapters 8 and 10.

§Despite apocalyptic prophecies at the beginning of the 1970s the world is not short of minerals. There are adequate, often vast, reserves of all but a few, relatively unimportant, materials in the earth's crust, and on the ocean floor. Substitutes can be found for those that are scarce, and, at a pinch, many minerals could even be gathered from the world's rubbish-tips and recycled. But exploiting minerals, by any means, requires energy—and if we exhaust the most accessible reserves, we will almost certainly have to use much more energy to provide the same amount of minerals. Besides, energy is needed in every industrial process, and once fuel is burned it cannot be recycled. Furthermore, the oil upon which we have based our civilisation since the Second World War is the only important mineral which really is running out. See Chapters 9–12.

poverty in the rich world, a decision which will have to be taken in any case, since growth does not solve poverty by itself.

Neither compassion nor justice are limited by boundaries, and a care for the poor both at home and abroad are complementary. As Roy Jenkins, who as British Home Secretary had a strong reputation for social reform, said: 'A society which says "to hell with famine and disease in Bangladesh, it's all their own fault isn't it?" is extremely unlikely to balance this with compassion and justice for its own pensioners and its own low paid.'

In fact what is being asked of us internationally is the same as what has been asked of us domestically by the champions of the poor—and we have long accepted it at home, at least in principle. I. G. Patel writes:

> What the developing countries demand is nothing more and nothing less than an extension on an international scale of what most modern states have come to accept on a national scale, viz: a basic minimum standard of living and a modicum of economic security for all citizens; a deliberate policy of developing as well as redistribution to achieve this; a sense of participation for all groups in a society; and a certain restraint on concentration of economic power per se so that it does not become the instrument of cultural or political domination.

Chapter 5

Towards a New Economic Order

How is the old order to change and yield place to new? It is harder to find convincing ways of changing the old system than to show up its injustices—and harder still to get international agreement on specific reforms. Indeed some say that the best approach would be for rich and poor countries to try to decide first of all how much extra wealth should be directed towards the Third World, and only turn to discuss specific measures once the general principle had been agreed. This would make it easier for practical proposals to be considered on their merits; rather than treated as punching bags in preparation for the real conflict. For so far that is how the negotiations between rich and poor have been carried out.

Generally speaking—like the changes that once took place within rich countries—the main proposals fall into two clear categories; one is to tax the richer to help the poorer; the other is to put a restraining hand on the blind operation of the market.

I. TAX

(1) *Aid*

At the time of the post-war Marshall Plan Americans were only two-thirds as wealthy as they now are, and then they gave more than ten times as much of what they had in aid. At present Britain spends more on her pets than on poor people overseas. Rich countries are still only half-way to the 1970 UN target of 0·7 per cent of GNP, and the World Bank reckons that at least 0·81 per cent is needed to give the poor countries any chance of reaching a reasonable economic growth rate. It is worth remembering when considering aid that in the past both Christianity and Islam decreed that one-tenth (not 0·7 per cent) of one's income should go to the poor, and that the rich in biblical times were generally much less wealthy than the average Westerner today.

There should be no debate about the need to meet—and surpass—the level agreed at the beginning of the decade. A more profitable question is what could be done with more generous aid. Generosity in aid at this stage could in the long run save a great deal even in terms of hard cash. By one estimate, a crash programme to bring the poor world to a decent standard by the end of the century would cost only about a third as much as a more moderate programme which ran from now until the year 2025; and only a fifth of a crash programme delayed until the turn of the century.

Some—limited—progress has been made over aid in response to the demands for a new order. In September 1975, and under pressure of a threatened major rise in oil prices, several rich countries undertook that they would reach the UN target ten years late—by 1980. It looks as if some of them will actually do it. Most aid-giving countries have announced their intention, at least, of directing their help towards the poorest countries. They have also agreed to ease the strings tying their aid, a start, if no substitute for the general untying that is needed. Meanwhile Britain has announced that in future all her aid to the poorest will be gifts, rather than loans. A valuable step would be to channel much more aid through international organisations, thus avoiding the favouritism shown by Western, communist and OPEC givers alike. Among other advantages this would lessen the use of blackmail, and the tying of aid. The disadvantage would be that, thanks to the snail's pace of international bureaucracy, the money would reach the people who needed it more slowly.

(2) *Tax on the Seabed*

Aid means dependence. It is the equivalent not of redistributive taxation but of charity. It is readily accepted within rich nations that poor people neither want to be, nor should be, beholden to charity; and poor countries feel strongly that the same applies to them. In negotiations over the new order they have therefore tended to reject proposals from the rich world which look like being merely aid in another form. Yet the poorest countries, at least, are going to need transfers of cash from the rich for a long time to come. The search for more automatic ways of transferring and redistributing wealth between countries therefore goes on. Ironically, it looks as if one of the best ways of doing this is going to be missed, through short-sightedness and narrow self-interest among both rich and poor.

The chance has come with the Third United Nations Conference on the Law of the Sea, which met to decide, among other important issues, the ownership of 70 per cent of the world's surface and the greater part of its unexploited resources.

Beneath the seabed, it is thought, are at least a quarter of all the world's recoverable oil reserves; they may be worth well over 20 trillion dollars. Meanwhile on the deep ocean floor lie potato-shaped 'nodules' containing manganese, nickel, cobalt, copper, molybdenum, aluminium and iron, several of which are scarce on land. Nobody knows the extent of the minerals in the nodules in the oceans of the world—only 3 per cent of the deep seabed has been surveyed—but the UN has concluded: 'Conservative estimates indicate that there are several hundred thousand million tons of mineable nodules in the high-grade areas of the Pacific', enough in themselves to last for thousands of years at present rates of consumption. Fascinatingly, the nodules are forming all the time out of sea water—at 10 million tons a year in the Pacific alone, by one estimate.

This wealth lay in international waters. It belonged to nobody—so perhaps it belonged to everybody. In 1970 the UN General Assembly unanimously agreed that the resources of the seabed 'were the common heritage of mankind', and that they should be mined according to international agreement and control. This offered the hope that the nations of the world just might agree on distributing the unexpected windfall of the ocean's wealth for the common good, giving the greatest proportion to the poorest countries. It seemed a unique chance dramatically and painlessly to narrow the gap between rich and poor.

But this hope has faded and faded. Almost all the oil and gas—at present, at least, by far the most valuable part of the seabed's wealth—seems to lie below the continental shelf. A 1958 treaty had laid down in principle that countries had the right to mine their 'continental shelves' but provided such a meaningless definition of where the shelves ended that a fresh start was both possible and necessary. During the early preparations for the conference several countries, including the U.S.A. and the U.S.S.R., proposed quite restricted limits to national jurisdiction, which would have left a large proportion of the shelves, and the oil and gas beneath them, to international control. But before long more and more countries, principally poor ones, were insisting that each coastal nation should have an exclusive right to all resources two hundred miles from its shores. It seems almost certain that the conference will agree, for the nationalistic pressures soon became irresistible; and this agreement will take away nearly all the continental shelf, all proved oil and gas reserves plus 87 per cent of probable reserves and, indeed, one third of all the oceans.* Hardly anyone expected such an enormous extension of national territory when the negotiations began, but by the time they finish even more of the seabed may be lost to the 'common heritage'. For it looks as if coastal countries will be given the right to exploit minerals to the edge of the continental margin, the almost indefinable spot at which the continental slope joins the abyssal ocean floor. This would give some countries—Britain included—vast new tracts of seabed, and because the limit is so hard to define could lead to more areas being gobbled up than the law allowed, and to extra disputes.

Although much of the drive for wide national control came from poor countries, the result will be that the main bonanzas are delivered irrevocably to the rich. The United States and Australia are by far the biggest beneficiaries from a 200-mile 'economic zone', followed by Canada, Indonesia, Japan, the U.S.S.R. and New Zealand—only one poor country among the top seven. In fact most of the seabed given away goes to developed nations. The vast bulk of poor countries, even coastal ones, thus stand to lose

*This remarkable figure is made possible by the numbers of islands in the ocean, and the effect of a 200-mile radius circle around even the tiniest of them.

more by this allocation than they would if the riches were exploited internationally and shared out around the world. Meanwhile, nearly fifty developing nations—either landlocked or with small or hemmed-in coastlines—will receive little or nothing; and most of them are among the poorest countries of all.

At one stage the United States made a proposal that would have created a much more just allocation of wealth. She suggested that almost all the area between the shore and the edge of the continental margin should be allocated to coastal nations; but they would only act as trustees, and would share out between half and two-thirds of the revenue gained from it, so that all nations would benefit. But this proposal met with a frosty reception even from developing countries—partly because it came from the U.S.A. By the end of the sixth session of the Conference in the summer of 1977 this imaginative concept had shrunk to an apparent agreement that there should be some sort of sharing from the much smaller and less wealthy area between the 200-mile line and the edge of the continental margin.

While coastal countries, the majority of the participants, quickly agreed that they should extend their jurisdiction far out to sea, the question of what to do about what was left of the 'common heritage of mankind' beyond the new economic zones went unanswered. After forty-one weeks of intensive negotiations rich and poor nations were still deadlocked over how to exploit the deep seabed, where the nodules lie. Delegates agreed that an international authority should be in charge and should have the right to carry out mining and share the revenues; but they were divided over the extent of its powers. Rich countries wanted their own companies, private or state-owned, to have a guaranteed right to mine as well. Poor countries, fearing that the authority would have little chance in competition with such industries, who alone have the technology to exploit the seabed, were determined to restrict their operations. In return the rich were extremely wary of allowing their firms to be tightly controlled by an authority representing the majority interest of the poor which would, after all, be a commercial competitor.

Despite real hopes of compromise, this atmosphere of mutual suspicion ensured that the fifth and sixth sessions of the conference, in the summers of 1976 and 1977, each ended with the delegates more divided than when they began. As session after session failed to produce agreement, the U.S.A. threatened to allow its companies to go ahead unilaterally. Already bills to this effect have been introduced in Congress and one of these companies has announced that it has taken possession of 23,000 sq. miles of ocean between Mexico and Hawaii. By the autumn of 1977 it looked as if the United States would carry out her threat, if there was no speedy progress to an agreement, and that the other developed countries with seabed interests would follow suit.

If the companies began mining with rich country consent before an agreement could be reached, the last of the common heritage would be lost. If, on the other hand, a reasonably strong authority came into being, and there were some revenue-sharing in the event of states being allowed to exploit minerals to the edge of the continental margin, some of the original promise of the seabed would be retained. There might still also be a useful redistributive 'tax', even if it was far less than we might once have hoped. But as the sixth session broke up, it looked as if the chance to use the windfall of the wealth of the seabed would be mainly a story of missed opportunities.

The story illustrates a fundamental difficulty in negotiating solutions to major world issues. What are needed are solutions which are in the interests of mankind as a whole; and such solutions are sometimes quite easy to discern in theory. But in practice they have to be worked out by the representatives of some 150 nations. Governments do not come to a conference with the object of co-operating with other nations in a disinterested search for a universal answer. They come to fight for their own interests, and assume at best that solutions will only arise out of a clash between all the interests represented.

One participant in the negotiations for the law of the sea put it like this: 'Your first loyalty is to your own nation; your second loyalty is to the group to which you belong; your third loyalty is to build up a viable and integrated system of law.' Another participant put it less diplomatically: 'The policies of virtually all the governments involved in the seabed negotiations have been directed to promoting the immediate interests of their own state, calculated in the most cynical and self-seeking terms, in the confident (and not unjustified) expectation that other governments would undoubtedly do the same for theirs.' This process is most obvious in the law of the sea negotiations because territory is at stake, but it is equally true of most of the discussions over the proposed new international economic order.

It is a natural enough process in a world made up of nation-states, many of which have good reason to distrust one another. But it means that the opportunity presented by conference after conference is lost in fractious bargaining. It means that even the successful conferences achieve their compromise in frantic last-minute negotiations, while days and weeks have been wasted defending positions that everyone knew would eventually have to be abandoned. Of course, it is not possible to achieve solutions other than by negotiating between nations—that is the way the world is made. All one can ask is that the attitude might change; that governments might recognise that co-operation may be more fruitful than conflict and that, in an interdependent world, the sectional interests of all countries are ultimately bound up with the common good.

(3) *Other Taxes*

There have been proposals for other taxes, but to become actual they will require a major shift in attitudes from those displayed over the Law of the Sea. One imaginative idea is to tax the use of the 'international commons' of air and water for transport and for pollution disposal. The Cocoyoc Declaration, issued after a top-level UN meeting of experts in 1974, calls for them to be 'taxed for the benefit of the poorest strata of the poor countries' as the first step in an international taxation system. Another suggestion—a tax on the use of non-renewable resources, such as minerals and energy—would have the valuable side effect of encouraging more economical use; yet another idea is a world-wide levy on luxury goods such as cars, pleasure boats, television sets and dishwashers. Savings from disarmament could provide the most beneficial source of funds of all. Eventually, says the Cocoyoc Declaration, these savings and forms of taxation should replace present aid systems, but in the meantime aid should be stepped up.

(4) *Paper Gold for Development*

Special Drawing Rights (SDRs) or 'paper gold', the new international money created by the International Monetary Fund, offer another opportunity for a more automatic form of aid. Ninety-seven per cent of the SDRs issued between 1970 and 1975 went to rich countries. But since their primary purpose was to add to world reserves so as to meet global monetary needs, why not, it is suggested, make the bulk available to poor countries? Then they could use the new money to buy more imports from the rich world.

The result would be twofold. The SDRs would end up with the rich world anyway—thus meeting their needs for reserves—and the wheels of development will have been oiled on the way. This could be one step in working out an orderly system of international credit in the place of one that tends to favour the countries that issue the main international currencies. Poor countries also want more votes in the World Bank and the International Monetary Fund to ensure that they get greater help in financing their trade and development.

(5) *Debt Relief*

In the short term, the lessening of their debt burden is a more important priority for developing countries than any of these. Their borrowing helped them achieve growth, but in the 1970s the end of the boom in the rich world brought about a collapse in the commodity prices that determine their income. Some estimates suggest that their burden may grow by 18 per cent a year until 1980. They say that as they have become the victims of an upset in the world economy not of their own making, they are entitled to an international solution. They have also insisted that they should negotiate a generalised solution, which would set down procedures for debt relief that would be applied automatically to all countries. Many poor nations fear that without this they will be picked off one by one when they ask for help and that their creditors will force them to impose tough economic policies which would make their people even poorer and thus provoke revolt; indeed harsh conditions imposed in the past, partly to discourage debtors from seeing relief as an easy escape, have ensured that few countries have sought this kind of assistance.

Easing the debt burden has proved to be one of the most difficult issues in the entire negotiations over the international economic order. The Third World has asked for the debts of the very poorest countries to be cancelled, and for more lenient repayment terms for richer developing countries. Both Sweden and Canada have indeed relieved their poorest debtors of their obligations, but they are relatively minor lenders, and the industrial world as a whole has refused to entertain the Third World demands, fearing that acceptance could provoke a banking crisis.

After eighteen months of hard negotiations the rich offered to lend the poorest developing countries an extra one billion dollars on extremely soft terms, a sum which the Third World dismissed as 'miserable' compared to the need. The rich also proposed new procedures for relief which, among other improvements, would enable poor countries to be helped before they reached the brink of bankruptcy; but they insisted that such relief should still only be applied to individual countries on a case by case basis.

Fears about interference in poor countries' economies were increased by another rich country initiative, the creation of a special IMF facility to lend money to developing nations in financial difficulties, a job that banks were becoming increasingly reluctant to do. The money will only be disbursed after the IMF has scrutinised a borrower's economy and laid down conditions as to how it should be run in future, conditions which, it is feared, might well prove socially and financially unacceptable; after all, only a few months before the facility was set up, the Government of Egypt had to abandon its attempts to implement IMF loan conditions after serious rioting in Cairo. In all, therefore, the various rich world initiatives failed to take the edge off the developing countries' demands, and by the summer of 1977 the two sides were as deadlocked as ever.

II. THE MARKET

(1) *Tariffs*

The World Bank reckons that the pulling down of the lowest tariff barriers, those against raw materials, would alone quickly result in poor countries getting half the extra foreign exchange needed to lift their growth rates to the UN target of 6 per cent a year. Producers of vulnerable raw materials would also demand that preference be given to their natural exports over domestic synthetics. And, of course, real development depends on bringing down the barriers erected against manufactured goods as well. At the start of serious negotiations on a new order, the Third World demanded that the barriers against goods from the poorest developing countries should be removed at once. However, there is strong commercial pressure on rich country governments to do as little as possible. Indeed, despite lofty resolutions from rich country leaders, protectionism grew during 1977. That summer, for example, Europe increased its restrictions on textiles. These are the most important Third World industrial exports, and make up one third of all the manufactures that poor countries sell to Europe—their biggest textile market.

Before this some progress was being made, particularly over the reduction of tariffs. The 'Generalised System of Preferences', whereby rich countries lower or remove tariffs on selected imports from poor countries in order to offer them an advantage, was adopted in 1964. But it was not until 1976 that the last—and most important—industrial signatory to the agreement, the United States, actually put it into practice. Its effects are limited. Often, for example, the amount of imports allowed preference is restricted by quotas, and one of the main criticisms of the system is that the products favoured under it seem to be those that are relatively unimportant to poor countries and pose little or no threat to the rich world's industry.*

For, of course, the point of having barriers is to protect industries and jobs at home from 'dangerous' competition. If they come down there will be changes, but these need not be nearly as traumatic as is sometimes feared. Obviously the Third World could not take over all the kinds of work that process its raw materials. Many of these industries would not be competitive there. The ones likely to do well in developing countries are labour intensive rather than capital intensive—which, of course, is precisely what they need.†

Manufactures of some processed foods and electrical goods, textiles, clothes and shoes, and basic wood products, would be among those best suited to the poor countries and most vulnerable in the rich ones. But removing restrictions would not mean that poor

*The system, of course, means that it is not in poor countries' interests to have a complete dismantling of all tariff barriers for everyone. Where the system actually gives them an advantage, their interest is to see that advantage maintained or even strengthened.

†See next chapter.

countries immediately swamped the market with cheaper products, putting rich country industry out of business. They would take a good deal of time to get their industries going and to improve their marketing abilities. Hopefully world trade would expand while this was happening, so that poor countries would be gradually winning a bigger share of a growing world market. This would reduce—if not eliminate—the eventual impact. The International Labour Organisation, which represents the trade unions, managements and governments of the world, reckons that at worst only a million people in all the rich countries put together would need to find new jobs. Nor would these jobs be lost immediately; the effect would be phased over ten to twenty years involving no more than one hundred thousand jobs each year. This is small compared to the effects of trade cycles and modernisation. Indeed, the ILO has found that even in the most affected industries the job losses would be less than those normally experienced in productive gains.*

Of course, a job lost is a job lost, for whatever reason, and a man is liable to suffer, whatever the cause. But the disappearance of these jobs does not mean that the people who held them would necessarily become unemployed. Studies show that the increasing world trade and prosperity brought about by the resulting development of poor countries would provide many more jobs in rich countries than were lost.† In theory, this should fit in with the desire of workers in rich countries to get better jobs and to avoid the dirty and bad ones, with the increasing skill of the workforce and with the development of more productive industries; developments which would greatly benefit both the workers and the economies of rich countries.

In practice, of course, you have to deal with flesh and blood people, not statistics. The vulnerable industries are often in depressed areas; the vulnerable workers are the unskilled, the low-paid, women and immigrants. Both industries and workers will need special help to adapt to more productive work.

*Similarly tiny figures can be given for the effect on agricultural jobs. The ILO worked out that the decline through the elimination of barriers would only be one-fortieth of the 'natural' decline that is already taking place.

†Britain, it is estimated, would be the rich country least affected by lost jobs if all tariffs were abandoned and the one most likely to benefit from the increase in trade. But even the U.S.A.—the country likely to lose most jobs—would stand to gain enormously from the change.

'Adjustment assistance', as it is called, has a poor reputation in many countries, but that is because it has been applied wrongly. When help is given at all, it is usually too late, because the industry is dying anyway. Then the help given is usually inappropriate; the government merely pours in money to try to keep the struggling industry going, increasing investment in an attempt to make it more competitive. Such indiscriminate help has rarely been successful, and disillusioned workers and management naturally prefer the protection of barriers to such 'assistance', but in some countries the story has been quite different. Governments have predicted which industries are likely to become uncompetitive, and then, instead of trying to shore up inefficient and failing production, have helped firms to switch to competitive and healthy lines and products. This has happened in the Japanese textile industry, while Sweden has painlessly halved her textile labour force in the last twenty years, retraining the workers who leave for new jobs and providing skilled, highly paid jobs on profitable lines for those who remain. Besides such retraining, assistance might involve subsidies to help firms change their products and to assist families when they have to move house because of a new job. Above all, workers must be convinced that the changes brought about by bringing down tariffs are in their own interest; that the government is really interested in seeing that they get better paid, more productive jobs. Otherwise, they may continue to fear that the lowering or removal of barriers will just allow cheap labour overseas to undercut their work. All this can be achieved. 'There is widespread agreement', writes Francis Blanchard, the Director-General of the ILO, 'that such structural changes in the world economy are ultimately in the best interests both of the developing and the developed countries.'

Yet, to be realistic, some people in the rich world are likely to suffer, however good the adjustment assistance, however much the new pattern of industry benefits the overwhelming majority. At the risk of seeming to trade one suffering against the other, it is important to see this in perspective. Rich countries do have the scope to adjust and plan to make such transitions as smooth as possible; poor ones have no room for manoeuvre at all. Rich country workers can fall back on some sort of welfare; when poor country workers cannot work, they do not eat. As many as twenty jobs could be created in the poorest countries for every one lost in the rich ones.

In trying to put right a long-running injustice—after all, between 1955 and 1970 the poor countries' share of world trade fell by the equivalent of 72 million jobs—the price of change is not so very great. An immediate abolition of injurious tariffs and other barriers may not be practicable, but there must be a firm commitment by the rich to do away with them and give guaranteed access to poor country goods on fair terms.

(2) *Commodity Prices*

It would be in the interest of rich countries, as well as of poor ones, to stabilise the swings in the prices of at least some commodities. This would make it easier for them to plan ahead for the costs of their manufactured goods, and would avoid the sudden price shocks which all too easily set the inflation snowball rolling. Indeed, Lord Kaldor, when special adviser to the Chancellor of the Exchequer, said that the instability of these prices could be blamed for triggering off both the recent world-wide rapid inflation and the onset of recession. And, he added—almost heretically, considering the traditional official ideology—that the market mechanism is 'highly inefficient' in regulating the supply and demand of raw materials.

Despite occasional outbursts of horror from rich countries at the thought of interfering with 'market forces', there is now general agreement that special arrangements will have to be made. Both the countries that sell the raw materials and those that buy them accept that they should together regulate prices. Buffer stocks would be a feature of some of these arrangements. Stocks can keep prices within range through the buying up of surpluses to stop prices plunging too low and through the selling off of part of the stores to stop them soaring too high at times of scarcity. Needless to say, such buffer stocks are expensive; and any agreement to regulate prices requires considerable co-operation, not only between the two blocks of consuming and producing countries, but also among rival consumers and producers who might otherwise undercut each other.

Of course, such measures are not enough in themselves to safeguard the earnings of poor countries. Some commodities, like fruit, cannot be stored in buffer stocks. When the price of a product is continually falling, the stock may just build up into a mountain. In some cases, where a commodity is fighting the challenge of a synthetic product, its exporters may have to lower its price to stay in business. Moreover, a regulated price does little to help a producing country that suffers a catastrophic harvest.

In such circumstances, poor countries will often need to be helped by a form of insurance or 'compensatory financing'. This too is a principle now largely agreed by rich countries. It was the most revolutionary aspect of the historic Lomé Convention between the EEC and forty-six African, Caribbean and Pacific countries in 1975. The convention introduced a scheme called Stabex to safeguard the earnings from the commodities that are important to these producers. When their earnings fall below an agreed level the EEC will compensate them by lending money to tide them over until things improve. The poorest countries do not have to repay the loan. This agreement has its drawbacks, but it has served as a model.

This progress, however, is only a beginning. Commodity agreements have still to be worked out in practice, and poor countries want the insurance scheme to be improved. More crucially, they believe that it is not enough for their earnings to be stabilised. They need to get richer. Indeed, stabilising their income will merely make them poorer so long as their imports continue to rise in price. They have therefore asked for the prices of their commodities and their imports to be linked, or 'indexed'.

This demand has been treated as anathema by the leading rich countries. It is a recipe, they say, for continued inflation. The poor reply that they did not cause inflation in the first place, have suffered horribly because of it, and need some security against recurrences—a view supported by, among others, the House of Commons Select Committee on Overseas Development.

The UNCTAD secretariat spent eighteen months preparing an 'integrated programme for commodities' for its Fourth Conference, in 1976. This included a system of buffer stocks and a common fund to finance them; the improvement of compensatory financing; the removal of tariff barriers and diversification of poor country economies; and the adoption of commitments to ensure that rich countries continued to get the raw materials they need. Prices would be indexed.

As the date for the UNCTAD IV conference approached, the poor countries put all their support behind the programme. Most of the rich were distinctly unenthusiastic. They were prepared from the outset to agree that compensatory financing should be extended —but this is only one part of the whole scheme, smacks of aid, and by itself is no real answer. They were not prepared to agree to an integrated system or a common fund, insisting that commodities were so different that agreements for each one should be made separately.

This insistence might seem reasonable enough, but in fact it struck at the very heart of the poor world's position. Developing countries and the UNCTAD secretariat were convinced that an overall framework for agreements, and the money to implement them, had to be settled before any realistic negotiations on individual commodities could take place. For a start, several commodities simply cannot be considered in isolation. Copper and aluminium (which is made from bauxite) can often be substituted for each other, and so there is little use in setting up an agreement for one mineral that bears no relation to the other. Similarly any agreement over tea must take into account arrangements for alternative drinks like coffee or cocoa. Apart from this, it is likely to be much easier to negotiate a satisfactory *package* of agreements than an adequate series of individual ones. Trade-offs can be arranged in a package, enabling countries who would lose through the regulation of one commodity to be compensated by gains from the arrangements for another. Besides, some commodities are more important to rich countries than others, and poor nations learned during the negotiations over the Lomé agreement that by sticking together the producers of weaker commodities can benefit from the bargaining power of the producers of stronger ones.

In fact, piecemeal attempts to create commodity agreements over the past thirty years have almost always been unsuccessful and such agreements as were made have failed largely even to stabilise prices. One of the main reasons for the failure to establish agreements has been the lack of finance, scarcely surprising as the producers of commodities have had to shoulder the burden of paying for buffer stocks. The proposed common fund, on the other hand, would eliminate this obstacle at a stroke, by providing money from both producer and consumer countries.

Against this background, poor countries interpreted the rich world position as evidence that industrialised nations were not really serious about commodity agreements—or were only interested in agreeing on stable prices for commodities where these were important for the health of their own economies. They countered by insisting that the rich should first agree to the establishment of the common fund as evidence of good faith.

Their decision to make the fund a test case meant that it dominated both UNCTAD IV and the negotiations that followed the conference. This was unfortunate as it diverted attention from the more important issue of trade barriers at a time of increasing protectionism, and it enabled rich countries to seem to make a major concession while hardly altering their position at all in practice. For when—after a year-long rearguard struggle—the last rich countries dropped their opposition to the principle of a fund, their idea of a 'Common Fund' resembled the poor world and UNCTAD secretariat proposal in little more than name.

While the original conception saw the establishment of a fund as an essential precondition to the negotiation of agreements, the rich countries insisted that one should be set up only *after* separate agreements were concluded. While poor countries wanted a fund of six billion dollars to finance a scheme of eighteen commodity agreements and provide some money for the diversification of their economies, the rich intended it to be a much more limited operation, restricted to supporting about six individual commodity pacts. These pacts, moreover, said the critics, would cover only those commodities for which price stability was as important to consumers as to producers; and rich countries refused to provide money for an institution which, they feared, would be used by the Third World to bid up the prices of its products.

So although the principle of a common fund was agreed in the summer of 1977, almost every other question concerning it was left open for discussion in yet more negotiations. And although it looked as if some sort of common fund might be established eventually, it seemed likely that it would fall far short of the original conception.

Meanwhile little progress had been made over other aspects of the commodity issue—and least of all over how to reverse the long standing trend of the terms of trade against poor countries. Rich countries might have grown more interested in stabilising the prices of some commodities—and continued to offer to study ways of stabilising the export earnings of developing countries—but they seemed to become no keener on ideas for maintaining the real value of poor country exports against the cost of their imports, let alone increasing it. Indexation, an essential part of the proposed integrated programme, continued to be rejected out of hand. That, in itself, may be no bad thing—for a crude form of indexation could well increase the risk of a recurrent worldwide inflation which would benefit no one in the long term—but rich countries put forward no specific proposals as an alternative. They might agree to some form of automatic review of the prices agreed in commodity pacts to keep them in line with those of manufactured goods. Up to the summer of 1977, however, they only suggested that prices of industrial products should be 'taken into account' when commodity agreements were reviewed, which was not nearly strong enough for the poor.

Some way of not only compensating for inflation but of increasing the earnings of poor countries must be an essential part of any agreement worthy of the name. The compensation, at least, may be necessary to ensure stable supplies of raw materials, for otherwise poor countries may suddenly cut back production to try to keep up prices. And if such an arrangement were to stop rich countries exporting home-grown inflation to the poor, and thus encourage them to tackle it more vigorously, it might be that the problem would actually be reduced.

Of course, any system of guaranteeing or raising prices is not cut and dried in its effects. The richer poor countries export more raw materials than the poorer ones and would therefore benefit more, while rich countries which are major primary producers—like Australia, New Zealand and Canada—stand to gain most of all. Rich countries insisted at UNCTAD IV that the poorest countries might end up worse off than before; but significantly this point was mainly made by those rich countries that would lose most from higher prices, while the poorest countries—who in fact are net exporters of the commodities that would be covered—supported the UNCTAD scheme. Richer poor countries would in many cases benefit the most from both higher commodity prices and lower tariffs for manufactures, at least initially, but that is no real argument against making the reforms, and a powerful reason for providing a much higher proportion of financial aid to the poorest developing countries than at present.

(3) *Multinational Companies*

Some people regard multinational companies as the least acceptable face, not only of capitalism, but also of the old economic order. The multinationals in their turn often present themselves as great benefactors of the developing world.

No one can deny that they are extremely important. For the last quarter of a century they have been growing two or three times as fast as the economies of the world's richest countries. By 1972 the sales of the top twelve of them came to more than the income of the world's thirty-five poorest states and their billion inhabitants. What is more, they tie up a large part of world trade in a closed system; internal buying and selling among different parts of individual companies accounts for at least a fifth of all international trade.

The truth is that they are neither universally beneficial nor universally harmful in developing countries. They can provide much-needed capital investment; but in doing so they can either increase the countries' foreign debts or mop up scarce native credit that might otherwise go to home industries. They can encourage the growth of local industries by giving them contracts to provide components; or they can stifle any chance of home-grown competition. They can take risks that smaller companies would not venture; or they can knock out weaker enterprises. They can provide the country with enormous export revenue; or they can concentrate only on local sales, raise the price of imports and restrict export possibilities. They can provide important tax revenue for poor countries; but by fixing the prices they charge each other in their closed trading systems they often ensure that disproportionate benefits pile up in the parent company in rich countries. They can import useful technology; more often they keep their technical secrets to themselves. They may help countries develop much-needed managerial and business skills; all too frequently they use their superior expertise to drive one-sided bargains with poor country governments. Some may act partly from a genuine desire to help; others not only practise sharp business but infiltrate politics and foster corruption.

Of course, some companies have far better images than others. ITT or Lockheed have gained bad reputations; others, like Philips, are getting good ones; but it is not easy to work out whether in the final analysis multinationals benefit or hinder poor countries. For example, a painstaking study by UNCTAD of the operations of 159 firms in six developing countries decided that in 55 per cent of the cases the firms had a beneficial effect on the countries' balance of payments; but three-fifths of these were so near the borderline that this could be only a tentative conclusion. Even so, this falls far short of the sweeping claims of the companies and their supporters; and in general much more positive results could be expected from a less exploitative relationship. A major UN study ended by praising the social responsibility practised by some companies, but found that in general the multinationals did not do enough to control exploitative practice. Senator Jacob Javits, one of those who took part in the study, concluded that the multinationals are 'just one more human institution, at the same time fallible and useful, whose benefits can be increased and drawbacks reduced by appropriate policies'.

The Senator's view may be rather too complacent; but since the world has to live with the multinationals, like them or not, the international community has spent much of the last few years trying to work out the 'appropriate policies' to bring about reform. The OECD has recently formulated a code of practice to try to control the worst abuses, ranging from bribery to the fixing of internal prices. This does not go as far as many would wish, and the UN is working on another one. Yet the greatest opportunity for controlling many of the abuses lies in the hands of the host countries, something they often seem to forget in their imprecations against the multinationals. Colombia tackled the price fixing without losing a single company. Other countries are compelling the firms to export more of their output, and to invest more of their profits in the local economy. Meanwhile the UN is preparing a service to give expert help to poor countries who might otherwise be tricked in negotiations.

Already there are signs that the companies are prepared to be more flexible in meeting the real needs of poorer countries. They seem ready to operate in countries with tough regulations, provided that the rules governing their conduct are stable. Once there, they are vulnerable to the threat of nationalisation. Many operations cannot be moved easily, if at all, to countries with softer regulations; and the widespread adoption of agreed standards by the countries which fear exploitation would limit even the operations of such 'runaway' industries. Another fundamental, and often forgotten, issue is the economic objectives of host countries—whether they are mainly interested in capital intensive industries to produce goods for an elite, or whether they want work which gives jobs to many people and produces goods that benefit the masses. (See Chapter 6.)

(4) *Transfer of Technology*

Only 2 per cent of the world's scientific research is carried out in the developing world, and only 1 per cent of the world's patents are held by it. Poor countries therefore lack both the technology they need and the resources to develop it. They have to buy technology from the rich. By the end of the 1960s they were having to pay one and a half billion dollars for the right to use patents, licences, trademarks and know-how; more than half the amount they were receiving in industrial investment. The amount was expected to increase sixfold during the 1970s. Furthermore, the technology developed in rich countries is often not what the poor countries really need. In striking better bargains with multinationals poor countries could demand freer access to their technical know-how and stipulate that part of company revenues should be used in local scientific and technical research. They also want to reform the patent system and use other ways of transferring technology. A measure of agreement on these aspects was reached at UNCTAD IV.

(5) *Other Trading Changes*

Poor countries pay for the shipping costs both on the manufactured goods they import from rich countries *and* on the primary commodities they export to them. Something like one-fifth of all the money they earn in exports has to be paid to foreign shipping owners for using their transport, and that proportion is increasing. As 90 per cent of all their trade goes by sea, they naturally want a fairer system—and to increase their own shipping fleets. India is one country which has successfully broken the bottleneck, now having the world's fourteenth largest fleet. They also want a better share in other lucrative areas of trade like insurance, marketing and distribution.

(6) *Inter-co-operation*

One way for poor countries to reduce their dependence on rich ones would be for them to increase trade and co-operation amongst themselves. At present this amounts to only a fifth of their trades and it usually goes through commodity markets and exchanges controlled by the rich. 'Collective self-reliance' is the new slogan. Small countries, often balkanised by the boundaries drawn in colonial times, would benefit from greater co-operation with their neighbours. The Third World as a whole would gain from strengthening the economic relationships between its members. The many ideas that have been floated include agreements on preference trading and an international marketing scheme, on regional co-operation in setting up transport networks and establishing industries to process raw materials which complement, rather than compete with, one another. Poor countries agreed at two conferences during the late summer of 1976 to set up a Third World Bank to reduce their dependence on the international reserve currencies. They also decided to form co-operatives to strengthen their bargaining positions by buying what they need from the West in bulk. The producers of several commodities have got together to form cartels, and the poor nations decided to establish a council to link them together. They also decided to study ways to increase trade amongst themselves.

In the past, attempts at 'collective self-reliance' have made little progress. They tend to favour richer areas, and so the weaker ones have been suspicious. Ideas of regional co-operation, which make economic sense, may be politically impracticable. How many neighbouring countries get on well with one another? An even stronger obstacle is that history has linked them so firmly with the West that it is extremely hard to break the dependence.* The rich countries are their main markets, and they are the ones with the most money to buy their products. They also are the ones who can lend the capital or sell the equipment that poor countries need. Tied aid and systems that give preferences to rich country imports in return for favourable treatment for commodities can make it even harder

*Until recently, for example, it was impossible to fly between the neighbouring countries of Senegal, Mali, Upper Volta and Chad unless you went through Paris!

for poor countries to think of looking elsewhere. And the people who run most poor countries would themselves find it extremely hard to break Western consumer habits. Finally, poor countries cannot greatly reduce their dependence on rich ones until they become much more self-sufficient in food.

Yet as Gamini Corea, the Secretary-General of UNCTAD, says, co-operation among poor countries 'must be a cornerstone of the new economic order'. Their political co-operation has already been vital in such progress as has been achieved. The power and money of OPEC gives them more hope of economic co-operation, as well as of putting pressure on the industrialised world.

Greater economic justice within industrial nations did not come without a struggle. The demands of the poor began as polite requests. They hardened through rebuff into cynicism, to emerge again backed with the threat of power. The threat would rarely be taken seriously until it was shown to be real. Then came the crucial period. Sometimes a more just social order came about relatively painlessly, sometimes there was chaos as economic force was used (and misused) on both sides. And sometimes the struggle turned into violence and even revolution. The same path has been followed internationally in recent years, and has now reached its crucial point.

For years the poor countries asked relatively politely—and in vain—for a fairer deal. This phase ended in the failure of the third UNCTAD conference in 1972. Disillusionment and cynicism set in. The change came on the day that OPEC unveiled the oil weapon in 1973. Of course, there had been a long build-up to that day, a build-up of nationalisation, lesser increases in the price of oil and growing solidarity among Third World nations; but that day marked the transition. For though the weapon was first used as a political one, it soon became the power behind demands for economic change. It marked the first great assertion of economic power against the dominance of the developed world.

The immediate reaction is well known. Panic-stricken rich countries, abandoning any serious attempt to find a common strategy, rushed to make private deals with the countries which controlled the export of their most vital raw material. They plunged into massive balance of payments deficits, and an incipient world recession deepened into the gravest slump since the 1930s. They accelerated into an inflationary spiral, which damaged poor countries even more than the rich.

Yet, despite all appearances and protestations, the oil price increases only involved a transfer of 2 per cent of the income of developed nations to the OPEC countries. The deep troubles which followed the price rises thus tell us much more about the vulnerability of the richest economies of the world than they do about the actual proportion of wealth involved.

The price rises revealed an embarrassing lack of foresight, planning and solidarity. They also had a psychological effect. For the first time for many years, the rich countries had come up against what is an everyday fact of life for the poor—lack of control over a vital part of their economic decisions. The Western leaders' emotional denuciations of the OPEC countries at the time show how deep this went.

Conversely, the poor countries who were far more devastated by the oil price rises hardly protested at all in public. The psychological effect on them was quite different. They realised that the coup brought off by OPEC challenged the old economic order and showed that it is based not on immutable circumstances but relationships of power which can change, and change rapidly. In fact, it offered an opportunity to demand a new way of doing things—so long as the OPEC states and the rest of the Third World could form a common front.

The opportunity was seized with remarkable speed and unity. Almost immediately after the shock of the price increase, the oil exporting and poor countries were together telling the rich that they must now negotiate on a new economic order. The following spring the majority at an acrimonious special session of the United Nations called for a new order. Developed countries tabled two hundred pages of reservations.

The common front has withstood the reactions of the rich, which ranged from attempts to break up OPEC to the U.S.A.'s threat to retaliate with food power and even with military intervention. Meanwhile the threat of the oil weapon has pushed rich countries further and further into talks. Time after time the negotiations have been near breakdown, but the rich world has made it possible for them to continue for fear of what might happen if they did not.

OPEC has shown that, while the rich world's dependence on its oil lasts,* it can do more economic damage than can be inflicted upon it. It has enough wealth at the moment not to be worried about the food weapon; it can pay top prices for what it needs. OPEC countries have said that they will blow up their oil facilities rather than have them taken over by military power.

Ever since OPEC's declaration of power in October 1973 there has been speculation about whether Third World exporters of other commodities can and will cause similar upsets. The answer is almost certainly not. Other cartels have been formed, but with the exception of the phosphate producers, no group of exporters has been remotely as successful. As far as can be seen, no other cartel will be as effective in the future. The only raw material which ranks with oil is food—and that weapon, if present trends continue, will be in the hands of the rich world.

Some of the raw materials that have been proposed for cartel action, like bananas or coffee, are scarcely vital to the future of Western economies. The copper, bauxite and tin associations are more significant—but none of these materials are exported entirely by Third World countries. To achieve monopoly—or even near-monopoly—control they would have to take aboard developed countries, particularly Australia who has made it clear that she will have no part in 'blackmailing' consumers. All of them, like the rubber cartel, face competition from substitutes or synthetics. Indeed, surprisingly few commodities originate, vegetable or mineral, overwhelmingly in poor countries. A German economics ministry report shows that more than two-fifths of non-communist world mineral production is in rich countries. And though poor countries are so dependent on selling commodities, industrialised countries actually export a greater total volume of primary products than they do.

This is not to say that some cartels cannot improve things for their members.† And while there is no chance that they will have

*How long this is will be dependent on many factors, not least the ability of the rich world both to conserve energy and to develop alternative sources. But all the indications are that most rich countries will be dependent on imported oil for many years yet (see Chapters 9–12). America, indeed, is far more dependent now than she was in 1973.

†Members of the International Tin Agreement were able to increase the price of tin by 50 per cent between 1973 and 1975 by cutting back their

the devastating effect of OPEC, they may be able to disturb and unsettle the all too fragile Western economies.

If growth, and particularly the waste of resources, continues to escalate in the West many rich countries may become more and more dependent on imports. By the year 2000 the U.S.A., once the richest storehouse, could become totally dependent on imports for about ten minerals, more than three-quarters dependent for another seventeen, and more than half dependent for over twenty more. Less well endowed nations like those of Western Europe and Japan can be expected to be much more vulnerable. Already more than half Britain's industrial raw materials are imported from the Third World.

Meanwhile, though the world faces no absolute lack of minerals, there may well be shortages in several specific ones, and these could cause some parts of our economies to undergo quite rapid and painful change. Even threat of shortage could strengthen the hands of new cartels. And although poor countries may not have any important monopolies besides oil, they could still use a major share of exports to unsettle economies at least for a short time. The world would not be turned upside down, but there could be a good deal of disorder.*

There are other weapons that could be used to make life uncomfortable for industrialised countries. For example, if after setting up co-operatives to buy materials in bulk from the West, the whole of Africa decided to buy trucks exclusively from Volvö, because of Sweden's record of support for a new economic order, what would be the effect on British Leyland, Mercedes or Toyota? More frightening, perhaps, poor countries might decide to default on their massive debts. While very few poor countries might wish to do this unilaterally and risk retribution, many more might be

---

exports. The International Bauxite Association agreed on a common pricing strategy, and some member countries were able to increase their revenues sevenfold by increasing taxes paid by the companies that mined their land.

*Poor countries will go on taking over foreign companies that exploit their resources. Indeed, they have voted themselves the right to do so, through the United Nations. Nationalisations were running at 93 a year in the early 1970s. Quite apart from other effects on rich countries, nationalisations and the uncertainty brought about by the threat of takeovers slowed down exploration for minerals and investment in their exploitation and this may be an important factor in bringing about shortages in years ahead.

willing to take part in a co-operative exercise. C. Gordon Tether, writing as the *Financial Times* columnist Lombard, described as 'catastrophic' the effects that this would have on the world's financial structure. Even relatively few defaults could cause severe disruption.

Of course, the greatest power remains with OPEC. The extent of this power tends to be obscured at present, for the stagnation of rich country economies and the production from new fields, like the North Sea and Alaska, have brought a short-term glut of oil. For a while, therefore, OPEC's bargaining position is somewhat weaker. But studies show that by the early 1980s the West will be utterly dependent on the OPEC nations again. Indeed unless OPEC members (particularly Saudi Arabia) dramatically increase their oil production to meet the West's soaring demand there could be an acute shortage by the middle of the decade. They might prefer not to do this, believing, for example, that oil in the ground is more valuable than cash they cannot spend. OPEC countries would not even have to use the oil weapon, as such, to create havoc. They would merely have to decline to undertake a major shift in their present production policies.

The biggest question for the future, therefore, is whether OPEC will stand by the poor countries in their demand for change. This will be increasingly important as the economies and interests of OPEC's most powerful members become more and more entwined with those of the rich world. Will they then want to shake the house to benefit their poorer protégés? We do not yet know.

OPEC politics are complex enough even now. Certainly a reluctance among more conservative members to do catastrophic damage to the West has been partly responsible for the price freezes and relatively small increases from 1974 onwards. So have other economic and strategic factors, and the Saudi Arabian hope that the U.S.A. may be encouraged to help secure a satisfactory Middle East settlement. Yet the West would have had to suffer had it not shown willingness to talk with poor countries, and it may eventually have to pay a price if it does not make significant concessions. For the OPEC countries, diverse as they may be, are at least united in a public commitment to continue to use their power in the struggle to get a better deal for the Third World as a whole. President Perez of Venezuela, feted in Britain at the end of 1976 in the hope that he might help keep prices down, put the view of an influential moderate early in the negotiations over a new order: 'We're not going to be too hard on you—we know you would not stand for it, and in any case it would bring the house down. But we are going to lean on you enough to make you talk to us on an equal basis about planning fair distribution of the world's resources and wealth.' And since then he, like other moderates has often repeated that 'petroleum will be used as a negotiating instrument.' And Third World support in, for example, the international lobby against Israel is very valuable to most of OPEC's members.

Confrontation would probably benefit nobody in the end; and it is certainly a much worse option than co-operation.* The OPEC–Third World front controls oil exports, but the rich countries control the export of food. The rich have overwhelming economic and military superiority, but their high technology life-style is particularly vulnerable to economic disruption and to terrorism and sabotage. Both terrorist groups and poor countries may soon have nuclear weapons of a sort.

Perhaps the rich would lose least from a confrontation, yet Dr Henry Kissinger has described 'a slide into economic and political warfare' between rich and poor as the gravest crisis facing the world. He should know, for it was he who at first tried hardest to break up OPEC and to promote hardline policies.

'The universal diffusion of common means of decency and health,' wrote Dickens 110 years ago, 'is as much the right of the

*A Club of Rome study compared the different effects of co-operation and conflict between developed countries and the Middle East over the supply and price of oil. In the first scenario the Middle East applied a squeeze. Its economies boomed, while the industrial countries suffered badly. In the second scenario the industrialised countries anticipated trouble by taking action against the oil-producers. The Middle East was hurt, though rather less severely, while the developed countries did well. The third scenario assumed co-operation, where neither side went out of its way to damage the other. As a result, the Middle East economies did as well as in the first scenario, and the industrialised countries did as well as in the second one.

It is easy in this context to doubt the ethics of the rapid oil price increases of 1973. But it should be remembered, as John Cole points out, that at the first UNCTAD conference, a decade before, the rich world was offered a deal on oil and laughed it out of court. Who can doubt now that it would have been much better to have worked out an orderly system of price increases on a basis of co-operation over that decade?

poorest of the poor as it is indispensable to the safety of the rich, and of the State.' What he wrote of the Britain of his day is just as true for the interdependent world of the last quarter of the twentieth century.

Since the big oil price rises and the acrimonious special session of the United Nations that followed them, the rich and poor worlds have swung precariously between co-operation and confrontation. The first trend was towards conflict. The United States led a drive to try to unite the rich countries in resistance to the demands for a new order, and to try to break up the Third World common front. It met with remarkably little success. The Third World remained united, and many of the rich countries were seriously reassessing their relationships with poor nations.

By the spring of 1975 it was clear that the attempt to head off the thrust for a new economic order had failed, and the trend was towards co-operation. The Lomé Convention—introducing the Stabex system of compensation, and giving duty-free access to the EEC to all industrial goods and most agricultural produce from forty-six developing countries—was an unexpected breakthrough. Meanwhile Britain was working on new policies in time for the Commonwealth Prime Ministers' Conference that summer. At the opening of the conference Mr Harold Wilson announced: 'The wealth of the world must be redistributed in favour of the poverty stricken and the starving.' His actual proposals were modest, but they led to the setting up of a committee of ten experts, including a British representative, which endorsed the Third World's demands. Simultaneously France was also seeking a rapprochement between rich and poor.

In the face of this reassessment by leading Western nations, the United States also shifted her position. At the same time poor countries were making some effort to modify their more extreme demands. As a result there was a totally different atmosphere when the United Nations again met in special session in September 1975. The session had been widely expected to be another shouting match. But the changes in attitude, and careful preparation, meant that agreement was possible. The session came perilously close to breakdown, but, led by the EEC, the moderates of the rich world worked with the moderates of the poor countries to produce a result that was an almost unanimous expression of political will to create a new order.

But this was merely a declaration of intent; when negotiations began on working out a new order in practice the trend swung back towards confrontation. Attitudes hardened and such little progress as was made came painfully slowly. The UNCTAD IV Conference barely reached agreement in May 1976, and even then only did so by leaving the major issues to be tackled by other conferences. For example it produced an ambiguous face-saving resolution binding countries to study the common fund in preparation for another meeting. When that conference met almost a year later rich and poor countries were almost as far apart as ever, and this time failed even to agree on a face-saver. Meanwhile talks in Paris between twenty-seven rich, poor and oil-producing countries, originally widely thought to be more promising than the UNCTAD negotiations, ran in fits and starts, through repeated deadlocks and revivals, for eighteen months—and produced virtually nothing. By the summer of 1977, nearly two years after the declaration of intent at the United Nations, the only significant agreement was that there should sometime be something called a Common Fund. Even that would depend on rich and poor countries reaching some compromise between their widely differing conceptions of what those words represented.

Of course there are moderates and hardliners among both rich and poor countries. Indeed, there is similar competition among those who form policy within individual countries—the Treasury and the Department of Trade in Britain, for example, have promoted tough policies, while President Ford's Treasury was outstandingly conservative. Failure to make progress can strengthen the hardliners on both sides.* It also strengthens the sideliners, the Russian Communist countries, who despite their own abysmal record on aid, can say that the old economic order is a product of imperialism and so has nothing to do with them. Agreements, as at the September 1975 Special Session of the United Nations, leave them isolated, for after all the Third World can still do its best deal with the West.

*Indeed, demagoguery by militant poor countries does much to forfeit the sympathy of rich world electorates, and arouses a political atmosphere in which it is more difficult for governments to make economic concessions.

The lack of significant progress in the first half of 1977 was all the more disappointing because there was a lightening in the international atmosphere. The new American administration, with a less rigorous ideological commitment to the 'free market' played a part in the change of mood. Britain, which had slipped from the van to the rearguard of rich countries between Mr Wilson's speech and UNCTAD IV, was embarrassed by the reaction into taking a rather more positive attitude again, and Germany also seemed affected enough by the shift in the wind to make a few gestures. All this encouraged hopes that there would be a good deal more progress than there was.

As a result the rich countries, which had delayed preparing their negotiating position until the beginning of the year, looked as if once again they were only ready to give as much ground as they thought necessary to avert total breakdown and influence the price of oil. 'We too often gave the impression of being hard faced and ruthlessly self interested' said one European Minister at the end of the Paris talks. Meanwhile poor countries were unwilling to depart at all from their original demands. But despite the deadlock and the disappointment, there was still general willingness on both sides to go on talking and to try to avoid complete confrontation.

Confrontation, if it comes, will not be the greatest tragedy; the real sadness will be the missed opportunity. For despite the rather cataclysmic sound of the phrase the changes needed to create the 'new economic order' are not all that great. Both the 'haves' and the 'have nots' stand to gain from a new system, at least in the medium to long term.

A return to healthier economies in the West is perhaps a precondition for a relatively painless transition to a new economic order; although a time of recession is in some ways a good time to prepare for change (even if public opinion may be less ready to accept it). An even more important precondition concerns the poor countries. The gap between the rich and poor in the poor world itself is as great as it is between nations. Until this is changed increased wealth will mainly end up swelling the bank-balance of the rich few, and this is unlikely to encourage the rich countries to be receptive to their argument. Redistribution within countries is just as important as redistribution between them. The two are inseparable if a true new economic order is to come about.

Chapter 6

Trickle-Down Dries Up

If you stand on the clubhouse terrace of an exclusive golf course near Lima, Peru, you can look straight out on the rollers of the Pacific. Turn the other way and there is an even more remarkable sight. No rain falls on Lima, but as you turn from the blue of the ocean you can see lush greens and fairways stretching out before you. On they roll until they come to an abrupt halt at a jumble of browns and greys, one of the unspeakably wretched shantytowns that are becoming the normal condition of urban life in the poor world.* Sprinklers play on the golf course, but in the shantytown beyond there is no running water at all.

You can measure destitution in gallons. Over half of the world's people have no safe, dependable water. They have to use whatever they can find, often foetid streams, rivers and pools; and this results in intestinal diseases, the chief cause of death among the poorest citizens of the developing world. Cholera, typhoid, dysentery and parasitic infections are endemic. Two hundred million people—equivalent to the population of the United States—suffer from bilharzia; over 250 million have filariasis, the world's greatest cause of blindness; more than 100 million people a year contract malaria.

Waterborne diseases kill 25,000 people a day, but more often they debilitate. The Venezuelan Government has calculated that to provide clean water in the countryside would pay for itself more than five times over because of the new energy that better health would give the nation's workforce.

*See Chapter 15.

The golf course by the Pacific is just one symbol of inequality within the poor world. In city after city water is piped into every home in wealthy areas, while the shantytowns do not even have standpipes to share among the community. Where these people are lucky enough to have water brought in by truck they can pay twenty times as much as the rich pay for free-running tap water for their homes, lawns and golf courses. Rural areas are almost always completely forgotten. The women often have to walk miles a day, breaking their health under the load, in order to carry even unsafe water to their homes.

Wealth, of course, is more generally measured in money. There is another golf club on the other side of the Latin American continent. Once again the shantytowns press up against the greens and fairways. Their people live on about £1 a week. To become a member of the club costs more than £1,500 a year. Over Latin America as a whole, such wealth as there is is concentrated in the hands of the rich few. The amount shared between the 6 million people at the top of the economic pyramid is the same as the amount spread out among the 140 million at the bottom.

It is much the same all over the earth. The bottom 40 per cent of all the people in the developing countries receive only one-eighth of the national income. The poorest fifth in most of them share only a twentieth of it.

One of the great shocks of the past few years has been to discover that this gap is widening, even as nations have been developing. Small though their share in the world's post-war bonanza might be, poor countries have managed to achieve growth after centuries of stagnation. During the 1960s, for example, growth rates in the Third World were actually greater than those achieved by rich countries when they were developing, while over the last twenty-five years their average income per person has approximately doubled. In the circumstances this is a remarkable achievement, but it has done almost nothing to touch the heartland of the world's poverty.

In almost every country inequalities have been growing as the fruits of development have accumulated overwhelmingly in the hands of those who were already rich. Almost everywhere the poorest people have become no richer, and in many countries they have actually become more destitute.

Still stranger to conventional thinking, this has been happening even in some of the most 'successful' countries of the Third World, such as Kenya and Pakistan. The poor also got poorer during at least part of Brazil's phenomenal 'economic miracle'.

Of course, the recession of the mid-1970s has recently accelerated this impoverishment of the poor. But the point is that it was happening even in good times; for the polarisation of wealth is the result of fundamental economic and social policies that need to be changed.

'The well-to-do citizens of underdeveloped countries, who are aghast at the cynicism of the super-powers which spend billions of dollars every year on their nuclear arsenals, have indeed no reason to feel self-righteous,' comments Sham Lal, editor of the *Times of India*. 'How many of them, when they drink a glass of Scotch in the evening, feel that they are snatching milk from the mouths of a score of poor children?'

Equally there is no reason for any of us in the rich world to feel self-righteous. Because demands for fairer shares between nations are usually presented by men who perpetuate deep divisions in their own societies, that does not invalidate the need for a new economic order. It simply underlines the necessity for both national and international change. Neither will eliminate poverty without the other. And before we are too quick to blame, we should remember that the structure of most poor nation economies was set up by Western nations in colonial days, and was designed to support a tiny minority in comfort at the expense of the great majority. This structure would in any case take time or revolution to dismantle, and, of course, the temptation of the new elite to step into the colonialist's shoes instead is enormous. Indeed it was only natural that they should have done for educated in western values and economic theory—often at western universities—many envisaged Independence as a continuation of the past, free of foreign rule.

Even in our own societies appalling, and often widening, divisions exist between rich and poor. In the United States, 0·2 per cent of the people own 30 per cent of the corporate stock while 26 million people live beneath the national poverty line. Absolute poverty in the rich countries may be infinitely less acute than it is in developing countries, but the growing inequalities both between and within almost all countries confirm that greed is a universal disease.

That conclusion is hardly news. What is new is the impact of the discovery that poor people in the developing world get poorer, even when the Gross National Products of their countries grow. For it has overturned the hallowed Trickle-down theory.

Trickle-down can be seen as an enshrinement of a comfortable view; that it is the duty of the rich to become as wealthy as possible because their prosperity will quickly and automatically trickle down to the poor. Only by making a minority predominantly wealthy, it was argued, could you obtain the incentive, savings and investment needed to get economies of developing nations off the ground.

So wealth and investment have been concentrated in the cities and in the modern industries which were encouraged to start up in them. As Louis Emmerij put it when he was Director of the International Labour Organisation's World Employment Programme:

> The 'modern sector'—the cities and the new industries—was to be the engine of development pulling along behind it the entire convoy of economic and social development. The 'traditional sector'—the agricultural and rural areas—was to provide cheap petrol for the engine in the form of an abundant supply of labour as the unemployed and underemployed of the rural areas migrated to the towns where they were supposed to become fully and productively employed in the expanding industries and services.

This strategy could be sincerely advocated by capitalists and communists alike, and by people concerned more with the best road to development than with either system. For it was by this kind of process that both the Western countries and the U.S.S.R. had become rich and powerful.

Modern industries were encouraged and conditions for them were made as easy as possible. Subsidies, favourable policies on foreign exchange, lowered taxes and periods of tax exemption were provided. Poor country governments arranged the terms of trade against agriculture within their borders, just as industrialised countries have kept the terms biased against third-world products on the world market. Food prices were held down to reduce the call for higher wages in industry with very little thought of how this affected the farmers in the neglected countryside. This policy may have looked good enough on paper, but it has not worked in practice. The engine Louis Emmerij described was pulling away steadily in the wrong direction.

You can see the result in the capital of almost any of the poor countries. In the centre of the city stand the international hotels, the offices of the big industries and the multinational companies, the fashionable shops, the headquarters of the professions. This is the territory of the wealthy minority. Cheek by jowl with this westernised capital is a city of shantytowns and slums woven in around the suburbs and shopping streets. Here most of the families will be living in hovels. They will probably have no sewerage or safe running water. The average yearly wage even among those who have some kind of steady work would not buy more than a few nights in the international hotels that dominate the skylines.

I once attended a multiracial conference in South Africa. By the law of the land the only place that black and white could eat, meet and stay overnight together was in an international hotel. For those of us from abroad and for the whites it was what you would expect from a hotel of its class, large, comfortable lounges, a swimming pool, and bedrooms with fitted carpets and small, tiled, private bathrooms. At the first meeting a tall, venerable lady from the Ciskie, a leader of her community, stood up. 'When I entered my room', she said, 'my first thought was that just the bathroom would be a good home for a whole family of my people.'

The shantytown city is the real capital of the poor country, for it truly represents the conditions of poverty that exist in the hinterland surrounding the 'modern sector'. This is where the people who were supposed to be the cheap fuel for the engine have ended up. The glamour and promise of the city compared to the countryside is sucking them in, as the Trickle-down policy intended. But this is happening far faster than expected, and the jobs which were supposed to open up for them have not materialised. The workforce of poor countries is growing up to four times as quickly as it did during the industrial revolution in the West, and it is being drawn into the cities very much faster. What is more, the Western industrial revolution, at least at the start, was labour intensive. The jobs might be appalling, but there were jobs—and jobs to match the lack of industrial skill and training of most of the people. Modern industry is capital intensive, and needs relatively few skilled men. There is no room for most of the people who want work.*

Urban unemployment in Africa is running at over 10 per cent. But unemployment, meaning people with no work, is a poor measure. Third-world citizens have to work if they want to eat, they do not even have workhouses to fall back on. So as the modern sector 'engine' cannot provide employment, they go about finding and creating miserably paying jobs outside it. Familiar sights to anyone who has ever visited a third-world city are the shoeshine boys on the street corners, the sellers of knick-knacks, the people who man foodstalls by the roadside, the office cleaners and street sweepers and a host of others in both legal and illegal occupations. This is often called underemployment. Nearly a quarter of the workers in third-world towns and cities have jobs that do not provide them and their families with enough to live on. And the position is even worse in the countryside.

According to one authoritative study, industrial production on the present pattern would have to grow by an unprecedented 18 per cent a year to absorb even the increase in the labour force. If it were to absorb all the people who are already unemployed or underemployed in the cities, towns and countryside, it would have to grow by an impossible 30–35 per cent a year for ten years.

Meanwhile, because the countryside is neglected and the potential of the small farmer ignored, insufficient food is produced. The most energetic people leave for the cities, and the areas which are supposed to provide food become even more demoralised. So the Trickle-down theory has not only failed to satisfy the two most basic needs of developing countries—for food and jobs—but it has been making the situation worse. Nor is this the only malevolent result of the once comforting theory. As the rich get richer, they spend more and more of their money on imported luxuries

*Between 1960 and 1970, only about 10 per cent of the surplus agricultural labour was absorbed by manufacturing industry in the towns. During the European industrial revolution the figure varied between 50 and 100 per cent.

and on goods produced by the capital intensive—and often foreign—industries in their own countries. This results either in more money going straight out of the country or, at best, to local industries which employ, and therefore spread the wealth among, only a few people. Meanwhile the poor, in both towns and the countryside, are left so destitute that they cannot form the home market which is essential for real long-term growth.

It is sometimes optimistically argued that these are relatively short-term disadvantages, and that the Trickle-down theory would work after several generations. But even if this argument were to be correct surely the short term should be the real concern, for in the long run an enormous number of people will unnecessarily be dead. Poor countries, and the world as a whole, cannot peacefully endure even one more generation of the mounting misery of the poor. Even Brazil, in many ways the arch exponent of Trickle-down, acknowledges in its present development plan that growth will not meet the needs of the poor, and has announced that one of the main targets of the next years must be the conscious redistribution of wealth.

The new philosophy of development involves a revolution in the true meaning of the word, for it turns the 'trickle down' theory upside down. Don't concentrate on increasing wealth at the top of the poor world in the hope it will trickle down, it says. Instead, get money and employment to the bottom in the first place. In this way the poor are cared for, the countryside is developed, food production is increased and the rush of people to the cities is slowed down.

The new approach is exemplified in the Cocoyoc Declaration. 'Our first concern,' says the document,

> is to redefine the whole purpose of development. This should not be to develop things but to develop man. Human beings have basic needs: food, shelter, clothing, health, education. Any process of growth that does not lead to their fulfilment—or even worse, disrupts it—is a travesty of the idea of development. We are still in a stage where the most important concern of development is the level of satisfaction of basic needs for the poorest sections in each society, which can be as high as 40 per cent of the popula-

tion. The primary purpose of economic growth should be to ensure the improvement of conditions for these groups.

This 'basic needs' approach received official sanction from the governments, employers and trade-unionists of the world in the summer of 1976. The decisions they took at the special World Employment Conference commit them—at least in theory—to change their development strategies for the 1980s to meet the new priorities.

The moral and human case for directing development to the poorest rather than the richest is unassailable. There are also good economic reasons, for a better distribution of wealth will promote growth. The new approach does not deny the importance of savings and economic incentive, but it says that the poor have at least as much potential to use them beneficially as the rich.

Money in the hands of the poor does a great deal of work in developing the country. Instead of spending their money on imported goods and on luxuries, they usually buy simple, locally produced items. Just as the rich tend to spend money on things produced by the relatively rich, so the poor tend to spend it on things produced by the relatively poor.

A poor farmer who makes a little more from his crops one year is not going to rush out and buy a television set, a refrigerator, a washing machine or an electric toothbrush. He is more likely to spend his increased income on better housing and basic household needs, on ploughs, pumps and implements for the farm, on clothing. Wherever possible he will buy them locally. His extra money thus passes into the hands of local carpenters, masons, blacksmiths, makers of textiles and clothes and other local artisans and village industries.

When the craftsmen and workers in small local industries receive the money from the farmer they too are likely to spend it locally, on better housing, on better implements for their work, on household needs, on clothing, and above all on food from the farmer. The farmer will spend the money that has come back to him on a need he did not satisfy the first time, and so on. The money spirals round, gradually lifting the standard of life in the whole area, working hard and reinforcing its effects all the time. In the process it increases self-reliance; it creates markets for goods, encourages the development of new skills to provide them, and makes available the resources needed to produce more of them. The need is to set the spiral working. This is why authorities like Professor Gunnar Myrdal and Mahbub el Haq say that if you pursue economic justice growth will look after itself.*

Agriculture is at the centre of the process, not only because everybody needs food but because four-fifths of the poorest people in developing nations live in the countryside. For many reasons it is the obvious place to start. The world food crisis, the past neglect of the poor farmer, the dependence of the people in the fast growing cities on the food they cannot grow themselves, are just a few of them. The need is greatest in farming, but so is the opportunity. In most poor countries agriculture seems to get two or three times as much extra production out of every dollar devoted to it as industry. And the small farmers, who most need encouragement, provide the greatest promise of all.

At present the small farmer almost always suffers from discrimination. Services, credit, essential supplies, subsidies and other forms of assistance go to the bigger and richer farmers. This needs to be reversed.

But the story does not stop at the farm gates. Hundreds of millions of the rural poor are landless labourers or have too little land to give them an adequate living all the year round. They too must have a chance to prosper. Even land reform, essential as it is, will not be able to help everyone. Already in much of Asia there is just not enough land to go round, and the situation will grow worse as population increases. Furthermore, the countryside needs more broadly based development than can be provided by food production alone. The need is not just for agricultural development but for the much wider concept of *rural* development. In this way, says the World Bank, large numbers of people can be benefited at only moderate cost.

Something of the Chinese achievement is now becoming known. We do not know the whole story, nor do we know what it may

*Of course there may be some distortion of these purchasing priorities in countries that emphasise income disparities and promote a consumer society. Poor people may want to ape the rich (or be persuaded to do so by advertising) by buying luxury 'status' goods instead of meeting all their needs. But a switch to the new strategy would itself mean that this emphasis and promotion would change.

have cost. But if even only a fraction of the evidence emerging is correct, what has been achieved must be one of the most hopeful developments of the twentieth century. This is not to praise any particular system. It is a tribute to the eventual success of rural development despite setbacks and mistakes. Of course, no such thing can be said of the administration of Russian Communism, as Stalin's two million dead peasants and the state of her agriculture will testify.

Mahatma Gandhi ranks with Mao Tse-tung as a pioneer of the new philosophy. His writings contain many of the ideas which have characterised China's success. These ideas range from intermediate technology, through the encouragement of rural industry, to the famous 'barefoot doctors' who provide basic medical help in the villages.

On the more general theme of rural development, much of what is now being hailed as a new truth was stated by Gandhi long ago :

> I regard the growth of cities as an evil thing, unfortunate for mankind and for the world. Unfortunate for England and certainly unfortunate for India . . . . The blood of the villages is the cement with which the edifices of the cities is built. I want the blood that is today inflating the arteries of the cities to run once again in the blood vessels of the villages.
>
> The reason why our average life-rate is deplorably low, why we are getting more and more impoverished, is that we have neglected our 700,000 villages.
>
> The real question is how to bring about man's highest intellectual, economic, political and moral development. In this there should be an equal right and opportunity for all. In other words, there should be equality between the town dwellers and villagers in the standard of food and drink, clothing and other living conditions. In order to realize this equality today, people should be able to produce their own necessaries of life, i.e. clothing and foodstuffs, dwellings and lighting and water.
>
> The villagers should develop such a high degree of skill that articles prepared by them should command a ready market outside. When our villages are fully developed there will be no

> dearth in them of men with a high degree of skill and artistic talent. There will be village poets, village artists, village architects, linguists and research workers. In short there will be nothing in life worth having which will not be had in the villages. The reconstruction of the villages along these lines should start right now.

Throughout Gandhi's writing runs a passion to see small labour intensive industries flourishing in the villages and to avoid a virtual monopoly of industry by capital intensive factories in the cities. This, of course, is a vital part of the rural development spiral, and indeed of the development of poor countries in general.

China is thought to have more than half a million village 'factories' employing from two people to several hundred, and producing up to one-fifth of the country's entire production value. Small-scale factories have been particularly successful in producing fertiliser. At least half of the country's total employment in manufacturing and mining is in rural industries. Similarly, in the early 1960s two-thirds of Taiwan's industry had been kept out of its main cities. In Pakistan scores of small diesel engine factories have sprung up to provide for the needs of tube-wells and grain mills. In Ghana two hundred small soap factories are to be set up around the country, instead of a single big one in a major centre. Japan has had particular success in rural development.

Tanzania has embarked on a bold experiment, in bringing previously scattered, often isolated, small farmers together in villages which can be organised into co-operatives. By 1976 effectively all of the rural population was living in them. The Government can help them establish basic services like clean water, education and health care. Agricultural production can be increased, and eventually small industries can be set up. It is by no means a flawless experiment. The move to the villages was carried out at breakneck speed and, there has been some coercion. No one knows if the experiment will succeed, but World Bank officials who have studied the system believe that family incomes can be doubled within ten years. Meanwhile a rural development programme covering more than half a million people in Malawi is expected to increase family incomes by 75 per cent by 1980, double maize yields and increase production of other foods as well.

As part of the general strategy public works—like installing irrigation or building roads—can fulfil a dual purpose by providing services much needed in the countryside and by giving more work, particularly during slack agricultural seasons. The Chinese are the main exponents of this, but there have been developments elsewhere; for example, in Kenya and Bangladesh.

A massive programme of public works was one of the first plans announced by India's new Janata government, which has committed itself to a comprehensive policy of rural development. The government has promised to reverse the nation's long concentration on the 'modern sector' and to switch the emphasis to the Mahatma's old priorities—poor people and the villages. It has set out to foster agriculture, to develop small-scale and village industries, to use labour-intensive processes wherever possible, and to improve welfare in the countryside. By the late summer of 1977 it had still to work out its plans in detail, let alone embark on the difficult task of implementing them; but, nevertheless, such a change of economic priorities in the world's second most populous nation is potentially as significant for the global community as the achievements in China.

Rural development is becoming more popular with third-world governments, but it is still the exception rather than the rule, and many opportunities have been missed. Barbara Ward tells how, by coincidence, two good ideas were put into practice simultaneously but clumsily. In the 1950s and 1960s in India about a thousand regulated agricultural markets were set up to help grade farm produce and stabilise prices. At the same time small-scale industrial estates were established. Lack of co-ordination meant that only a quarter of the new estates were built to overlap with the markets. She argues that there should be integrated planning, so that regional market centres would be provided with co-operative banks, light industries that serve the simple needs of the farmers, facilities for warehousing and storage, secondary schools, a small hospital with a mobile clinic attached, and all-weather roads to link them up with the villages they are supposed to serve. This kind of planning has been done in Israel, where there is a regional centre for every six villages.

Regional centres could support and be supported by regional cities, equipped with larger industries and facilities. The cities can not only help the rural economy, but they can also take some of the pressure from the capital cities and other conurbations which are being so inundated by the refugees from the countryside. It is important to realise that rural development cannot be a complete strategy for the growth of a country. Poor countries must industrialise, and some industries *have* to be concentrated in large units. Not long ago the Chinese tried to develop their steel industry on a 'back-yard' basis—and found it far too expensive, and very polluting. While there is considerable potential for small mines, ores have to be mined where they are found, and it will usually be wisest to process them nearby. Besides, there is already great poverty in the cities, and this must be tackled in any development strategy worthy of the name.

All over the Third World the new city-dwellers are showing themselves to have remarkable ingenuity and determination, and in this there is room for hope despite the degradation of the shantytowns. People show great enterprise in finding jobs outside the modern 'formal' sector. These are not necessarily the miserable jobs associated with 'underemployment'. All over the shantytown cities little, often shaky, businesses proliferate. In this 'bazaar economy' a man may set up a small shop on the front of the shack that he has built himself as a home. Others set themselves up as shoemakers, carpenters, tailors, launderers, repairmen, even house-builders. There are estimated to be at least 140,000 such mini-businesses in Calcutta alone.

The people of the shantytowns generally find it a struggle to keep alive, and the spirit of many may be despair rather than vigour. Nevertheless, they have enormous resilience and an entrepreneurial spirit which is a considerable unused resource. Given a chance the small farmer can produce far more food than the big one. Given a chance, too, the poor city-dweller might be able to perform equal prodigies.

Once again, co-operatives can do a great deal to help. Also, the small man must be able to get credit from a better source than the traditional moneylender. 'He does not need credit in large amounts, nor does he need it at unrealistically low interest rates', says Robert McNamara, President of the World Bank. 'But he needs it without excessive bureaucratic obstruction and he needs it without procedural delays.'

Above all, just like the small farmer, the poor entrepreneur needs a change from policies which discriminate against him to those that help small businesses and industry. Colombia, as part of a 'basic needs' development strategy, is encouraging small and medium-sized industries in the cities. Japan's phenomenal economic development included one method of helping the mini-businessman that could be particularly useful in Third World countries—sub-contracting.

Most components of a bicycle can be made very well by small, labour intensive workshops and industries. But its design, its final assembly, the making of some of the parts, and its marketing are better organised on a large scale. The same can be said of many products. The Japanese therefore evolved a partnership between big 'formal' industries, and small 'informal' ones. The big industries sub-contracted the suitable components out to the small men. Both benfited—and so did the economy as a whole. The World Bank argues that industrial estates should be specially laid out with space for 'formal' and 'informal' businesses to work side by side, so as to make such sub-contracting as simple as possible.

The small man may need a less tangible kind of help from the culture and values of his country. The poor countries which have the most vigorous small-scale producers are usually those which, like the Japanese before them, have clung most tenaciously to traditional clothing, foods, housing materials and implements. By contrast most developing countries are being swamped by the uniculture of international advertising, media, and fashion—scarcely the best stimulus to indigenous production.

Helping the small man is not a matter of charity, or even merely of realising that a country's best interests lie in meeting the needs of its poor. As the Japanese found out, it is good business. A study in Taiwan concluded that small industries produced twice as much as giant ones for each new dollar invested.

Clearly there must be both large and small firms, but the large ones should be sited so that they are accessible to people who have no transport but their feet, and wherever practicable they should be labour intensive. Modern technology, so capital intensive that it can cost $50,000 or more to provide one job, is generally out of place. It can be destructive, even when it is much less expensive. Robert McNamara gives the unhappy example of a plastic shoe factory which might cost $100,000 to set up, provide 40 modern jobs, but knock out 5,000 traditional shoemakers and their suppliers. Many jobs, including construction, earth-moving, road building or electrical assembly, may best be done by labour intensive techniques.

At the same time it is oversimple to call for every process to be as labour intensive as possible. Some industries, like steel, may have to be capital intensive. And, in fact, much of the work done by the poorest people, both in agriculture and in 'informal' workplaces, needs *some* mechanical help to make it more productive.

The answer, said Dr E. F. Schumacher, is to find the appropriate technology in each case. In many situations, particularly where the poorest are concerned, this may be intermediate technology. It is far more productive than traditional techniques, and yet employs many more people than the imported 'modern' Western technology which was, after all, developed for countries where labour was scarce but capital and energy relatively abundant. Dr Schumacher maintained that people would accept intermediate technology because it often improves on existing practices instead of making a complete break with tradition. The Intermediate Technology Development Group, based in London, works on developing these techniques and putting them into practice. It has a long enough chain of successes in developing countries to convince the most practical man and to lead him to wonder why many more research institutes, and governments, are not doing the same. Much depends on the multinational companies whose techniques and priorities are generally highly inappropriate. Some, like Philips, do already use labour intensive technology. The World Bank states that when these companies are made to pay realistic rates for capital instead of rates subsidised by third-world economies they tend to create many more jobs.

Despite its advantages, some people in developing countries denounce intermediate technology. They say that to endorse it would be to accept second best, to provide a level of technology lower than that of rich countries. Their sensitivity is understandable enough in the light of the exploitation of their countries, but the people who raise this objection are not those who suffer from the so-called 'first-class' technology, they are the elite whom modern techniques best serve. And even they might consider that the choice of technology decides who will provide it. Choosing Western techniques will make their countries all the more dependent on the West; developing new ones gives them a chance to be more self-sufficient, as well as finding the best technology for the job. Moreover, as capital and energy, the powers behind modern technology, become scarcer, and structural unemployment increases, they may find developed countries eager to learn from *them.*

Time after time reports emphasise that the lack of trained people and stimulated minds is the greatest obstacle to development; and they remind us of how much productivity is lost through the endemic debilitating diseases of the poor world. Poor countries have developed their health and education systems rapidly, but they have generally failed to reach the people who need them most. This is a result of Trickle-down thinking as well as of international inequity.

There is no shortage of doctors for the relatively rich, and almost every capital city has sophisticated hospitals equipped to cope with modern diseases. Yet in many third-world countries less than 15 per cent of the rural population and the urban poor have access to any medical services at all. Ill health is so widespread among them that at any one time a third of the world's entire population is suffering from one tropical disease or another.

In many ways, it is understandable and praiseworthy enough for poor countries to want to have highly trained doctors and modern hospitals. The idea was to increase them until they covered the whole population. Unfortunately, like the rest of the Trickle-down philosophy, this has not worked. Instead, in most developing countries, the system created to serve a colonial elite has been consolidated. The countryside has been particularly badly affected. In Kenya, for example, the towns enjoy a doctor for every 800 people: in the rest of the country there is only one among every 50,000 people. In the words of one World Health Organisation official: 'Seventy-five per cent of the diseases are in the countryside and seventy-five per cent of the doctors are in the towns.'

When the provision of a single bed in a sophisticated modern hospital may cost ten times the average income of a member of the country, when it may cost more than $30,000 to train a doctor, how can poor countries possibly ensure more equitable services, even if they want to? The answer lies in the nature of the diseases afflicting the majority of the people and in the nature of the help needed to deal with them.

The main diseases of the poor world can often be prevented quite easily. Digging wells for safe water, constructing adequate latrines, even fly-swatting campaigns are much more to the point for most of the people than building modern hospitals. This reflects the experience of developed countries during the last century, when clean water supplies and proper sewage disposal were far more important for public health than the development of new cures.

Highly trained doctors and nurses are not needed to give vaccinations against such plagues as TB, diphtheria, tetanus, whooping cough, measles, meningitis, or yellow fever—let alone to administer oral polio vaccine. Nor does it necessarily take a doctor to diagnose and treat such widespread debilitating diseases as bilharzia, hookworm or malaria. This kind of work can be done by simply trained workers chosen from among the people themselves.

The best-known example of this approach followed Mao Tse-tung's realisation—nearly twenty years after his revolution—that China's medical services served less than a sixth of the people. He sent doctors out to the countryside. Even more important, China began its system of 'barefoot doctors'. There are now more than a million of them; young people, who usually come from the villages or communes in which they serve. The Chinese say that they are chosen by their own people; in practice political conformity is likely to be a more important qualification than local popularity. They work part-time in the fields and in the community alongside their patients. They are helped in simple diagnosis and cures by regular refresher courses, and simple textbooks and manuals. More difficult problems are referred to rural clinics staffed by better qualified people, and, if need be, to the regional hospital. A similar system is being developed in Tanzania, where it is found that village 'para-medical' workers are able to handle 85 per cent of cases as competently as a fully trained doctor. And successful experiments among the 400,000 traditional 'doctors' of India suggest that these people—and their counterparts all over the world—could meet the basic health needs of the rural population after proper training in a few short refresher courses.

As one UNICEF report puts it: 'An untapped reservoir of

human resources exists from which a body of primary health workers can be drawn and trained more rapidly, less expensively, and in far greater numbers than doctors or nurses can be trained.' The 'barefoot doctor' strategy provides jobs for many people and makes it much easier to involve the whole community in looking after its health. It is not the whole answer; obviously more fully qualified doctors are needed, and research on tropical diseases must be vastly increased,* but it must surely be a major part of any attempt to bring medical help to the masses in developing countries. Both UNICEF and the World Health Organisation have put their weight behind it.

The ill effects of Trickle-down thinking on education are just as dramatic. True, there was remarkable growth in the 1960s—the number of school places in the poor countries almost doubled. And yet, with governments spending nearly a fifth of their small budgets on education, more than half the children of poor countries are still receiving no education at all. Governments can hardly afford to spend any more, and it looks as if education will no longer keep pace with growing population.

The education system, like the medical one, is inherited from colonial days and angled towards an elitist society. Instead of concentrating on giving everyone at least some basic training, it is tilted towards producing more and more high school and university graduates. This is an understandable aim; but once again the Trickle-down approach has betrayed the real needs of these countries.

The 'three Rs', which more than half the children never get a chance to acquire, are still the passport to modern life. Literacy and some skill are essential for development; vocational training and simple accounting skills are important for making the most of the small man's potential. While rural development is starved of people with the training that is needed, the cities are clogged with unemployed graduates and high school students who often

*At present research into tropical diseases receives little attention—a reflection of the fact that most of the peoples who can afford to pay for medical research are not directly threatened. At present some 30 million dollars a year is spent on all of them put together—one-fiftieth of the amount devoted to investigations into cancer, *one* rich-country disease. An extra $15 million needed to intensify the work is equivalent to the cost of a few miles of motorway.

possess totally inappropriate skills. The unemployment rate of young people with secondary education is double that of those who stopped studying at the primary stage, and two and a half times that of those who received no schooling at all. And yet public expenditure is running at up to twenty times as high for every student in secondary school and further education as for children in primary school, and the more advanced the education the faster it is being expanded.

Obviously poor countries need urgently to put more emphasis on spreading literacy, numeracy and the skills needed for development. Countries as diverse as Botswana, Thailand, Kenya, Guatemala, Upper Volta and Afghanistan have launched imaginative programmes aimed at doing this. But changing the education system cannot solve the problem by itself.

Education is universally seen as a way of escaping from rural poverty. The reason that the cities are full of the educated unemployed is that there is at least some chance of getting a well paid job in them. There is no opportunity at all in the countryside, so even after only four years at school, children turn their backs on agriculture. So long as governments continue to neglect rural areas and concentrate pay, prestige and career prospects in the cities, young people will leave home in the hope of landing an urban job and their parents will encourage them to do so. Education that seems designed to keep them down on the farm will be resisted.

The whole Trickle-down philosophy has to be changed, not just the system of schooling. The same applies in almost every field; changing one or two parts of the old system without thorough reform is no answer. A comprehensive new strategy is essential, for only a major, broad and continuing attack on poverty and inequality has much chance of succeeding.

Such an attack, moreover, must also concentrate on one of the most basic of inequalities. Among the poor, women usually suffer most. In most rural societies they are the last to be fed—and so receive the least nourishment—even when pregnant or breastfeeding. And yet they have to work hard; besides child-bearing and child care, cleaning and domestic tasks, they must labour in the fields—in Africa, indeed, they do more than half the farm work. Theirs are usually the long, heavy jobs of fetching water and firewood. The work that is assisted by animals or some form of machinery is almost always reserved for the men, and most of the intermediate technologies devised so far lighten the male, not the female, load. Almost everywhere girls have much less chance of an education than boys. And in societies where they have less earning opportunities—or need dowries on marriage—female children are regarded as liabilities; so desperately poor people can be driven to pay less attention to their nutrition and medical needs, ensuring that only the sturdiest survive. In general women are treated as little more than working and breeding animals, and often are allowed no satisfying part in community life. 'The women who listen and remain silent', say one African tribe, 'are the ones whose opinions we most respect'.

There can be no real development where the requirements of half the people are made subordinate, or where so much potential is unrealised. The new strategies for growth through justice must embrace everyone.

As it becomes clearer that the Trickle-down system is not working, development experts, economists and even some governments are turning increasingly to these new priorities. If they are implemented properly they do offer real hope of success. One Third World study estimates that, given reasonable economic growth, the basic needs of everyone in Latin America and Africa could be met within a generation, and those of the people of Asia by the year 2020.

Of course, these methods are not fool-proof, nor are they proof against malevolent or lazy men. Neither is it suggested that any blueprint can be applied to all peoples, or that any one country has worked out the answer for all the others. The Cocoyoc Declaration, after defining development as placing first priority on meeting the basic needs of the poorest, puts it like this: 'The development process varies considerably from one country to another, for historical, cultural and other reasons. Consequently, we emphasise the need for pursuing many different roads of development.'

The apparent achievement of the Chinese in meeting the basic needs of all in a country where the average level of income is still among the world's lowest is amazing in itself. It becomes even greater when 'all' means more than 800 million people—over one fifth of the population of the globe. Yet other spectacular examples come from countries as different from China in ideology as Taiwan and South Korea. Tanzania is perhaps the country which has most closely followed the Chinese pattern of rural development, but its President and guiding light, Julius Nyerere, says bluntly that the Chinese system would not work in Tanzania, even if it was desirable. Few countries have the historic tradition of discipline and self-reliance of China. And development has other sides as well. As the Cocoyoc Declaration adds: 'Development includes freedom of expression, the right to give and receive ideas and stimulus.'

Clearly by that measurement both China and South Korea, to take two examples, are less developed than many nations with much poorer economic records. And those who believe that the poor are faced with a choice between food and freedom might do well to consider that when Mrs Gandhi ran an election campaign, on the basis that her government alone could ensure stability and economic growth, she was ignominously ejected from office by an electorate that was mainly concerned with the way it had been treated during her 'emergency'. Fortunately, of course, the 'choice' between economic justice and freedom is a false one, as, indeed, it was in India where the new government's priorities were much more concerned with improving the condition of poor people than were Mrs Gandhi's. Some countries have, after all, achieved balanced development without dictatorship; authoritarian governments, cut off from popular reaction, are naturally more likely to perpetuate economic inequalities than to tackle them; and even China and South Korea can trace a good deal of their success in transforming desperately poor and dispirited economies to a considerable degree of self-determination permitted at village and community level.

It is, of course, infinitely easier to work out what should be done, or to report the new thinking, than it is to do it. Few governments would find it easy to adopt a 'basic needs' strategy, even if they wanted to. Although it would benefit most of the people of the country, almost every organised and influential interest is likely to be against it. Even the trade unions, which mainly represent the industrial elite in the modern sector, would feel that their members stood to lose, at least in the short run. The ILO has called for the rural poor to form their own unions and exert pressure, but usually only a fraction of 1 per cent of the rural workers belongs to a union; their dispersion and insecurity, their very poverty and illiteracy, make it hard for them to organise or apply constitutional pressure. Often such organisations as are formed run into intense opposition.

Yet the world's governments have committed themselves to the new approach, and some have actually begun to put it into practice. With frustration mounting among the poor, and with some violent revolutions already on the record, the establishments in developing countries would be well advised to accept the need for change, just as rich countries would be wise to accept a new order.* Just as in the international system, change may require only small short-term sacrifices from the rich, and is likely to be in their own long-term economic interest as well. There are already signs that these points are being taken.

The rich world can help. Increased aid, for example, would probably be needed to help countries through the short-term shocks resulting from changing their economic strategy. Changing the way aid is provided is even more important. Tied aid can hinder the process, by making it cheaper, for example, to build a road with machinery bought from the donor country than with the hands of the unemployed. Aid would also need to be directed less at prestige projects and more to assist strategies which really meet the needs of the poor, particularly in the countryside. Agencies like the World Bank and UNICEF are directing their aid at the poorest people in poor countries, and most aid-giving countries have also announced their intention of shifting their assistance in this direction. The actual performance of rich countries has yet to match their words, and certainly there are enormous political and diplomatic difficulties involved. To adopt the principle too enthusiastically, as some have suggested, by making the giving of aid conditional on policies that really redistribute wealth in the receiving country would be to embrace another set of dangers. It would also be both hypocritical and arrogant, unless the rich country

*Ethiopia provides one example of how an entrenched and intractable elite can be brutally and quickly overthrown. The fact that one elite is often replaced by another does not invalidate the force of this argument on those who would stand to suffer from violent change. They are likely to be more worried about whether they will hang, than whether they will hang democratically.

involved was itself ready for a new international economic order. It is all very well for President Carter to say that aid is a subsidy from the poor in rich countries to the rich in poor ones; but the old economic order has long ensured that the *poor* in poor countries subsidise the *rich* in rich ones far more.

The fact is that a 'basic needs' strategy and a new economic order are inseparable. There is not enough wealth in developing countries to meet the needs of the poor, even if it were equally distributed. The economies of the Third World need to grow faster if a basic needs strategy is to succeed, even if they do not have to accelerate at the impossible rate which would be necessary to make Trickle-down work. But in the inseparability of national and international change lies hope of a tacit deal among the nations of the earth. Rich countries and their people may be much more ready to accept a fairer international system if they feel that the poor—and not the elite—of developing nations will benefit. And poor countries may agree to implement basic needs strategies as the price of a new order.

What, a critic may ask, about the growth of population? Does that not make nonsense of fancy theories, even of such successes as there have been? A new consensus, however, has thrown up some surprising results.

Chapter 7

The Impotent Pill

In the spring of 1976, somewhere in the world, a historic child was born. It was only the fourth of its kind in the history of the planet.

No baby like this one appeared for the first three million years after man arrived on the earth—not, in fact, until the early part of the eighteenth century. More than a hundred years passed before there was another, born towards the end of the 1920s, on the eve of the Great Depression. This child was in his early thirties when the third appeared, in 1960. And now there is a fourth. The arrival of each one marked the point when the number of people living on the earth reached another thousand million.

Three of the 'Billion babies', whoever they are, are probably still alive—for even the second should still be in the prime of life. In his or her lifetime the world's population has doubled; and if the same rate of growth were to continue it would double twice more in the expected lifetime of a baby born in the West today. Before he or she died, therefore, there would be another three worlds of people on top of the present one.

Population has been growing at a tremendous rate. A graph of the number of people in the world from the birth of Christ until today looks not so much like a curve as a slightly rounded right-angle. For the first thousand years the line remains almost exactly horizontal, and then it slopes upwards almost imperceptibly to show a slowly rising population. In the mid-seventeenth century it suddenly rears dramatically upwards. By 1900 it has turned the corner, and today the line is almost vertical.

By official estimates world population is growing now by 1·9 per cent a year. This seemingly innocuous figure suggests that our numbers are doubling every thirty-seven years or so, and that every year we have to feed the equivalent of a new nation about the size of Bangladesh. Whereas the population explosion began in the West, more than 90 per cent of the increase between now and the year 2000 is expected to take place in poor countries.

Although this explosion is a powerful driving force behind the various crises with which the world is faced, it is not the cause of them. The depletion of cheap sources of energy and the pressure being put on the planet by pollution, for example, arise much more from the explosion of wealth in the parts of the world where population is growing most slowly. Inequality has human, economic and social roots, not demographic ones. The food crisis is the one most tied to population growth. The issue for the foreseeable future, however, is not one of an absolute shortage of food but of distributing the sufficiency we grow, and of devoting enough resources to producing more in the right places. Above all, this means enabling the poor to buy food. China has twice as many people as India to feed from every acre of arable land, but she feeds them adequately, while India does not. The same goes for Taiwan and Bangladesh.

However, if the people of the poor world are to be fed and raised to a decent standard of living, the proliferation of population will inevitably make heavy demands on the world's resources. As it is, it has already cut away much of the ground gained. The increase in the amount of food produced by poor countries has been impressive, but in two-thirds of them it has been overtaken by population growth, so that production per head is lower than before. The same is true of development. Had India's population remained static since Independence the country would, it is said, stand on the edge of prosperity; but, since then, at least 60 per cent of its increased income has been cut away by population growth. Increasing population helps to keep people poor, by weakening the bargaining position of labour and hindering any increase in productivity per man. And if it goes on increasing at its present rate, every facility in the poor world will have to be doubled in thirty-one years and quadrupled in sixty-two years merely to keep conditions at their present low level. It is a matter of having to run faster and faster just to stand still.

Population growth in the developed countries is much less often discussed, but it, too, intensifies the crises. This is less a matter of numbers than of impact. The average North American consumes five times as much grain and—by one estimate—uses fifty times as much resources as the average Indian or West African. So while the vast majority of babies to be born in the rest of the century are expected in the poor world, those that are born in rich countries will have more impact on the world's resources.

Some time soon population growth will slow down drastically by our voluntary decision to decrease the number of births; or it will happen through an increase in deaths, by famine, pestilence or war.* But we shall have to be prepared to look after a world with many more people than we have today, anyway. For even though population growth cannot go on indefinitely, it cannot—short of real disaster—be stopped at once. It has its own momentum, like a car driven at speed. Rapid growth produces a high proportion of young people who have yet to have families of their own,† and this 'bulge' takes time to work through. Even if the brakes went on tomorrow and every couple in the world decided to limit themselves to two children, the population of the planet would go on increasing well into the next century. In fact, of course, it also takes time to apply the brakes, and this underlines the need for starting to tackle population growth as fast as possible.

One set of detailed calculations shows that if we had embarked on policies in 1975 which would arrive at an average of two children per family over thirty-five years we would eventually end up with a stable population of just under eight billion. If we waited until 1985 before starting the transition, population would rise to 9½ billion. If we delayed another ten years the world's population would reach nearly 12 billion, and if we waited for fifty years there would be 20 billion people before stability was reached. To put it in more human terms, the same researchers analysed what would happen in the next years in South-East Asia, assuming that

*Several experts reassure us that the earth is able to carry many times its existing population. But the question that concerns us is not how many people the earth can *theoretically* sustain in the future, but whether we can produce enough food fast enough to meet the needs of such a rapidly rising population. The problem is particularly acute in countries with extremely rapidly growing populations which threaten to quadruple their people in 46 years or so.

†At the moment some 30 per cent of the population of the developed nations and nearly 50 per cent of the population of the developing ones are under eighteen.

the area relied almost entirely on its own resources to support its growing population. They found that an effective population policy begun in 1975 instead of 1990 would save the lives of more than 500 million children.

The population explosion in the Third World arose out of one of the greatest achievements of our century—the fight against killer diseases like cholera, smallpox, and typhus. The average length of life in poor countries has risen from 32 years to about 50 since the Second World War. Although birth-rates have actually declined by about 7 or 8 per cent, this has not been enough to compensate for the fall in the death-rate. As Peter Adamson, of the *New Internationalist*, says, the reason for the population explosion is 'not that we've suddenly started breeding like rabbits. It's just that we've stopped dying like flies.'

Something like this happened in the now rich countries during the nineteenth century, when improvements in sanitation, public health and medical knowledge—together with more food and other resources—brought down the death-rate at a time when birth-rates remained fairly steady. As they got richer the birth-rates declined in parallel, and now population is growing in developed countries generally by well under 1 per cent a year—about a third of the rate in poor countries. Several even have stable or declining populations.

This is the classic pattern known as the demographic transition. First both birth-rates and death-rates are high, making population growth small. Then comes the period of rapid growth when death-rates fall but birth-rates lag behind. Then birth-rates fall to levels near the death-rate and there is another period of slow growth, which may turn to stability or even decline. The Third World is now in the period of rapid growth, but this does not mean that the pattern will automatically complete itself. There are several different factors.

The death-rate in poor countries has fallen much more rapidly than it did in nineteenth-century Europe; and it has not been accompanied by the development which took place there. It has not been preceded by an equivalent agricultural revolution, and there are no colonies to take the overflow. In fact, by reducing the death-rate we changed some of the conditions of health in the Third World without changing very much else.

In these circumstances, it was natural enough for people to feel that we could help the demographic transition along. If death-control had brought down the death-rate, so, the logic ran, birth-control could bring down the birth-rate. And just as medical technology had brought about the first, so it could provide the means for the second. Family planning programmes were enthusiastically started in many countries. Millions of dollars, many millions of contraceptives, and thousands of experts were poured into them. The interest of the rich world in the programmes sparked off a widespread view that the developed nations were trying to reduce the populations of the poor for their own aggrandisement. It is sincerely held, but ignores the intense and long-standing interest of many poor countries in population control.

Many people who wanted smaller families welcomed the facilities offered, but the numbers were much fewer than expected. In country after country vigorous campaigns brought about only marginal falls in the birth rate, at best. The fact is that, for very good reasons, most poor people want large families.

The Sukuma people of the village of Mwamashele, Tanzania—like the old aristocracy of Europe—have a strong attachment to dowries. When they marry the dowry is paid on the hoof. The going rate for a bride is high, between thirty and forty cows, depending on the state of the animals (and the state of the girl). But the Sukuma are a canny people. If the bride does not produce babies the dowry has to be returned. Children are so important that no bride is sold without a cattle-back guarantee.

'Everywhere in the poor world, in the large feudal agricultural communities', says Tarzie Vittachi, Executive Secretary of the United Nations Fund for Population Activities, 'there is a popular saying that "every additional child brings along its additional fortune".' An Indian proverb says, 'Each extra mouth to feed means two extra hands to work.'

In the rural areas of the poor world, where 70 per cent of the people live, children play an important part in making the family's living from an early age. They will fetch and carry water from the well, firewood to the home, meals to the fields—jobs that can take at least four hours a day. They will help in household work. The young sons may look after the livestock, help with the tilling, sowing, weeding and harvesting; they provide unpaid labour for fathers who are craftsmen. Their cost to the family is small. The arrival of a new baby does not mean moving to a bigger house or buying expensive clothes and toys as in rich countries. Their requirements are modest. As the family is likely to be producing its own food, little extra work is needed to feed a child. 'By the age of 10', writes James Kocher, author of *Rural Development, Income Distribution and Fertility Decline*, 'children are often producing more for the family than they are consuming.'

On small farms incomes can be so low that the cost of hiring one man is prohibitive. One farmer told a researcher, 'Why pay 2,500 rupees for an extra hand? Why not have a son?'

In the shanty-towns children are also an asset. Apparently it is not until parents move into apartment blocks, right into urban life, that they begin to think of limiting their families.

There is, too, always a chance that a child may prove to be clever and get a well-paid job. Or, more usually, he may emigrate to the city in the hope of finding paid employment so as to send some money home. A quarter of the rural families in one part of India were found to be supplementing their income in this way, hoping that the son in the city could help them build up savings and possibly extend the land worked by his parents, brothers and sisters at home.

Children also provide security. In old age, or illness, or unemployment, having children who are fit and working is vitally important—something we may forget in our welfare state.

It is particularly important to a poor couple to have a son, and prudent parents may well aim to have two of them. One might be shiftless and lazy and fail to look after his parents in their old age. Or he might die of malnutrition. An Indian family needs to have more than six children to be sure of having one surviving son. For although some of the great killer diseases may have been beaten back, infant mortality, like general ill-health in poor countries, has remained appallingly high, and largely neglected.

Partly perhaps for all these reasons, there are strong religious and social customs that stress the importance of children. If these were not reasons enough, there is quite simply the pleasure and satisfaction that children bring to lives that have little else to brighten them. In many countries most women are denied any satisfaction in life other than child-bearing. So while a rapidly growing population may be against the interests of poor people en masse, it is overwhelmingly in the interest of each couple to have a big family.

Tarzie Vittachi writes: 'It is perhaps a measure of the condescension inherent in the approach to the population problem so far, that the biggest lesson that has had to be learned is that poor people are not stupid.'

In fact poor people exercised birth control when they did not want children long before the arrival of modern campaigns. Professor Paul Demeny, Vice-President of the U.S. Population Council, writes: 'Effective means of fertility control have always been known and available in all societies.' Traditional African societies might expect up to a three-year interval before the next baby, and couples abstained from intercourse over the whole period. 'Women', writes Sue Tuckwell in the *New Internationalist*, 'were expected to plan their families and went through considerable self-denial to do so—backed up by great social pressure to conform.' She says the safeguards against pregnancy were often swept away by the 'modernising' social atmosphere brought about by the colonial powers.

Other practices have included marrying older men to younger women, using herbs as contraceptives and forbidding the remarriage of widows; they have also, in extreme circumstances, included infanticide.

If people want children, and for good reasons, then birth control becomes barren. You can hardly expect a couple who pray for many children to share the enthusiasm of family planners from the cities and the rich world.

In fact, the planners received a surprise or two. Trucks covered with telling posters were driven into villages. The posters showed two families. One family consisting of mother, father and two children, was obviously well fed and happy: the other, a family with six children, looked starving and miserable. The posters were visually effective, and they brought people rushing to the vans. The only trouble was that the people came to ask how they too could become like the enviable couple with six children.

Despite such setbacks, the family planners managed to give

advice and dispense large amounts of birth control equipment—only to find that the birth-rates remained much the same. Mahmood Mamdani went to the villages to investigate the failure of India's first major field study in birth control—one which lasted six years and cost a million dollars. Hakimjee, a traditional village doctor, explained to him why so many people had accepted pills but never used them:

> But they were so nice, you know. And they came from distant lands to be with us. Couldn't we even do this much for them? Just take a few tablets. Ah! Even the gods would have been angry with us. All they wanted was that we accept the tablets. I lost nothing and probably received their prayers. And they, they must have got some promotion.

In one hut Mamdani saw a religious sculpture made out of boxes and bottles. He was told: 'Most of us threw the tablets away. But my brother here, he makes use of everything.'

Some villagers in Bangladesh were even more ingenious. They accepted the pills offered and fed them to their chickens. This fattened the birds, improved their food supplies and alleviated their hunger.

In 1972 the United States Agency for International Development gave 22 million cycles of oral contraceptives to Bangladesh. It is thought that less than one million of them were actually used in the next two years or so. During the 1960s Pakistan, one of the developing countries to pioneer birth control campaigns, carried out an enormous family planning programme—only to discover that the fertility rate in 1972 was not significantly lower than it had been eleven years before.

India, the first country of all to undertake a national programme, found that in 1976 (twenty four years after the policy was adopted) less than 4 per cent of its fertile couples were using contraceptives. Three times as many had accepted voluntary sterilisation—often after being given money, transistor radios or some other inducement—but even so five-sixths of the nation's young couples had resisted all the blandishments and propaganda and were using no birth-control whatsoever.

From the Government's point of view sterilisation has the

advantage of security. For while people may decide not to use contraceptives they accept from planners or may stop using them after a while, the operation only has to be performed once. Unfortunately for the proponents of sterilisation, however, the pool of people who actually wanted the operation, (or who could be persuaded to have it by incentives or publicity) was quickly mopped up and the numbers of volunteers came crashing down. Indeed offers of the equivalent of up to 20 days wages failed to induce even the unemployed to come forward, and within six months of Mrs Gandhi's assumption of emergency powers in June 1975, compulsion was part of the programme.

Government employees were given high quotas of the number of people they had to 'motivate' to have the operation. People who failed to fulfil them could have their salaries stopped. Inevitably, abuses were rampant. Sometimes 'acceptors' were not told what was happening to them. People were clubbed down in the street, crowds herded forcibly into the clinics, villages raided and their people driven off by the truckload to fill up the quotas. Even teenage boys were sterilised. Workers were told that they would not be paid unless they had the operation. Rickshaw drivers and other small entrepreneurs were refused licences unless they produced sterilisation certificates. The issue of ration cards and obtaining of bail were both linked with the procurement of 'acceptors'. One hospital turned away people with TB and malaria unless they were already sterilised or were prepared to go through the operation *before* being treated for their disease. Besides, Joseph Hanlon and Anil Agarwal report in *New Scientist*, in the obsession with quotas no follow-up was provided for people who had undergone sterilisation. So hundreds died from tetanus and other complications.

Almost all the suffering was borne by the poorest people. It was they who could be most readily rounded up and most conveniently coerced. Indeed more prosperous people due to be sterilised were let off, sometimes on condition that they provided poor 'acceptors' to take their place. Professor D. Banerji, who was in charge of a study of the sterilisation drive, reported that it was 'a most blatant manifestation of class repression'.

The campaign seems to have been enormously inefficient as well as monstrously unjust. In the rush to fill quotas the suitability of people was ignored. Many were sterilised more than once; many others were far too old to have children. In one district 60 old age and widow's pensions were held up and the applicants told that they must be sterilised before they got the money. Dr Hanlon and Mr Agarwal report: 'In practice, the key target population—people of child bearing age with several young children—was almost completely missed out.'

Nevertheless the Gandhi Government proudly announced that seven million operations were performed in just ten months. Meanwhile the state of Maharashtra passed a bill to compel people with more than three children to have the operation, and other states began drawing up similar legislation. The Maharashtra bill also proposed compulsory abortion of pregnancies that would result in a fourth child.

While some Indian family planners—and Western intellectuals—spoke sternly of the need for these measures, others warned that, among other consequences,* the campaign would create a backlash that could wreck any hope of reducing population growth through any means of birth control. And, sure enough, the reaction came. Poor people rioted, and were shot for doing so. Family planners were murdered. Irresistible political opposition built up in the country, and was a major factor in Mrs Gandhi's landslide defeat in the 1977 elections. The whole issue of family planning was discredited through being equated with terror—just as the more farseeing experts had warned it would be. Indeed, the sterilisation campaign seems to have inspired a deep distrust of doctors and health care. And even several months after Mrs Gandhi's departure from power, menfolk would flee to hide in the fields when a strange vehicle drove into their villages.

People are bound to reject measures that will deprive them of children they see as vitally important assets, sorely needed to alleviate their poverty. It is cynical as well as dangerous for any government to force a reduction in the number of children without also reducing the need for them. On the other hand, if the need is reduced the numbers will necessarily fall. It would seem that, as

*One had warned in 1973 that compulsory sterilisation was mad, because 'it would wreck the mental health of the population, it would ruin individual families and the social climate of the country'.

happened in developed countries, the desire and need to have big families decreases as poor people become more prosperous.

Of course, a rise in national wealth that merely increases the prosperity of a small minority will have little or no effect on the birth-rate. What counts are benefits that affect the majority of the people.

Some family planning programmes in poor countries have succeeded spectacularly, often with only minimal expert assistance from overseas. In some countries birth-rates plummeted down even before family planning programmes began.

Alex Marshall of the United Nations Fund for Population Activities writes:

> Certain countries have noted steep declines in birth-rates since the early 1960s. Some of these countries have higher gross national products and higher growth rates than others. But what they all have in common are high rates of literacy, good access to health and education services, low unemployment and a low ratio of ownership of wealth as between the top 20 per cent and the bottom 20 per cent of the people. Infant mortality is low, effective land reform has been carried out, most of the farmers belong to co-operatives. In other words, the benefits of economic growth find their way back to the ordinary people.

An illustration of this during the 1960s is the experience of Mexico, Brazil, South Korea, Taiwan and the Philippines. Mexico and Brazil began as the richest of the five and remained so throughout the decade, with Mexico ending up almost twice as wealthy as any of the others. The rest started out much poorer. Korea and Taiwan achieved very rapid growth; the Philippines did not.

Despite their riches, Mexico and Brazil had the worst record in the distribution of wealth. In Brazil, for example, the income of the top 20 per cent of the people in 1960 was twenty-two times greater than the income of the bottom 20 per cent, and this rose to twenty-five times as much in 1970. The Philippines was no better at distributing wealth, though she had less to share.

However, in Taiwan the story was quite different. The income of the top 20 per cent was fifteen times the income of the bottom

20 per cent in 1953, but this was cut to only five times in 1969. In South Korea, too, the ratio became only five to one. In Taiwan the income of the lowest fifth trebled over twenty years, in South Korea it more than doubled, but in the other three there was little rise.*

The population figures reflect this record. During the 1960s the birth-rates in the Philippines, Mexico and Brazil fell only marginally. In South Korea and Taiwan, where the increased wealth had been redistributed, the fall was dramatic.

Other countries have shown similar success, including Singapore, Costa Rica and Barbados. Although they, like Taiwan and South Korea, have imaginative and successful birth control campaigns, redistribution of their varied economic growth is again accepted to be the determining factor.

The great example is China. Like Indians now, the Chinese once wanted big families.† The Government's family planning programme, which started later than India's, was twice halted for long periods during the 'Great Leap Forward' and the 'Cultural Revolution'. Yet today China feeds her people, and—though no official figures are published—her population growth rate may be as little as 1 per cent a year, which suggests that she is completing her demographic transition. During the Chinese campaigns there was intensive pressure to cut the birth rate by encouraging, and partly enforcing, later marriage and pre-marital chastity; by Party-backed community pressure through special local committees,

*If these figures are broken down further, unemployment and gross under-employment in Taiwan and Korea stood at a fraction of the level of the others. These two countries, unlike the others, had carried out effective land reform. Both of them had nearly 200 people working on the land per 100 hectares (247 acres) compared with 71 in the Philippines, 43 in Brazil and 35 in Mexico. And as a reward the yield per acre were much higher than in the other three—nearly treble in Taiwan, and more than double in Korea. In both countries virtually 100 per cent of the farmers were in co-operatives as opposed to lower percentages in the other three. Infant mortality rates per thousand births were 94 in Brazil, 72 in the Philippines, 66 in Mexico, 41 in Korea and 19 in Taiwan.

†Like India, too, China was once written off. As late as 1960 one expert wrote: 'China quite literally cannot feed more people . . . the greatest tragedy China could suffer at the present time would be a reduction in her death rate. There can be no way out. These men and women, boys and girls, must starve as tragic sacrifices on the twin altars of uncontrolled reproduction and uncontrolled abuse of the land resources.'

by developing the 'paper pill'—a perforated scrap of paper like a postage stamp impregnated with contraceptive.

The pressure that a dictatorship can put behind a policy may be repugnant—though not more so than the forced sterilisation practised under Mrs Gandhi's avowedly democratic rule in India—but there is much more to China's success than that. It does seem that the Chinese have carried through the sort of measures which reduce people's wish for children. The Government has striven hard to reduce income differences, to set up rudimentary social security, to provide schooling for every child, to feed and clothe everyone. There has been land reform, emancipation of women, health care at the village level. The people are not rich, but apparently they have sufficient.

Ironically, at the United Nations World Population Conference in Bucharest in 1974 China played the maverick, denouncing (maybe for ideological reasons) policies that it is known to practise itself. But the conference, chaotic as it was, marked a general acceptance of the new view, at least in theory.

One of the most heartening things about the practical successes of the widely varied countries that have cut their birth-rates heavily is that they have been able to do this at a relatively early stage in development. The rates only began to collapse in rich countries when average incomes reached the equivalent of about $600 to $1000. By sharing their wealth more evenly these poor countries have been able to achieve success at average incomes of only about $150 to $300. The kind of development strategies outlined in the book so far, therefore, offer a remarkably good chance of defusing the population explosion much earlier than might be expected.*

Of course, effective birth control does not stop at increasing the wealth of poor countries and distributing it more fairly. Other 'basic needs' measures that reduce child mortality, provide health services, increase literacy and appropriate education, and expand job and other opportunities for women can have an effect over and above the general rise in prosperity. Local nurses, barefoot doctors and community advisers seem better able to persuade poor people

*Ironically, implementation of the New Economic Order might help to prevent extra population growth in the rich world as well. For there is evidence that there is another development beyond the demographic transition—that families begin to grow big again when people become *very* rich.

to plan their families than Western or city-educated 'experts'. Once again different measures will be particularly important in different countries, and there can be no universal blueprint. But it is clear that the greatest successes have been achieved by countries that have adopted as many of these economic and social benefits as possible and combined them with birth control campaigns.

Contraceptive techniques are important, but clearly they have their major role to play only after people decide they want fewer children. According to the International Planned Parenthood Federation only one third of the world's people has sufficient knowledge of even one form of contraception. The fact that abortion may now end a third of all the world's pregnancies shows that there is a considerable need for less drastic means of birth control. If cheap and acceptable methods and advice are available at the same time as attitudes towards family size change, then birth-rates can fall sharply. But modern techniques and campaigns are no answer in themselves. Rafael Salas, Executive Director of the United Nations Fund for Population Activities which has taken part in the birth-control programmes of more than 100 countries, reports: 'It has been made clear that even the broadest family planning campaigns *on their own* are largely ineffective in producing a lower rate of population growth.'

In the past family planning has been applied with scientific tunnel vision, as was the Green Revolution, while the basic point is that population is about people, and their wishes, their hopes and their fears. 'Take care of the people', ran one UN-distributed slogan for Population Year, 'and the population will take care of itself'.

The question remains whether attitudes and cultural traditions which demand big families can be changed quickly enough. Tarzie Vittachi says, 'There is plenty of evidence to show that the inner responsiveness to change in outer circumstances is swift.' Experience in Tanzania, for example, suggests that a demand for smaller families and for contraception follows only five years after people begin to believe that most of their children will live: and certainly few people had such deep cultural veneration for big families as the Chinese, whether they lived on Taiwan or on the mainland. Moreover, we simply have no option but to embark speedily on this strategy. The short cut of applying birth control without changing circumstances has turned out to be a dead end.

What is more, economic and social changes are already having an effect in slowing down the world's rate of population growth. Thanks particularly to the slowing birth-rates in China and in Western countries, demographers are scaling down their predictions. At the beginning of this decade it was usual to expect a population of eight billion by the year 2000. By the spring of 1976 the accepted wisdom was that there would be rather less than seven billion people on earth by then. Since then the United Nations has reduced its estimate to six and a quarter billion, and other projections suggest that even the six billion mark will not have been reached by the turn of the millennium.

Unfortunately, there is also an ominous side to the slowing of population growth. While most of it is due to falling birth-rates, part of it comes from rising death-rates, particularly as a result of the poor harvests in the first half of this decade. This points up our choice, for at whatever level world population reaches stability, it is certain that population growth will return to near zero before many more generations have been born. Will this happen the easy way, through declining birth-rates or will it come through a catastrophic rise in deaths?

On the one hand there is the prospect of development, and sharing both internationally and within countries. That would not only reduce population growth but also look after the people already here. The more population grows, the more this approach will be needed. The alternative is neglect; and that is likely to lead not only to famine and disease but to social breakdown and maybe war of unprecedented destruction. After all, people do not blame themselves for being born.

Chapter 8

The Armageddon Factor

The doors of the world's most exclusive club have been opening recently. Ever since it was founded during the Second World War, its membership has grown only slowly; and although some of its members are bitter enemies it is bound together firmly by its motto—'mutual deterrence'. From 1964 to 1974 its membership was limited to the United States, the U.S.S.R., Britain, France and China. Then the world learned that India and Israel may have joined the nuclear weapons club. Pakistan and Egypt threaten to follow.

Other 'nuclear threshold' powers include South Africa, Spain and South Korea. Argentina has announced her candidature, saying that she can now build a bomb whenever she wants one. Brazil, Taiwan and Yugoslavia are other prospective members. Australia, Indonesia and Iran are sometimes mentioned. Libya's Colonel Ghadafi is also in the membership queue. By 1985 thirty-five countries are expected to be able to make nuclear weapons.* Naturally, if one country goes nuclear its enemies and neighbours may feel bound to follow. Indeed, quite probably, if only a few more nations acquire the Bomb 'the dam will break and the world will go nuclear'.

There is no guarantee that the new members will abide by club

*Of course, no new nuclear power is going to be able to build up an arsenal to rival the superpowers. Israel, for example, has been variously estimated as having enough nuclear explosives for between eight and eighteen Hiroshima-size blasts, compared with the U.S.A.'s estimated armoury of more than 600,000 Hiroshimas. But the prospect of even eight Hiroshimas in another Middle East war is no more tolerable; and, of course, the use of only one of the Israeli bombs might bring the armouries of the superpowers into operation.

rules. Professor Bernard Feld, one of the world's leading authorities in the field, reckons that this proliferation and the continuing arms race of the superpowers mean that there is one chance in three that a nuclear weapon will be used before 1984, and a fifty-fifty chance of nuclear war before the end of the twentieth century. Professor George Rathjens, another top authority, reckons that by the year 2000 the fatalities from nuclear conflict could have reached one billion.

The danger does not come only from the spread of nuclear weapons among states. While the drama continues on the threshold of the club, smaller and more ruthless groups (against whom the rules are unenforceable) may be breaking in at the back door. Terrorist and possibly criminal groups may soon have nuclear arms.

Neither terrorists nor nations without advanced technology are likely to produce the sophisticated weapons that are in the armouries of the big powers. But it seems that producing crude bombs with the explosive power of the one that destroyed Nagasaki will be well within their scope. Nor would the bomb necessarily have to work properly. Even a 'fizzle' could be enormously destructive.

By some calculations, radiation from a nuclear blast no larger than that from ten tons of chemical high explosive could kill as many as 100,000 people. In addition to those killed quickly by radiation, others would die later in life by contracting cancer. Others still might suffer genetic damage that could cause descendants to be born mutilated or with incurable disease.

Nor would nations, let alone terrorists, need to develop the complex strike forces of the superpowers. Even some poor countries could probably afford the cruise missiles now being developed, and find them ideal vehicles for their warheads. Metereological or sounding rockets might be adapted; and in some ways the less sophisticated the means of delivering a bomb, the harder it will be to detect. A civilian airliner capable of carrying one would not be suspected despite defences adequate to intercept the speediest missiles. It would surely be harder still to spot a truck driven into a city carrying a nuclear weapon. And all the nuclear armouries of the major nations are powerless against home-based urban guerrillas with a bomb. Indeed, states might well use terrorist groups or other sympathisers within their target nation as a means of delivery.

Presumably the bomb would initially be used as a blackmail weapon. Clearly, if the demands were made directly the source of the threat would be obvious. Even if the threat were made by a terrorist group on behalf of a state, the source might very well be traced. However, in a world where nuclear weapons of a sort were widespread, bombs might be let off without warning in desperation or revenge—and considerable damage might be done without the source ever becoming known. Retaliation would be next to impossible. What happens to 'mutual deterrence' then?

So, despite the huge disparities between the armouries of the superpowers and those that any other nation could develop, the spread of the Bomb heralds a major change in the distribution of power in the world. Small groups and nations will have a capability for destruction far beyond any weapon they have ever wielded before.* No nation or group that has nuclear weapons, however crude, can be safely ignored.

Nuclear proliferation will almost certainly arm unstable, irrational and belligerent governments. And nuclear weapons might well be used for 'rational' reasons too. Israel, for example, may well imagine herself forced to use them even at the risk of her own destruction, through what strategists have called her 'Samson complex'. Others might wish to use them in revenge or in desperation against even a 'conventional' attack. 'We may be on the verge of a world where political confrontation anywhere could be nuclear armed,' Mr Charles Yost, the former US Ambassador to the United Nations, told a Congressional hearing.

If the present talks between the rich North of the world and the poor South break down into conflict, and if nuclear weapons become widely available, might not the two developments come together? If the gap between rich and poor continues to widen, if the food crisis develops while the rich continue to live indulgently, may poor countries not come to feel that their only effective weapon is nuclear? Some of the more bitter spirits may feel that already. Might not a clandestine nuclear attack be seen as revenge for sufferings inflicted by developed countries? And would not the growing instability of poor countries, as their crises deepen,

*They could, of course, wield comparable power with chemical and biological weapons. But these are not about to be spread about the globe in the same way as the nuclear weapon materials arising from nuclear energy.

make unreasoning and desperate nuclear attacks more rather than less likely?

Rural and decentralised countries would be far less vulnerable to retaliation than developed states. Their societies might survive nuclear attack on their main centres, whereas the complex and urban societies of developed countries would not. This view, right or wrong, might encourage a variation of the 'Samson complex'—a 'David complex', if you like—among bitter or bellicose poor governments.

Robert Heilbroner, the philosopher and social scientist, has already said, 'Wars of redistribution may be the only way in which the poor nations can hope to remedy their condition.' Barbara Ward and Rene Dubos write:

> If developing nations were as ignorant as Pharaoh's slaves of 'how the other half lives' they might toil on without protest. But the transistor and satellite and worldwide TV have put an end to that kind of ignorance. Can we hope that the protest of the dispossessed will not erupt into local conflict and widening unrest?

The Club of Rome agreed, and added: 'Unless this lesson is learned in time, eventual nuclear blackmail and terror will paralyse further orderly development . . . Ten or twenty years from now it will probably be too late.'

In the end nuclear blackmail would cease to be an effective weapon of wars of redistribution. Some retaliation, however random, would be made. The result would be likely to be nuclear anarchy. The breakdown of relations across the world would be only one basic cause of the holocaust. Another would be the spread of nuclear weapons among groups and nations, and nothing is more likely to bring that about than the wide distribution of 'the peaceful atom'.

Once upon a time the barriers in the way of making nuclear weapons were virtually insurmountable to most countries. But now, according to a study carried out for the Ford Foundation by Professor Mason Willrich and Professor Theodore Taylor, one of the most brilliant bomb-designers America has employed, there is enough information published in the open literature on nuclear technology to tell anyone how to make a crude bomb.

Much more important has been the new availability of explosive materials needed to make a bomb. Obtaining them, say Willrich and Taylor, was always considered to be the most lengthy phase in building a nuclear force; it involved the setting up of a costly and complex system of plants, which was beyond the reach of most governments, and impossible for terrorists. Now, they say, 'more than enough fission explosive material will be available immediately to a government that decides to acquire a nuclear force if it has access to a civilian nuclear power industry'.

In America and Britain nuclear energy developed out of the production of nuclear weapons. Now the process is likely to work in reverse. Professor Edward Teller, the 'father' of the H-bomb and an advocate of nuclear energy, says bluntly, 'The operation of any reactor produces materials which can be used to make nuclear explosions'.

Nuclear materials suitable for weapons have been mainly confined to the military installations of a few nations. Now the rapid growth of nuclear energy threatens to spread similar materials to hundreds of power stations and other plants all over the world.

Three materials used for nuclear fuel could also be employed to make a bomb—plutonium, highly enriched uranium, and uranium 233. By common consent, only small amounts of any of them would be needed.

Plutonium, created by any reactor which uses natural uranium, is by far the most common of the three. At one time all the plutonium in the world was kept in a cigar box in a storeroom next to the office of one of the men who had discovered it. Already it is being produced by the ton from civilian nuclear power stations. Soon there will be more plutonium in the hands of industry than there is in all the weapons of NATO.

Normally, however, the plutonium owned by industry will be different from what is in the warheads. The best plutonium for making nuclear weapons, we are told, is plutonium 239. If the plutonium is removed from a reactor soon enough, that is what it will be; but the longer it remains in the reactor the more it is vitiated with other isotopes, such as plutonium 240. Generally it becomes quite heavily affected. Since for all practical purposes the isotopes cannot be separated, nuclear optimists come to believe that the plutonium produced by power stations could not be made into bombs. This myth has long bred complacency about the consequences of producing plutonium.

People who actually know how to make bombs, however, have been warning for years that such complacency is out of place. Dr Taylor said in 1973, 'There is, good, better and worse, but there is no non-weapons grade plutonium in the nuclear industry'. The Ford Foundation study he co-authored concluded that the other isotopes could make bomb-making more difficult and even more risky, but would not prevent the plutonium being useable in fission bombs very likely to produce explosions in the kiloton range. Dr Carson Mark, Director of the Theoretical Division of the Los Alamos Laboratory, where bombs are designed for the United States' nuclear armoury, added his voice to the warnings, and a study at another leading US nuclear weapons centre, the Lawrence Livermore Laboratory, concluded that 'an entirely credible' national nuclear arsenal could be produced from power station plutonium. Perhaps the United States may have finally convinced those who stubbornly stuck to their illusions. She recently tested—and exploded—a bomb made of nuclear industry material.

Willrich and Taylor concluded that illicit bomb-makers would need only 24lb. of highly enriched uranium, 10 lb of uranium 233, or 9 lb of plutonium, if these materials were in their most suitable, metallic, form. Expert bomb-makers—such as a nation could employ—might need 'significantly less'. Amateurs, it went on, could produce a Nagasaki-sized explosion from about 22 lb. of plutonium oxide, the principal form of the element used in the nuclear power industry.

Contrast the tiny amounts needed for making bombs with the huge quantities that will soon be turned out by the world's nuclear power industry. Dr Frank Barnaby, Director of the Stockholm International Peace Research Institute, estimates that the industry is already producing about 20 tons of plutonium every year and has accumulated about 100 tons. The rate of production is rising rapidly, and by 1985 we are likely to have 500 tons in stock. So by then we would be sitting on stocks that could produce some 50,000 Nagasaki-sized explosions, even through the work of amateurs. More than a third of this plutonium, Dr Barnaby goes on, will be owned by countries that do not now have nuclear weapons.

Just because this material is produced, it does not mean that it is going to be stolen by thieves or diverted by governments for bomb-making. But even if only one ten-thousandth of the world's stocks got into the wrong hands the prospects would be terrifying.

Building an atomic power station may be a nation's first big advance to the nuclear club. A typical reactor produces enough plutonium every month to build a bomb with the yield of the Nagasaki explosion. At the end of 1975, nineteen countries had nuclear power reactors. By 1985 nearly forty nations may have them.

Fortunately, the current generation of nuclear reactors present no real danger in themselves. You cannot just take the plutonium out of the back end of a reactor and put it into a bomb, for it is mixed with other radioactive products, including highly toxic wastes. A separation or reprocessing plant is needed. With one of these and a power station, however, you have the main facilities to be a nuclear power.

Once it was thought that the separation of plutonium would be an obstacle to proliferation, but now it is accepted that nations would have little difficulty in setting up a simple reprocessing plant. The necessary information was made public as long ago as the start of the unfortunately titled American 'Atoms for Peace' programme in the 1950s. Countries, including India, Argentina, Spain and Yugoslavia, have already built them. Nearly half of the countries expected to have nuclear reactors by 1985 are hoping to have their own reprocessing plants as well.

Although reprocessing was developed to produce plutonium for weapons, it is the key to the next stage planned for the development of nuclear energy—the so-called 'plutonium economy'. Once the plutonium is separated, it can itself be used as a fuel for nuclear reactors. It can be recycled through some of the present generation of reactors, and it is expected to come into its own with the fast breeder reactors which are now being developed as the long-term basis of nuclear power generation. These reactors, which have so far only been operated as prototypes, are not only fuelled by plutonium, but actually produce more of it than they consume.

There are therefore strong commercial pressures to go ahead with reprocessing, even though the plutonium economy would make raw material for bombs widespread as fuel for power stations.

Other developments promoted by the nuclear industry may open up another route to the weapons club, through highly enriched uranium, which can be used not only to make atomic bombs but also to act as a trigger for the much more difficult and secret H bomb. Natural uranium, which is a fairly widespread element, or low-enriched uranium which is used for most nuclear reactors, can be enriched still further for making bombs.

A civilian uranium enrichment plant produces fuel for power stations, not material for bombs. At the moment almost all the uranium passing through these plants is taken out after it has had only a low level of enrichment; for the current generation of nuclear reactors do not use more powerful material than this. Limited amounts of highly enriched uranium are used in research, and some proposed fast breeders and the high temperature gas-cooled reactor (HTGR) would use it as fuel. The HTGR which is being developed in Germany would produce uranium 233, the third dangerous material. But while the nuclear industry is set on reprocessing plutonium, it is far from convinced about developing these other reactors, and they may well never go into production. More serious is the danger of the proliferation of the uranium enrichment plants themselves.

In the past uranium enrichment has been extremely complex and secret. This has held up the spread of nuclear weapons. But already less complicated processes, more easily used for producing weapons-grade material, are being developed. And what will happen to secrecy as the commercial demand for highly enriched uranium grows?*

Much the most worrying work is being done by the Soviet Union, Israel and the United States on using laser beams to enrich uranium. Experts say it will be very much cheaper, quicker and easier than any other method. Indeed, it may even become so

*Already there has been some proliferation of knowledge. One nuclear threshold power, Iran, has a major stake in an enrichment plant being built in France. Some details of a new German process have been published and Germany reportedly helped South Africa, another nuclear threshold power, to develop a variation upon it.

simple, says one energy analyst, that 'a generation hence an exceptionally ingenious schoolboy will probably be able to enrich significant amounts of uranium in the cellar'. Quite apart from the dangers which this would present in the hands of terrorists or criminals, it would give every country with either stockpiles or deposits of natural uranium the ability to make weapons-grade material for itself. It is likely, however, that the laser will be developed commercially. 'Who', asks Sir John Hill, Chairman of the United Kingdom Atomic Energy Authority, 'is going to ignore a process which might conceivably be so much cheaper?'

Fortunately, considering this kind of attitude, one means of uranium enrichment might actually make the world safer. In May 1977, the French Atomic Energy Agency announced that it had developed a fairly simple chemical process which enriched uranium to the low levels needed for nuclear fuel, but which could not be adapted to produce the highly enriched material necessary for bombs. We do not yet know whether the process will be practical (the French say that it will not be proved commercially until the end of the next decade), and it is only one positive line of development among several which increase the risk of proliferation. But, if it works, it could offer nations another chance to keep the uranium route to the bomb under control—if they adopt responsible policies.

Until recently virtually nothing had been done to prevent a rush of new members into the nuclear club. As Dr David Owen, U.K. Foreign Secretary, admitted in the summer of 1977, 'politicians have allowed the urgency and dangers to be swamped by commercial interests and bureaucratic indifference'. Indeed, governments have strongly supported the unintentional contributions of their nuclear industries to the risk of atomic war.

Nuclear reactors are the merchandise of a handful of technologically sophisticated nations. The United States has been the most successful exporter. Russia and Germany have both been selling. Among Canada's sales has been the reactor which helped India to produce its bomb; among France's potential customers is Libya, one of the last countries of all to seem to need nuclear energy for peaceful purposes. Britain might have pulled off exports recently too if she had had a reactor design that anyone had wanted to buy.

Nor have sales been confined to reactors. In 1975 France agreed to sell reprocessing plants to South Korea and to Pakistan, whose President at the time, Mr Bhutto, once said that his people would make the bomb 'even if we have to eat grass'. And West Germany agreed to sell Brazil a complete 'nuclear kit', including both enrichment and reprocessing facilities as well as reactors—a deal which would seem to offer Brazil a choice of either the plutonium or the uranium route to nuclear weapons.

Germany included these two dangerous technologies as 'sweeteners' in a multibillion dollar contract for reactors. Meanwhile all Western nuclear exporting governments have been offering concessionary financing to promote reactor sales. The more an industry's expansion is delayed at home the keener it will be to sell abroad—preferably, one suspects, to authoritarian governments where opposition is unlikely. And at least the small nuclear industries, like those of France, Germany,—and Britain, for that matter —depend on exports to achieve economies of scale. The same pressures would be likely to require the export of fast breeder reactors if they are developed—indeed these nuclear industries are already determined to sell them abroad. This means that customers would either need reprocessing plants as well or would have to be provided with plutonium for fuel. The export of the fast breeder would be particularly ominous for another reason too —part of the plutonium it produces is almost pure plutonium 239, and so particularly useful for weapons.

While the nuclear salesmen enthusiastically circled the world with their wares, there was only a feeble international agreement aimed at stopping their ploughshares from being beaten into swords. This was the Nuclear Non-Proliferation Treaty, first agreed in 1968 and still in force. Under this treaty countries which do not have nuclear weapons promise not to obtain them, while nuclear powers agree that they will aim to move towards disarmament. Countries without nuclear weapons can be provided with nuclear technology, equipment and material so long as it is subject to international 'safeguards'.

More than one hundred nations have signed and ratified the treaty. However, and more important, the list of those that have not done so includes half the countries with the technology to make the bomb* and several more of the countries who plan to get it soon. Most of these are unlikely ever to accept the treaty, and are, indeed, the nations most likely to divert nuclear materials to weapons. This by itself ensures that the treaty is powerless to stop proliferation.

Moreover, such value as the treaty does possess is being undermined by the nuclear exporting powers. With a curious blend of cynicism and naïveté, they have continued to sell nuclear materials and technology to countries like Pakistan, Brazil and South Africa which have neither signed nor ratified the treaty. Why be party to the treaty when the service is available anyway?

Also, what assurance is there that even those who have agreed to it will not make bombs? There could be a change of mind, a change of regime or a change of circumstances. A reprocessing plant may still be operating in twenty years' time. Which country, particularly in the Third World, can be sure that it will not have at least one revolution or political upheaval during that period? Diplomats are usually reluctant to make predictions of political behaviour more than five years ahead. The Lebanon once seemed an unusually stable Middle East country—but what might have happened if she had had a reprocessing plant at the time of the 1975–6 civil war?

It would not take necessarily a dramatic change of regime or circumstances to make a country change its mind. The Canadian equipment that gave India her start on the road to producing a nuclear bomb was acquired by the peace-loving Pandit Nehru. It is unlikely that either party would have been perturbed had they known that in twenty years the ruler of India was to be Nehru's own daughter. Yet it was under her rule that the country produced its first nuclear explosion.

Nations can legally renounce their membership of the treaty at three months' notice; and since the treaty allows nations to research and develop nuclear weapons so long as they do not actually make them, non-nuclear countries can lawfully go to the very brink. Experts agree that if the material and parts are ready

*Nor have the nuclear powers, France and China, signed, though France, with Gallic individuality, has agreed to behave as if she had.

the final assembly of the weapon may take a week or less. A nation might even continue to be a member while making her own weapons in secret. Tests might not be necessary; the Hiroshima bomb was never tested.

The treaty's defence against such covert action is international inspection. All non-nuclear powers that sign and ratify the nuclear proliferation treaty agree to accept safeguards enforced by the United Nations' International Atomic Energy Agency (IAEA). But, at best, these safeguards can only detect the diversion of nuclear material away from peaceful purposes, not guard against it. That is all they are designed to do. To prevent diversion there would have to be an international agency which, in effect, ran part of a country's security system, and was able, if necessary, to resist force from the host country. As Professor Taylor and Dr Willrich write, 'The interest in safeguards in the international community is nowhere near that strong.'

The safeguards are based on adding up, checking and accounting for all strategic materials. They rely partly on information provided by the country itself, checked by occasional inspections, which the national authorities could prevent. All this means that it could take weeks or even months to detect the disappearance of plutonium, by which time weapons could be built. Indeed, a diversion might *never* be detected. Accountancy systems are never perfect,* and have margins of error built into them. When the amounts of material needed to make bombs are so small, a margin of error which is statistically acceptable may be strategically dangerous. At present, at least a 1 per cent margin of error for plutonium is said to be unavoidable. Even if this could be cut to a tenth all over the world within a few years, so that the accountancy was 99·9 per cent effective,—'an impossible task'—enough plutonium could still hypothetically be diverted without detection to produce a nuclear weapon every week.

What happens even if the International Atomic Energy Authority does find out that a country under its inspection is diverting nuclear

*The amount of plutonium that has been created in each fuel element that goes for reprocessing is generally not known precisely. Then no process ever achieves 100 per cent conversion—there is always some loss or gain of material that cannot be fully explained. Even after conversion, materials get stuck in the machinery. No means of measurement are perfect, either.

materials? Dr Rudolf Rometsch, the agency's inspector-general of safeguards, replies, 'I would refer it to the Director-General of this organisation. He would refer it to the board. They might order an additional investigation or, if the case was crystal clear, would refer it to the Security Council of the United Nations.' It seems a cumbersome, and far from reassuring, procedure. More than one third of the countries on the agency's board have not ratified the non-proliferation treaty themselves; indeed several of them are among the nations thought most likely to develop nuclear weapons. And even if all the countries on the board do manage to agree that a serious infringement has taken place, we can expect no more from them than a report to the Security Council—scarcely the world's most decisive or effective body. The Agency itself has no authority to recapture materials.

Hitherto very little atom-bomb material has been produced in non-nuclear countries, and so the shakiness of the safeguards system has not been crucially important.* Now the planned proliferation of nuclear power and the enthusiastic salesmanship of the countries with nuclear technology have made this a very urgent issue indeed. But a conference held to review—and hopefully strengthen—the Non-Proliferation Treaty in May 1975 achieved virtually nothing.

At about this time the nuclear exporters at last became concerned. The United States, the Soviet Union, Britain, West Germany, France, Japan and Canada began a long series of secret meetings. But the talks failed to prevent the crucial deals between France and Pakistan, and Germany and Brazil.

By September 1977, after over two years of meetings, the nuclear exporters had achieved two things. They had expanded the talks to include eight other nuclear nations, all from the developed world and agreed to widen membership so that customer nations could also take part in future; and they had concluded a gentlemen's agreement on safeguards. On the whole the agreement does more to show up the inadequacy of the old regime than to inspire confidence in the new one. For example, the exporters have agreed to sell important nuclear equipment to nations that

*The material that is thought to have provided India and Israel with nuclear weapons was made in plants not subject to safeguards.

have not ratified the Non-Proliferation Treaty only on the condition that it is covered by IAEA safeguards; to seek 'assurances' from purchasers that the equipment would not be used to make any nuclear explosives, even 'peaceful' ones;* and to obtain agreement that similar rules and safeguards would be applied to any of the technology re-exported to other countries.

Although the agreement does include some new requirements, its safeguards are even weaker than those applied under the Non-Proliferation Treaty. Parties to the treaty have to place all their nuclear facilities under inspection. But under the agreement clients are only obliged to submit to safeguards on the facilities they import or derive from imports. Anything they design and construct themselves is exempt, and it may be hard in practice to decide what has been derived from imports and what has not. How do you regulate knowledge, particularly when so much is already known about reprocessing technology? Furthermore even a plant directly copied from an imported one is likely to be only subject to safeguards during a limited period, and the IAEA has anyway no authority to search for or inspect such plants.

The whole approach to safeguards does not seem particularly promising. Presumably, more rigorous checks could be devised if nations were interested enough in them. But they could do little more than stop up some of the more obvious loopholes. They could, for example, provide resident international inspectors at nuclear plants instead of relying on occasional visits. A uniform set of rules would also be important, for at present each safeguard agreement is negotiated individually between the IAEA and the country concerned; the results vary allowing nations to stand out for minimal surveillance. An instant system of sanctions against offenders is also essential. Even the best arrangements can provide no real security against national diversions in themselves, however, and in fact members states of the IAEA are increasingly resisting proposals for strengthening the feeble ones we have got.

Stricter safeguards—arranged, perhaps, through the nuclear exporters meetings—must be an essential part of any strategy to

*'Peaceful nuclear explosions' are earth-shifting blasts indistinguishable from nuclear weapons. Signatories to the Nuclear Proliferation Treaty agree not to make them, but nuclear powers are obliged to provide them—under international control—to those that want them.

combat proliferation, but such a strategy needs additional lines of attack. Professor Enrico Jacchia, a former director of nuclear safeguards in the EEC, writes: 'Safeguards are not safe. It is unrealistic to believe, and dangerous to let people believe, that nuclear safeguards may become the adequate instrument to prevent the proliferation of nuclear weapons. The ways to cheat international safeguards are innumerable, like the ways of the Lord.'

While other nations were insisting that safeguards provided adequate protection, the United States was developing a more realistic policy. She has altogether refused to export enrichment or reprocessing plants and she increasingly tried to convince other countries to do the same. She persuaded South Korea to cancel her order for a reprocessing plant. Finally, after repeated rebuffs, her policy began to be taken up. France and Germany, while insisting on fulfilling their agreements with Pakistan and Brazil, indicated that they would not make any more like them 'for the time being'. Hope grew that there might be an internationally agreed moratorium on the export of these particularly dangerous technologies.

Some people, particularly advocates of nuclear expansion, argue that stopping such exports is a useless and even counter-productive gesture. They say that any nation that is determined to have a nuclear bomb can have one, and no amount of commercial self-restraint will alter that. They point out that countries can now build their own reprocessing plants, and argue that it is better to sell them ones with safeguards than force them to build their own facilities free from inspection.

Up to a point they are right. Many nations can build their own simple plants to separate plutonium, although they may need help from abroad to build bigger, commercial-sized ones. But it will take them time to do so, and time is all-important.

If a country already has a reprocessing plant—and has secretly prepared itself, experts agree, she can have a nuclear weapon in days, if not hours. No safeguards can prevent nations switching plutonium from civilian use to bombs, or detect the diversion in time to give any warning. But if she has to start from scratch by building her own reprocessing facilities, and maybe a small reactor, the process is likely to take several years. This gives her neighbours and the international community time to find out what she is doing and to try to stop her. It gives them a chance to apply diplomatic or political pressure, to try economic or even military sanctions. It also makes it easier for them to discover her intentions, for with a civilian reprocessing plant she can seem to have a purely peaceful nuclear industry until the last moment.

More important, the very availability of plutonium is likely to influence the nuclear decision. Many governments would think carefully before embarking on a long and costly bomb programme. They could expect their enemies to retaliate, probably by setting out to get nuclear weapons themselves. They could expect international pressure. And they themselves might well be out of office before their bombs were ready.

But if the plutonium were already available in a civilian industry, the arguments for having a bomb would be very much stronger. Governments might think it prudent to have contingency plans for switching the plutonium to weapons, should there be a threat to national security. Any such threat, real or imagined, could lead to the rapid acquisition of the bomb. So could the whim of a belligerent government or a madman. And, fearing that this might happen, the neighbours of such a country might also think it wise to have access to nuclear arms. Thanks to mistakes in the past there is no absolute security against proliferation. But we can at least refuse to compound these mistakes by selling dangerous nuclear plants around the world.

There is, however, a more compelling argument against a ban on exporting reprocessing or enrichment plants than the one deployed by those who say that proliferation is inevitable anyway. Such a 'solution' would be seen to be unfair, and would therefore be unstable, for it suggests that only a few rich countries are responsible enough to have sensitive technology. One of the main reasons why countries have failed to become part of the Non-Proliferation Treaty is that it seems to endorse a similar inequity, attempting to stop history at a point favouring a few powers who already have nuclear weapons. Indeed, American pressure to rescind the agreements with Brazil and Pakistan has already increased third-world determination to use plutonium as a fuel.

Such an arrangement seems to threaten the independence of the second-class nuclear nations as well as their dignity. For if they are to have neither of these plants they will be dependent on the few first-class nations for their nuclear fuel. At present most reactors need enriched uranium, while the fast breeders that are so confidently expected to form the next generation will need plutonium as well. If nuclear power is going to be as important to poor countries as the nuclear exporters have been telling their governments for the past twenty years this arrangement would mean they were placing an important part of their economies at the mercy of foreigners.* European countries have been developing their own enrichment plants to break dependence on the United States. The spate of agreements to export enrichment and reprocessing in 1975 is sometimes ascribed to a temporary halt in United States supplies of enriched uranium in 1974. And Brazil has made it quite clear that she wanted the complete 'nuclear kit' so as not to be beholden to other countries for fuel. For these reasons no two-class system can be imposed for ever, and a moratorium on exports, though necessary to slow down proliferation at present, cannot provide more than a breathing space.

So in 1976 the United States, the International Atomic Energy Agency and some independent experts proposed various kinds of international reprocessing and enrichment centres. On the face of it, these promised several advantages. International control would ensure that safeguards could be enforced more easily, and should secure supplies. Moreover, the number of plants would be limited. The idea that these could be established by regional co-operation, however, soon began to look shaky. Imagine the difficulty in deciding which country in a region should have the plant on its territory, particularly when there is little that could be done to stop that nation moving in its army so as to embargo supplies to an enemy or make materials for bombs. And, naturally enough, the nations giving most cause for concern about their nuclear intentions are those least likely to collaborate with their neighbours.

All the same, some kind of system of international centres for enriching uranium might work. So far, at least, the technology has remained sufficiently expensive and secret. Most countries might well be glad to forgo the cost of building a plant if only they

*In fact nuclear energy may not be nearly so important to them (see Chapters 11–12), but this fact is not appreciated by more than a handful of poor country governments, and so does nothing to assuage their sense of outrage.

could be sure of their supplies of fuel; and maintenance of secrecy could make certain that they had no option. Alternatively the new French process could be safely exported if and when it proves practicable. Either way the international community could make sure that countries got material enriched enough for power stations but not for bombs.

This cannot be said of international reprocessing centres. The point of reprocessing is to separate out plutonium for use in fuel and so eventually will be sent out to reactors. It makes no difference whether a country reprocesses its own plutonium or imports it from an international centre. Indeed, the very existence of international facilities would probably spread the material to countries that would never have reprocessed it for themselves.

It is sometimes said that mixing the plutonium with uranium, either in powerstation fuel elements or even during reprocessing, will be a safeguard. But nations could easily separate the two materials again.

The establishment of international plants may give reprocessing false encouragement, for the need to reprocess spent fuel and embark on the plutonium economy at all is coming increasingly into doubt. The technology of big commercial plants,—much more complex than that of simple separation ones—is proving more difficult than expected, and the economics of it are looking less and less favourable. This means that a new and unexpected opportunity is arising which offers an equitable way to slow proliferation. Reprocessing could be halted everywhere, at least for a time.

At Easter 1977, President Carter grasped this opportunity. He announced that reprocessing would be deferred indefinitely in the United States nuclear industry and made it clear that he hoped the rest of the world would follow his lead. He promised to increase his country's output of low enriched uranium to ensure adequate supplies of nuclear fuel—an essential goal for any strategy to prevent the spread of dangerous nuclear facilities—and suggested that spent fuel elements could be stored under international control with the plutonium still mixed in with the intensely radioactive wastes.

The rest of the world had to take his proposals very seriously, for the United States can force compliance with her reprocessing policies. She supplies almost all the non-communist world's enriched uranium fuel and can lay down what happens to it after it has been used in power stations. She will probably retain this near-monopoly for about a decade, and shortly after the President's announcement she showed that she was ready to use the power it gives her. She told the world's nuclear industry that she would only allow her nuclear fuel to be re-exported for reprocessing in exceptional circumstances, when reactors were threatened with closure because of 'extreme congestion' in spent fuel storage. And she delayed Japanese plans to start testing a small reprocessing plant of her own. Since no country had yet begun reprocessing modern nuclear fuel on a large scale, and since plans to do so, as in the proposed expansion of the British facilities at Windscale, depended on secure supplies of imported fuel to be viable, this seemed to be an attempt to halt development altogether. Meanwhile Canada, who, with the United States, provides more than two thirds of the West's uranium ore, was taking a similarly tough line.

Almost all the other main industrialised countries, however, strenously opposed the new policies. Europe and Japan felt that they needed plutonium much more than did the United States, as they had smaller energy resources. Many of these countries also believed that, as pioneers of the plutonium-using fast breeder reactor, they had won a rare lead over American technology—and they had no intention of giving this up. Several defiantly announced that they would go ahead with both reprocessing and fast breeders—and the Russian communist bloc said that it would do the same. And bit by bit, as the summer went on, President Carter had to modify his approach.

Presumably the United States can still have her way if she is determined to do so. But if she vetoes reprocessing she will cause a breach with most of her principal allies, so long as they remain in the same frame of mind as in the summer of 1977. A tough unilateral policy also risks provoking chauvinistic reactions that could endanger such fragile progress as has already been made over such matters as the export of dangerous technologies. Furthermore, the power given by a near monopoly of enriched uranium supplies is a double-edged weapon. Using it, or even threatening to do so, can encourage the proliferation of both enrichment and reprocessing plants as a counter-measure.

So while President Carter's initiative has provided a remarkable chance for the world at least to pause before entering the plutonium economy, a great deal depends on the attitudes of other countries —and of their public opinion. They should consider not only the dangers of proliferation, but the threat of nuclear terrorism.

Ever since the great powers started stockpiling nuclear weapons there have been grave fears of thefts by terrorists. Indeed, an article in the 'alternative' magazine *Undercurrents* has even suggested that the troop and tank movements around Heathrow and other European airports in January 1974 may have followed just such a theft. But it would be the increasing availability of bomb materials through the spread of *peaceful* nuclear power which would make the danger of the 'People's Bomb' really serious.

Experts say that even the strictest precautions cannot eliminate the risk of theft. In these days of international terrorism, the defences against terrorist action are only as strong as the security precautions of the least vigilant country. Unfortunately, there is plenty of evidence of the ability of governments, and the firms and people handling the materials, to fail to take the risk seriously enough.

Naturally, countries wish to keep their security arrangements secret:* little is known, for example, about the arrangements in Britain. They have been most publicly examined in the United States. The U.S.A. has more than half the world's nuclear power capacity, and is no stranger to organised crime or urban violence; so it would be natural to expect her to take the greatest care.

Yet Professor Willrich says that as he and Dr Taylor worked on their Ford Foundation study they became convinced that the

*Indeed, it may be thought irresponsible to write about the subject of nuclear terrorism as I do in the following pages. But I decided to do so for two reasons. The first is that the risk from nuclear terrorism is small at present, but threatens to increase with a nuclear programme and to be with us for a long time once it has become established. Were it only a temporary danger, or one which could not be almost entirely averted by a change of policy, it might be right to say nothing. As it is the public has a right to know about it before the decisions are taken that would commit us to a world where the threat was really serious. The second reason is that the people who might misuse the information given in this chapter (which is widely available) are already aware of it, even if the public as a whole is not. Furthermore, this chapter gives none of the basic, or detailed, information needed for obtaining materials or making a bomb; indeed I do not know any of this myself.

United States Government had examined the problem only superficially and sporadically, and that much of the nuclear industry was largely unaware of the seriousness of the risks involved. Indeed, as recently as 1973 the United States Atomic Energy Commission, —then responsible for the nation's nuclear industry—had itself admitted, 'Almost no standards exist in the materials protection area and in many cases such standards have not been developed.'

During that year Congressional investigators visited three plants containing atom-bomb materials—a small fraction of the number in the United States. They reported many disturbing features at two of the three, including unlocked windows and vents without alarms. In one plant they found that they could break into a storeroom for these materials in fifteen seconds, without needing to use any tools but their hands; in another they found the job would take one minute and a wrench. USAEC inspectors had reported security in both plants as 'good'. Indeed, until regulations were improved at the end of the year hundreds of pounds of plutonium or highly enriched uranium could be stored in a locked building, checked by an unarmed watchman only once every four hours.

In 1974 alone nine companies in the United States nuclear industry were fined for breaking or failing to implement security regulations against theft, intrusion or sabotage. And the United States Atomic Energy Commission produced its own report which confirmed the insecurity of strategic materials.

In Britain the Royal Commission on Environmental Pollution noted a lack of attention to security when visiting nuclear installations. Anthony Tucker, Science Correspondent of the *Guardian*, reported that a press visit to Windscale—where British reprocessing is done—'revealed a number of obvious security weaknesses'. He added:

> An 'inside' operator could certainly 'divert' plutonium pellets and even carry them out of the plant without serious risk of discovery under present security arrangements. Unless there exist hidden security forces which are adequately armed, a group of twelve well trained guerrilla troops could certainly force an entry into the plant and, with relatively little advance knowledge of the storage system, make off with an incredibly potent haul of plutonium.

It seems that governments have begun to wake up to the dangers only recently. Though it is generally admitted that attackers would be heavily armed, it was only at the end of 1975 that guards were authorised to carry weapons routinely in Britain. Similarly that same autumn when a lovesick girl climbed the fence of the Kerr McGee plutonium plant in Oklahoma City with a shotgun, Congressional investigators were told that if the weapon had been loaded she would have had the two guards 'outgunned'.

Fortunately, so far as we know, no terrorist or criminal group took advantage of such conditions, and lately both Britain and the United States have paid far greater attention to the matter.

Security has been strengthened in both countries. The precise measures taken are kept secret, but we are told, for example, that in early 1976 some two million pounds was spent on strengthening fences, vaults and alarms and communications systems at British sites. The authorities admit, however, that these can only 'deter and detect' a serious attack, holding the fort until reinforcements can be called up. Clearly, details of such reinforcements are generally not made public either, but some inquiries have elucidated that it might take over an hour to reach a remote sight under attack, and we can only hope this time has since been reduced.

United States reports show, however, that security arrangements still need to be increased considerably, in that country at least. Its nuclear authorities recently found that only about half the licensed facilities handling significant amounts of plutonium and highly enriched uranium could resist an attack by just three armed men. This kind of vulnerability can surely be reduced, but it is hard to imagine how any system could guarantee security against a determined, well-armed force without being enormously expensive. It may be that the few sites that use nuclear materials at present *could* be (and, for all we know, now may be) adequately guarded, but if these were to proliferate with the coming of the plutonium economy, the danger of weak spots would surely increase and the cost of effective security could prove prohibitive.

The problem of preventing theft by employees seems even more intractable. This is because measures to stop such diversions are at least partially dependent on the same kind of accountancy as international safeguards and are subject to similar margins of error. Indeed the U.S. has said that it is already 'missing' 8,437 pounds of plutonium and highly enriched uranium, within this margin enough for some 300 bombs. Most of this 'material unaccounted for', here and in other countries, is certainly only 'missing' statistically or is locked up in pipework and machinery, and from time to time nuclear authorities give assurances that none has been stolen. But they have no way of knowing that their confidence is justified.

As long as an inside operator took only small amounts—and, after all, only small amounts are needed for bombs—the theft would be unlikely ever to be detected. One graphic illustration of this turned up at the beginning of 1976. One day an audit in a Tennessee plant showed that sixty-six pounds *more* of weapons-grade uranium had come out of a process than went in. It seems that this occurred because of an insurance scheme operated by workers. For some time, apparently, they had been collecting a secret cache of uranium during processing to safeguard themselves in case an audit ever showed that too much of the material was missing. One day the computer showed that sixty-six pounds had gone, so the workers put in uranium from their cache to make up the difference. Unfortunately, the computer had made an error, and so the excess turned up. Presumably, what could be done to set up an insurance scheme like this could be done to steal uranium altogether. Indeed, a thief need not even be that subtle, for since it takes time to work out accounts it could be a while even before quite a large theft was discovered.

Of course, other safeguards beyond accountancy can be implemented; but one expert, given the job of keeping track of plutonium at a reprocessing plant, put the problem simply. 'If you are not able to employ trustworthy people', he said, 'then you can design no physical materials system that can override them—because there is always some way to work around it.' And the methods for ensuring that people are trustworthy seem far from foolproof. Kerr McGee hired as one of its first guards a convicted bank robber, Leonardo Crusher, operating under an alias. When a credit card company uncovered his past, the firm fired him. Six months later he was arrested again and is now serving a 103 year jail sentence for armed robbery and attempted murder. When asked in the summer of 1977 how Mr Crusher could have been given such a job, an expert at the Nuclear Regulatory Commission, the body in charge of security for the US nuclear industry, replied: 'There were, and at present are, no requirements that guards have security clearances'. The Commission, he said, was proposing that this should be done in future, but if someone were to falsify his records he could 'conceivably' get through such a security screen. In Britain, we are told, employees are screened by procedures that have been used for many years in the Civil Service and defence organisations. This provides some comfort—but not much when one recalls some of the great spy scandals of the past decades.

Employees are also searched, though apparently there were complaints at one American plant that the automatic monitors used to detect whether workers were carrying plutonium were sometimes just not turned on. Despite the precautions, some nuclear material does seem to have been taken out of American facilities without authority.

Miss Karen Silkwood, a 28 year old technician employed by Kerr McGee, died in a car crash in 1974. She had complained about safety conditions in the plant and died on her way to see a *New York Times* reporter. Her flat, more than 25 miles from the plant, was found to be contaminated with plutonium, and the Nuclear Regulatory Commission has admitted this shows that small amounts of the material could be taken from the facility. A worker at a different plant walked off with 50 lbs of uranium in 1969. According to Mr Peter Stockton, a Congressional investigator, the worker was apparently merely interested in taking a box and only found when he got home that it contained the uranium. Scared to admit his discovery he had put it in his cellar. Nobody seemed to notice the disappearance, and the uranium was only found two years later when company officials went to the worker's home on a totally different mission. The same plant was allegedly unable to account for more than 350 lbs of highly enriched uranium in 1965. According to a report in the *Washington Star* the CIA concluded that most of this ended up in Israel.

Yet nuclear plants are, at present at least, supposedly the strong points of the system, far more secure than the transport links between them. Some years ago John McPhee spoke to William Brobst, whom he describes in his book *The Curve of Binding Energy* as the chief of a United States Atomic Energy Commission department dealing entirely with transport. Brobst said:

> In trucking there is constant pilferage, day-to-day theft, 'shortages.' Of all the freight of any kind that is shipped in this country, one to two per cent disappears. Holy mackerel! Is this going to happen to our nuclear materials? The trucking business is a mass of crime. Eighty-five per cent of its thefts are by authorised people—that is, by people who belong there. Four out of five truck hijackings involve collusion—the drivers are in on it. The nuclear business has vaults, fences, alarms. They have great machines to count atoms. Then they take all these atoms, lump them into a drum and toss them out into crime.

At about the same time, another expert announced that amounts of nuclear material sufficient to make dozens of bombs were lost as a matter of routine. One shipment had been unloaded at the wrong airport and left unattended. Another bound for St Louis from Ohio turned up nine days later in Boston under a load of shoes.

In 1977 the world learned, nine years after the event, that 200 tons of uranium ore bound from Amsterdam to Genoa under Euratom safeguards had disappeared on the high seas. The ore itself could not be used for bombs, but officials suspected that it had been taken to Israel's reactor, which, of course, could use it to produce plutonium. It provided a foretaste of the dangers that would accompany the export of plutonium itself, whether from national or international reprocessing plants, for, as Mr Hans Schleicher, Euratom's safeguard director, commented: 'Safeguards cannot prevent such a thing'.

Even if by some magic we could eliminate crime and negligence in transport and ensure that everyone who took a key part in transporting nuclear material by road, rail, sea or air was scrupulously honest and careful, or completely covered by similarly trustworthy security officers, we would still be in danger. Any form of transport, particularly a truck, must be harder to guard from attack than a plant or store. It will probably be staffed by fewer men. It should be easier to penetrate; and even if armed guards or the design of the container can hold off an attack for long it may be very much harder to get reinforcements to the scene fast enough.

At present, says the United Kingdom Atomic Energy Authority, *occasional* shipments of plutonium, made into fuel for the British prototype fast breeder reactor at Dounreay are carried in secret from Windscale in bullion vans; such vans have not proved impregnable when containing mere money. Yet if fast breeders spread as hoped there will come a time early in the next century when hundreds of such shipments will be needed every year. The Authority might decide to replace the vans with the massive armoured casks that carry the highly radioactive 'spent fuel' from reactors to the reprocessing plants in the first place. This would probably be advisable, for it must be much harder to break into them to steal plutonium. On the other hand, the amount of shipments would have to be doubled, and terrorists might still be able to use them to create immense damage.

The Authority sometimes suggests that it could eliminate the danger of theft in transport by making the shipments protect themselves. Spokesmen say, for example, that the fuel could be 'spiked' with radioactive wastes or irradiated in a special nuclear reactor before it ever left reprocessing or fabrication plants. In this way it could be made so radioactive that it would kill any terrorist that tried to handle it. This might work—after all, highly radioactive *spent* fuel is already transported from reactors to reprocessing plants. The Authority began a costing exercise in 1977. But a study carried out for the United States Nuclear Regulatory Commission earlier concluded that any method of irradiating the fuel or 'spiking' it with radioactive materials would be far too expensive and hazardous ever to be practicable.

The United Kingdom Atomic Energy Authority argues that the fuel would be unattractive to the malefactor anyway. Fast breeder reactors or conventional power stations using plutonium would be powered by a combination of plutonium and uranium, and the two are mixed in each pellet of fuel. These, it is said, would have to be separated again if terrorists were to obtain the material needed for a bomb. Unfortunately, the Ford Foundation study concluded that the separation could be 'fairly easy' for a terrorist group.

The Authority can advance these 'solutions' because in Britain the same site is designed both for reprocessing old fuel and for making the new fuel needed for fast breeder reactors.

There is obvious sense in minimising transport of dangerous materials, and it is even suggested that it could be eliminated altogether. This would involve grouping fast breeder reactors on the same sites as reprocessing and fuel fabrication plants. But although it is an attractive idea there would be enormous practical difficulties in putting it into effect. Although the Atomic Energy Authority has often suggested it, the British electric power utilities have rejected it as uneconomic; and when the Ford Foundation study put forward the idea in the United States it was rejected even more vehemently.

Although many security measures can be taken to reduce the risk of theft it seems that none, singly or in combination, can eliminate it. As Sir Brian Flowers, Chairman of the Royal Commission on Environmental Pollution and a member of the United Kingdom Atomic Energy Authority, concluded after a long study: 'Plutonium offers a unique and powerful weapon to those who are sufficiently determined to impose their will. In these circumstances, I do not believe it is a question of *whether* someone will deliberately acquire it for purposes of terrorism or blackmail, but only of when and how often.'

His Commission recommended accordingly that, if possible, the development of plutonium as a common fuel should be avoided altogether. At present this development has yet to take place and relatively little of the material has been produced, so the Commission was satisfied that existing security measures rendered the risk small. But it did not hide its concern that Sir Brian's fears could be realised if the plutonium economy came about.

Proliferation may ensure that a terrorist group in a country with good safeguards may never have to go to the trouble of stealing bomb material. Rather a black market may begin. It would be a lucrative business for a criminal group. The price of plutonium is comparable to the black market price of heroin, and the open market price of highly enriched uranium is even higher. The black market price of both would certainly be higher still. A uranium smuggling ring has already been uncovered in India—after it passed materials worth £1 million out of the country through Nepal.

If the laser technique for enriching uranium is as simple as has been suggested, and if it becomes widely known, terrorists will have no difficulty in making their own bomb material. It is going to be hard enough to protect the dangerous material produced by industry. How can we possibly hope to guard every deposit of uranium ore on the face of the earth?

How much does it matter if terrorists do get hold of plutonium, highly enriched uranium or uranium 233? Will they be able to do anything with it? Unfortunately, the answer appears to be that they will.

The Ford Foundation report calculated that terrorists—and conceivably just one person working alone—could design and build a bomb within weeks. After this conclusion was challenged, a television producer commissioned a 20-year-old chemistry undergraduate to design one in five weeks. The student, who remained anonymous, had no previous knowledge of nuclear engineering. He worked alone, and was allowed access only to public books and documents. It took him three weeks to master the elements of nuclear engineering to his own satisfaction, and another two to design a bomb which he reckoned would need some 15 lb. of plutonium. A nuclear scientist at the Swedish Ministry of Defence* said that there was 'a fair chance' that, if the bomb were built, it would go off, though with a relatively small yield for a nuclear explosion.

The student said, 'I have come to feel that designing and building a bomb—assuming you had the plutonium—would not be much harder than building a motor cycle.' Apparently he was constantly refining the design even while writing it up, and, it is said, would have come up with a much more credible version in another few weeks. Since then there have been several similar exercises in the United States and Britain. One of the British ones, carried out for the *Guardian*, specifically took one fuel rod for a fast breeder reactor as its starting-point. The success of such crude designs may not be guaranteed; but as the Swedish expert who reviewed the first one commented, 'the fact that the bomb *might* go off is the important thing'—particularly when the purpose is blackmail, perhaps the most likely terrorist or criminal ploy.

Professor Feld says:

'Let me tell you about a nightmare I have. The Mayor of Boston sends for me for an urgent consultation. He has received a note

*It was first sent to leading weapons experts in the United States. They refused to comment in case they violated their security clearances.

> from a terrorist group, telling him that they have planted a nuclear bomb somewhere in Central Boston. The Mayor has confirmed that 20 pounds of plutonium is missing from Government stocks. He shows me the crude diagram and a set of the terrorists' outrageous demands. I know—as one of those who participated in the assembly of the first atomic bomb—that the device would work. Not efficiently, but nevertheless with devastating effect. What should I advise? Surrender to black-mail or risk destroying my home town? I would have to advise surrender.

In 1970 the nightmare nearly came true when the authorities of Orlando, Florida, received a threat for money accompanied by a drawing of the much more secret H-bomb, so convincing that they had to take it seriously. It turned out to be a false alarm, and the hoaxer to be a 14-year-old boy.

Some experts insist, however, that it is very difficult to *build* a nuclear bomb. A spokesman for the National Radiological Protection Board, one of the main watchdogs on the British nuclear industry, told me that the possibility that a nuclear bomb could be made of the plutonium used in nuclear energy was 'one of the myths of the business'. 'It is bloody difficult to make the bomb,' he said. 'Your problem of a bomb is not one that really worries us.'

But on the other hand, the old United States Atomic Energy Commission, before its demise, accepted that someone with 'a moderate knowledge of high school chemistry or physics' could produce an explosion that could kill as many as 50,000 people.

In Britain the Royal Commission on Environmental Pollution, concluded that a 'crude but very effective' weapon could be made with equipment little more elaborate than that already used by criminal groups to manufacture heroin. Indeed, the British Government has also conceded that making a bomb would be possible.

When eminent bomb-designers are also among those who are convinced that terrorists can make a nuclear weapon the burden of proof that it cannot be done rests with those who promote and defend the 'peaceful' use of nuclear materials. There is no sign of this proof; indeed, it seems to be more and more unlikely to be forthcoming. All experts say that the process would be difficult, but nobody should underestimate the ingenuity and determination of terrorists.

And even if the optimistic ones were right after all—even if terrorists could not explode the material they stole—we would have small cause for comfort. For plutonium is dangerous used as a poison as well as an explosive. A ball of plutonium the size of a grapefruit would be sufficient for a nuclear bomb. It would also be sufficient, if it were possible to distribute it evenly,* to kill nearly all the 4,000 million people alive today. Comparisons of poisons can be extremely misleading but, to give some guide, the Ford Foundation study said that, in terms of the total weight needed to give a lethal dose, plutonium 239 was at least 20,000 times more toxic than cobra venom, and 1,000 times more poisonous than heroin or modern nerve gases, if less toxic than some biological weapons. So any terrorist, criminal—or lunatic—who gets hold of plutonium has a fearsome weapon even if he chooses not to try to make a bomb.

The dispersion of only a small amount of plutonium could have the most devastating results, not only on people but on the environment. 'The ubiquitous nature of such contamination,' declared the USAEC, 'absolutely defies description.' An area that has been contaminated would either have to be abandoned indefinitely or cleaned up at horrendous cost. When a mere teaspoonful of plutonium was blown out of an American nuclear plant everything in the area had to be sprayed with paint to keep the deadly material from spreading further. Even after this, so one description goes, 'it took eight months of vacuum cleaning, scrubbing, scraping, chipping, acid-burning, digging, burying and asphalting to "relocate" the plutonium and restore the site.'

Plutonium 238, which is even more poisonous than the material used in bombs, is also becoming available. While it will not explode, it is three hundred times more toxic even than plutonium 239. Tiny amounts of it—less than a fifth of a gram at a time—are already being used to power new heart pacemakers. In the future, some say, people may be fitted out with nuclear powered hearts, containing up to 60 grams of the stuff—enough, in theory, to contaminate 400 square miles a time. If plans to do this are realised could terrorists, criminals or lunatics, resist the lure of so

*Of course, it is *not* possible to do this, and so this figure serves merely to illustrate the extreme toxicity of plutonium.

much plutonium? And while it is unlikely that they would go to much trouble to get hold of the tiny amounts in present-day pacemakers, these do seem to present an unnecessary risk, however small, to their wearers and to the public. For non-nuclear pacemakers are being developed with all the advantages but none of the drawbacks of the plutonium ones.

We can no doubt expect such a compact power source as plutonium to be used for other 'unconventional' purposes. If these are developed the would-be thief would have more and more sources to choose from—sources which, like nuclear powered hearts, might be impossible to guard.

Plutonium is far from being the only poison produced by the nuclear industry. Highly radioactive materials are carried from nuclear power stations to reprocessing plants. These would be dangerous for terrorists to handle. But might they not mine a truck or railway wagon carrying them? The New York Department of Health has barred the transport of nuclear wastes through the city precisely because of this risk. Dangerous radioactive wastes have already been used maliciously; in April 1974 carriages on the Vienna–Rome express were contaminated with radioactivity by a self-styled 'justice guerrilla'.

Another possibility altogether is that terrorists might sabotage a nuclear power station or factory. This would presumably take some skill to accomplish. Nevertheless, a former director of the USAEC has warned that 'a band of highly trained, sophisticated terrorists could conceivably take over a nuclear power plant near a major city and destroy it in such a way as to kill thousands—perhaps millions—of people'. Already there have been some disturbing incidents. In the summer of 1975 there were three bomb attacks on French power stations and workshops, while in Germany an MP carried a bazooka past guards and detectors at a reactor and presented it to the director. Two years earlier a band of fifteen terrorists occupied a nearly completed nuclear reactor in Argentina for twenty-four hours.

'Terrorists will not resort to nuclear arms so long as they can make enough impact with more conventional tactics.' 'They will be reluctant to provoke international co-operation against themselves by using nuclear weapons.' 'If I were a terrorist I would not be interested in nuclear power because other things like chemical factories or tankers present much easier targets.'

There is a strand or two of consoling truth in all these theories, but they are slender threads on which to hang our security. Unfortunately, terrorists must innovate to be effective. The main aim of most groups is to publicise their cause, and this is best done by grasping hold of public attention. If the world's imagination can be seized with an impressive coup, the strength of the group and the importance of their cause will be exaggerated in the public mind. Nuclear power offers a unique potential for doing precisely that. No weapon would be more dramatic than a nuclear bomb, none would have more of an effect on public emotion. Sabotage of a nuclear power station, or the dispersion of nuclear poisons, would also be likely to pose much more dramatic threats than those based on 'easier' targets.

Wide enough international co-operation to deter nuclear terrorism seems enormously unlikely, particularly when several countries may well find it convenient to use terrorist gangs on their own behalf.

Perhaps the biggest flaw of all is that these theories choose to disregard the irrational in human nature. The people who advance them assume that terrorists choose their methods by reasoning similar to their own, uninfluenced by emotions such as hatred, the wish for power and the desire to cause maximum sensation or effect.

By the same reasoning you might expect terrorists to be put off by the dangers of handling nuclear material. These dangers would be considerable—by one estimate you would run a 50 per cent death-risk during the theft of plutonium, followed by a 30 per cent risk in making a bomb.* But the threat of losing their lives has not proved an effective deterrent to terrorists in the past.

Anyway the argument is becoming academic, for, as recorded above, there have already been minor attempts at nuclear terrorism.

*It could be a particularly horrible death: Walter Patterson tells the story of Harry Daghlian, a physicist who accidentally allowed a sample of fissile material to go critical while he was handling it. 'His hands and body were raked by a massive burst of radiation . . . . Admitted to hospital within half an hour, Daghlian lost sensation in his fingers, then complained of internal pains and finally became delirious. His hair fell out. His white blood cell count surged as his shattered tissues tried vainly to cope. It took him twenty-four days to die.'

The sober fact is that governments—and nuclear industries—are at last accepting that sooner or later terrorists will turn their attention to the atom, and are taking precautions.

Ironically, these precautions pose a new danger of their own, a danger to some of the most fundamental freedoms of democratic societies. For the thought of nuclear terrorism is so horrific that the public may be ready to submit to enormous constraints to their civil liberties to try to avoid it.

This may already be happening. A slim four-page Act slipped almost unnoticed through the British Houses of Parliament in the spring of 1976. It met no really serious opposition, for both main parties accepted that it was an unpleasant necessity. Yet for the first time in Britain the Atomic Energy Authority (Special Constables) Act armed a private police force and empowered it to go anywhere and arrest anyone on suspicion of having committed a crime. Since the special constables are just another technical service of a nationalised industry, it looks as if the Government cannot intervene in their normal affairs or be responsible to Parliament for their activities. Although this was pointed out during the passage of the Act, the Government fought off amendments that would have created a clear line of accountability. It may well be that Government responsibility was deliberately avoided because it would interfere with the paramount task of guarding nuclear materials; that flexibility and furtiveness may have to be so essential a part of the constabulary's job that the public knowledge of its activities gained through parliamentary questions and the like could inhibit it in its work.

In the light of these developments it is worth considering what further freedoms might have to be sacrificed to the cause of avoiding nuclear terrorism. For this disturbing situation has been created to cope with the security of a nuclear industry which is still in its infancy at a time when the threat of terrorist action is only beginning to emerge. At the moment plutonium is essentially an experimental fuel; what further measures would be necessary for when it was in widespread use as the basic source of our electricity?

Quite extraordinary measures will surely have to be taken. Constant and secret surveillance of the public is thought to be inevitable. Wide powers of general search might have to be granted for use in an emergency, for the rapid recovery of any stolen material would be essential. Habeas corpus might have to be suspended, and the public might not be particularly squeamish about the means used to interrogate people suspected of being able to give information.

Much of this might take place even if no incident of nuclear terrorism ever took place, for some of these powers would be necessary to prevent an incident, and others would have to be granted in advance to cope with the emergency when it arose. The very presence of plutonium and other dangerous materials in large quantities would be sufficient. And if there *were* an incident, the public outcry for even stronger measures might be irresistible. If our energy supplies had begun to become dependent on dangerous nuclear materials, we would not have the option of stopping their use, but would just have to tighten security. However, as we have seen, even the tightest security would be illusory, for there seem to be no measures that could prevent theft, and none that could eliminate the human error and corruptibility that can negate the most careful precautions. Indeed, the kind of authoritarian society that might have to be created could provoke the very social upheavals that might lead to the use of nuclear weapons. We could be caught in a particularly vicious circle.

In the summer of 1976 the Royal Commission on Environmental Pollution took the British Government to task for not taking this danger seriously enough. Indeed, Sir Brian Flowers, its Chairman, said, 'The Government seems to have preferred that we should not be made aware of these problems.' Yet, as he also added, 'in the end the kind of society we have is more important than the amount of electric power we have got'.

What ways are open to us to reduce both the opportunities and motives for people to use nuclear weapons? The most obvious way to restrict opportunity is to stop the development of nuclear technology all over the world. David Ennals, when Minister of State at the British Foreign Office, said as much. But even if it were wise completely to close this option for producing energy, it would be extremely unlikely that this could be achieved. So much momentum has been built in, so much capital and interest and so many careers and reputations are at stake—and so much knowledge is now available so widely—that it would take an unprecedented pressure of opinion all over the world to call a halt. Ironically, almost the only thing that might bring that about is a nuclear disaster—and that cure would be far worse than the disease.

But we could decide not to go ahead with particularly dangerous nuclear technology. The laser method of enriching uranium is one example. Its promise of reducing uranium enrichment costs will be of small value to the public, for such costs make up only a small fraction of the price of electricity from nuclear power. Its dangers offset this advantage millions of times over.

We could also decide at least to defer the development of reprocessing and the use of plutonium, whether in current or fast breeder reactors. These are the technologies which at present pose infinitely the greatest danger of proliferation and nuclear terrorism. At this stage they are still in their infancy, but if the few countries that are developing them do bring them to fruition they are bound to spread around the world and present irresistible opportunities to the terrorist. They may well prove to be entirely unnecessary for the provision of our future energy supplies. They may prove to be uneconomic. At the very least we can afford to wait for a decade while we explore the alternatives. President Carter's new approach has given the world the best chance it will ever have to pause and think about them. For example, safer ways of developing nuclear power may be practicable. Several of these have already been put forward and, as a result of Mr Carter's initiative, the nuclear nations have begun a two-year study of them. The most widely canvassed alternative is a different system of fast breeders based on the use of thorium. These could be considerably less dangerous for the spread of nuclear weapons, though far from hazard-free. But it may be that there are more promising non-nuclear alternatives that would be better beneficiaries of the huge sums of money needed to develop such a system. Certainly alternatives to plutonium have been so little researched in the past that it has been easy for its proponents to shoot them down.

It is also certain that there will never be such an opportunity to pause again. For while a decision to wait can be reversed, should dangerous technologies prove necessary, a decision to go ahead will soon be irrevocable.

Yet stopping the development of the plutonium economy, though the most important technical step that can be taken, is not enough.

As long as nuclear reactors proliferate—and even the United States is still keen to sell them abroad—there will be the danger that nations will secretly separate out plutonium from the spent fuel and use it in weapons. So as soon as they leave the reactors fuel elements should be stored, without reprocessing, under international control. Enrichment technology that could be used to produce atom-bomb uranium must also be tightly restricted.

Nevertheless, no restraint on technology will provide complete security. Nations that are determined to get nuclear bombs will always be able to get them, albeit with much more difficulty. Any strategy therefore to limit the spread of nuclear weapons must also address itself to the motives for acquiring them. There is no hope of stopping nuclear proliferation while the attitude of the present nuclear powers remains the same. Proliferation may seem a horrific prospect to people living in a nuclear weapons state or in a country under the protection of one. People living in other countries, however, naturally have a different perspective.

It is, for a start, the height of arrogance for certain nations to claim a right to nuclear weapons while demanding that others should renounce them. This position is made much worse when the superpowers fail to implement their side of the Nuclear Non-Proliferation Treaty—to aim to move rapidly towards disarmament—and continue an arms race instead. It becomes worse still when the nuclear states refuse flatly, as they did at the review conference in 1975, to promise not to use or threaten to use nuclear weapons against non-nuclear parties to the treaty.

Total nuclear disarmament may be impracticable at this stage; for one thing the nuclear umbrellas of the superpowers have prevented allied nations from getting weapons of their own. But a start needs to be made. The powers could signal that they are serious about nuclear weapons by agreeing on a comprehensive test ban as a first step. But President Carter grasped the essential point. While running for the Democratic nomination, he told a United Nations conference: 'I believe we have little right to ask others to deny themselves such weapons for the indefinite future unless we demonstrate meaningful progress towards the goal of control, then reduction and, ultimately elimination of nuclear arsenals.'

The President also enunciated an even more important principle.

'As long as the more powerful nations exploit the less powerful, they will be repaid by terrorism, hatred and potential violence. Insofar as our policies are selfish or cynical or shortsighted, there will inevitably be a day of reckoning.'

While it cannot be said that creation of a new world order will end the threat of nuclear weapons in new hands, it is clear that failure to do so will greatly increase the chances of it. History is studded with examples showing that the failure of talk leads to violence, and that the failure of men of reason is often succeeded by the action of men of hate. The fact is, as Willrich and Taylor end their report, that 'The widespread use of nuclear energy requires the rapid development of near perfect social and political institutions. That is the unprecedented challenge before us.'

Chapter 9

The Ending of the Oil Age

We are just emerging from the Oil Age. As eras go it has been lightning-fast; more of a spurt than an age; more of a wild fling than a steady progression. Yet it has had a profound effect on the history of the planet.

In the Middle East oil virtually bubbles out of the ground and can be produced much more cheaply than any other form of energy. This created a freak situation. During the 1950s and 1960s oil's already low price declined even in absolute terms, as well as in real terms that take account of inflation. The surprising element in the history of oil is not the abrupt sixfold increase of price between 1970 and 1974 but its cheapness until then. Even now it is competitive with other sources of energy. When it was a sixth of the price it was irresistible.

The OPEC countries never had a monopoly of energy, though as 1973 turned into 1974 one might have been forgiven for thinking that they did; what they had was a monopoly of *cheap* energy for export. Since there was plenty of it, coal-mines were shut down all over the rich world, nuclear energy programmes were all but shelved, research on other forms of energy was forgotten. Conservation seemed absurd. It was generally assumed, despite repeated warnings from many authorities, that cheap oil would flow forever.

Western Europe and Japan became dependent upon it. The United States, blessed originally with huge reserves of her own, was expanding demand and burning her oil with equal disregard for most alternatives or for conservation. So she too became more and more reliant on imported oil, and in doing so played a large part in turning the oil business from a buyer's to a seller's market in time for the OPEC price rises.

Plentiful energy creates wealth, and cheap energy can bring bonanzas. Cheap coal fed the furnaces of the major part of the Industrial Revolution. Cheap oil has been one of the important factors in the wealth explosion in the rich world since the Second World War. The age of cheap oil altered the ways of life in developed countries. It brought mobility. It even changed the face of the earth as cities grew and prairie agriculture spread. It also added greatly to the world's burden of pollution. Above all, it brought prosperity to the minority of mankind that lived in the parts of the world that were already relatively rich. It did not bring wealth to the poor world, which could not afford enough of the energy needed for development even when it was cheap. The end of the bonanza may have shaken the rich world, but it played even greater havoc with the economies of the poor countries.

During the oil age, from 1950 to the Yom Kippur War of 1973, the world's use of all energy grew by about 5 per cent a year, which means that our use of energy was doubling about every fourteen years. If that long-term trend were to continue we would need to quadruple our annual energy supplies by the early years of the next century. That is something we cannot do. This is not because of any lack of energy resources as such. Our problem is rather how to find the money, evolve the technology, build the installations and produce the hardware needed to get at them. We cannot do all these things fast enough to sustain the growth of energy we are used to. In the past it has taken about half a century to switch over to a new source of energy.

Furthermore, if the use of energy is to increase rapidly the development of each new source must be able to grow faster than its predecessors. Nothing is available that can grow faster than oil and gas. It will also take increasing energy to exploit most resources. Indeed, drawing up a balance sheet of the energy required to produce new fuel and power—'energy analysis' as it is sometimes called—is going to be increasingly important. Except in certain specialist applications, for example, there will be no point in putting more energy into building an installation or mining a fuel than can be got out of it.

The world's system may provide the most important limit of all to energy growth, for there are mounting fears that burning conventional forms of fuel will heat up the planet. In theory people living in cold or temperate countries might welcome the idea of a slightly warmer climate, but in practice quite small changes in temperature can have devastating results. A two-and-a-half year study carried out by more than twenty of America's leading authorities for the National Academy of Sciences concluded, for example, that a rise of just a few degrees Centigrade could have dramatic effects on farming and fisheries. The world's agricultural zones would shift towards the poles; one result of this could be to push the great north American corn belt off the productive soils of the Mid West and on to much less fertile ground in Canada. Rainfall would increase; but as it would also change position, crop producing areas would become deserts or semi-deserts. Fisheries would be reduced and shift location. And the polar ice-caps could be so affected that the sea level would rise by nearly 20 feet, inundating coastal cities. Even this dire warning from America's scientific establishment is optimistic compared to hypotheses, current in the early 1970s, that the ice-caps might disappear altogether, shifting climatic zones by hundreds of miles and raising the sea-level by some 250 feet or more—enough to make a small scattered archipelago of the British Isles, and to submerge a large part of Northern Europe.

Burning fuels can increase the earth's temperature in two main ways—by producing heat and releasing carbon dioxide. Carbon dioxide makes up less than one three-thousandth of the atmosphere, but it plays a particularly important role in the climate. The gas acts as a sort of two-way mirror, letting sunlight through but intercepting and reflecting much of the heat radiated back from the earth. This has been called the 'greenhouse effect', for the gas traps heat in the same way as glass does in a greenhouse.*

Over the last fifty years or so we have increased the concentration of carbon dioxide in the atmosphere by about a tenth through

*In fact the 'greenhouse effect' seems to work better in the atmosphere than in greenhouses. The main reason for the warming up of greenhouses, it is suggested, is the restriction of ventilation.

burning fossil fuels—oil, gas and coal. If we were to continue to increase our consumption of these fuels as we have done in the past we might swell it by another fifth by the end of the century. The World Meteorological Organisation has warned that a build-up of carbon dioxide could result 'in a very significant warming of global climate' by several degrees Centigrade—a warming that would persist 'for many centuries after fossil fuel reserves had been depleted'. It was once thought that the dust that is also put into the atmosphere by burning fossil fuels might counteract such a warming. But this is now in more doubt, and evidence has been emerging that other pollutants may reinforce the greenhouse effect of carbon dioxide.

This might seem to be a good reason for phasing out our use of fossil fuels in favour of nuclear power. Recent research has suggested, however, that a radioactive gas released during reprocessing could seriously affect the climate by the beginning of the next century. And nuclear power, whether fission or fusion, shares the other main climatic drawback of fossil fuels. Releasing the energy in coal, gas, oil, uranium or other nuclear fuels inevitably puts extra heat into the atmosphere. This is a much smaller problem on a global scale than the release of carbon dioxide, for the heat added to the atmosphere by burning fuels seems to be much less than that caused by an increased greenhouse effect. But its local and regional effects—which nuclear fission may particularly enhance—could prove in practice to be the greatest hazard of all.

Because the use of energy is spread unevenly over the globe there are local concentrations of heat, often called 'heat islands', around cities and other gross users of energy. The centre of London is already several degrees Centigrade warmer than its surroundings, and the heat released in Manhattan is more than 2,500 times the United States average. Power stations inject massive doses of heat into the atmosphere from a small area,* and the nuclear industry often proposes grouping power stations together in massive energy parks, partly for security reasons. Many authorities fear that these concentrations of heat may severely upset the balance of the climate locally and regionally, although it is not yet possible to predict the effects with much confidence. There is already evidence

*For the reasons for this see below, Chapter 12.

of more rain, more fog and less sunshine in cities than in their surroundings. It is feared that increasing local outputs of heat may have more serious results, interfering with the pattern of circulation and rainfall even on a global scale. Slight shifts in such patterns can have profound effects on agriculture. There is also evidence that high local concentrations of heat may bring on hailstorms and tornadoes. The effects of heat islands would be likely to be felt before the effects of the global release of heat or carbon dioxide, and so in practice may prove to be the more severe limiting factor on patterns of energy growth.

Of course, we are still only beginning to learn about how the climate works naturally; let alone about how man may affect it. Some calculations suggest that the greenhouse effect might melt the ice-caps some time during the next century; some scientists say that the extra heat would create more clouds which would cool the earth instead; others doubt whether man can seriously affect the climate at all. In fact the Northern Hemisphere has been cooling for the past thirty years, despite our increasing use of energy. But there does seem to be a growing conviction that developments in the future may be different, and, indeed, that man's actions, if unchecked, may seriously affect the climate in the next century. In our ignorance we are wise to be cautious. As two experts from the U.S. National Center for Atmospheric Research, Dr Stephen Schneider and Mr Roger Dennet, summed it up,

> Evidence exists that continued energy growth to the year 2000 and beyond has the potential to cause climatic changes which could be both global and irreversible. Knowledge of climate theory will for many years remain insufficient to eliminate fully the most pessimistic of the present estimates of the climatic consequences of energy use, let alone dismiss the possibility that even these estimates could be conservative.

Population growth, increased affluence in the rich world and the drive for development in poor countries have been strong thrusts behind our growing demand for energy. Increasingly energy-intensive technologies and waste on a gigantic scale in the rich countries have added to the strain. Anyone who cares about the situation in the world and who appreciates the danger of the widening gap between the rich and poor countries will surely conclude that energy needed to relieve poverty and to fuel development should take priority over energy used to gratify extra affluence. This, coupled with the possibility of climatic disturbance, is a powerful argument for spreading the load, for increasing energy consumption where it is low rather than where it is high. Unfortunately, the blind laws of the market generally create exactly the opposite effect.

The effects of these laws, and the legacy of history, are easy to see. North America, with 6 per cent of the world's population, consumes more than a third of its energy. The Soviet Union and Eastern Europe take 22 per cent of the world's energy, and Western Europe uses about 20 per cent. Latin America takes 4 per cent, Africa 2 per cent. An American consumes on average more than 330 times as much energy as an Ethiopian.

These bare figures do not portray the full extent of the imbalance. During the last decades the rich countries have consumed vast amounts of the most easily accessible resources, the fossil fuels, stored sunlight laid down millions of years ago. The best of that store has been raided in a few decades. Thus even in 1970 it could be calculated that about half the coal mined during the world's history had been burned in the previous thirty years, and about half the oil ever produced had been consumed in the previous decade. A gallon of oil took millennia to form. Today a fast car burns that amount of fuel in ten minutes, Concorde in one tenth of a second.

As far as we can tell, fossil fuels will be expensive from now on, and again it will be the rich countries, who benefited most when they were cheap, who will best be able to afford the increased price.

Meanwhile at least half of the people on the planet have scarcely raised their energy demands above those of stone age man. The smell that greets you in an Indian village is not that of the petrol fumes of modern cities but the odour of burning dung. Nine-tenths of the people in the poor world depend on firewood for their chief source of energy. The burning of wood, dung and grass roots tends to degrade the soil, cut food production and encourage the onward march of the deserts.

So, while growth in the use of energy in the world as a whole cannot go on as it has done, no rational man will believe that energy growth everywhere must stop. In most of the world it needs to improve and increase; in fact, there is still enough unexploited energy to provide everyone on earth with a comfortable, if not extravagant, life.

At the moment there is a rush to discover more oil. Some nations have had their lucky strikes. Indeed, Britain's North Sea oil, with the country's large reserves of coal and natural gas, has given her the promise of an exceptional short-term abundance of fuel that tends to obscure the fact that she faces the same long-term problems as everyone else. India, Brazil and above all, Mexico, are among those that have recently found fields while there are major reserves in Russia, the United States and China.

However, the geologists say that there are no more Middle East size bonanzas to be discovered. The size and number of the new discoveries will not be sufficient for production to go on doubling every ten years. Besides, most of them are being made in areas where it is difficult and expensive to extract the black gold. The Canadians, the Americans and the Russians have scaled down their expectations from new discoveries—the United States by as much as three-quarters. The search for new fields has been accompanied by government appeals throughout the world to use less oil.

If the historic rates of growth continue, oil production will almost certainly peak well before the end of the century and will then begin to decline, running out completely in perhaps seventy or eighty years.* Not all analysts agree, but even if the consensus estimates are much too low it would make little difference. Simple mathematics show that if the production of oil continues to double every ten years the discovery of even as much oil as there is in reserve would only extend its life by a decade. What *would* affect the lifetime of the reserves is a major and early cut in the growth of demand. Rising prices forced by dwindling supplies should eventually cut demand and extend the life of oil somewhat, but we would be much wiser to apply conservation and to develop other sources of energy as soon as possible. At present the chance to take these measures is being allowed to slip, for the short-term glut of oil has created a totally unjustified complacency. Despite it, the threat of shortages in the 1980s lies ahead.

*Estimating the size of reserves is difficult; but techniques have been evolved for making an informed guess of even undiscovered reserves.

Of course it still makes sense to look for oil, and it would also help if we could get a higher proportion of it out of wells. At the moment only about 40 per cent of the oil in a reservoir is brought to the surface. The wells are then capped because companies find it cheaper to move to the next one. Generally it is far too difficult and costly to open the old ones again. However, it is possible that some of what is being written off could be exploited in future, and as prices rise this may be done.

There are other reserves, quite different from the conventional oil wells which are expected to run out soon. Enormous amounts of oil lie in the tar sands of Alberta, Canada. Mr G. B. Mellon, the Alberta Minister for Mines and Minerals, said in 1974 that soaked sandstone contained some 120 billion tons of oil, which would be more than twice the proved reserves in the Middle East. Optimists say that some 40 per cent of this may eventually be recovered, but so far the attempts to exploit it have run into formidable technical and financial difficulties. Two tons of the sands, which are sticky in summer and frozen hard in winter, have to be excavated to produce a barrel of oil. A private firm often accumulating big losses and extracting relatively little fuel is only now making marginal profits. A largely government-backed consortium is struggling to crack the problems with a bigger plant, but its cost has quadrupled in three years and stands at over 2 billion dollars. If it works it will dig out a quarter of a million tons of material a day, but still will not be able to meet more than 5 per cent of Canada's oil needs in the 1980s. Most of the major oil companies have acquired interests in the sands, but they—and the real potential of the area—await the development of really effective ways of exploiting the reserves. The same is true of other enormous tar sand deposits in Venezuela, Angola, Malagasy, Colombia and elsewhere.

There is much more of the precious liquid in shale. By one calculation suitable rocks scattered around the globe contain a thousand times as much oil as can be recovered from the world's wells. The richest and best-known deposits are in the Green River Formation of Wyoming, Colorado and Utah, where the Ute Indians were using the oil to light their fires long before the white men came. Shale oil was produced in Scotland for more than a century until the early 1960s, and China reportedly produces millions of tons of it a year.

Again, it is extremely difficult to squeeze the oil from the stone. The scientists who estimated the huge extent of the world's resources warned that less than a ten-thousandth of it could be recovered under prevailing economic conditions. That was in 1965, and the economic prospects have greatly improved with the ending of the age of cheap oil; but there are still other big difficulties. Huge amounts of rock have to be quarried or mined and then heated to liquefy the oil. With our present technology it may not be worthwhile to exploit any but the richer rocks—for most of the shale may yield less energy than has to be used in the processing. Enormous amounts of water are needed. There would be considerable effects on the landscape. Indeed, a Federal Government project in Colorado and Utah began with high hopes at the beginning of 1974, only to be hit by a series of delays brought by legal and technical problems and environmentalist opposition. In the autumn of 1976 both the Government and two private companies suspended operations for a year, and others were still wondering whether it was worth continuing; during 1977, however, hopes rose again and the prospects for exploitation improved.

One way of getting round some of the technical and environmental problems would be to develop a way of heating the rocks without removing them from the ground. But this, too, is by no means easy, though developers are reporting rapid progress. Russia feeds the rock directly into power stations, and some say that this may be the major area of development in future. But neither the shales nor tar sands will provide cheap oil, and they are not likely to surrender much of it soon.

Very much less is known about natural gas reserves. The use of gas has been growing even faster than oil, and some experts estimate that its production will peak at about the same time. Others are more optimistic, and researchers have recently been reporting findings of other forms of natural gas that might multiply our resources many times over. But gas, while it is an excellent, clean fuel, needs an intricate pipe network for its distribution. This disadvantage and the cheapness of oil have caused gas to be flared off and wasted when it occurs at oil wells. Now there is considerable impetus behind liquefying and shipping the gas, but this may result in one of the nastiest environmental hazards. A standard tanker shipping liquid natural gas will hold energy equivalent to fifty-five Hiroshima bombs in highly inflammable form. If spilled the liquid natural gas would boil off very quickly. This would then form a huge, easily ignitable and possibly asphyxiating gas cloud. What might the result be if an accident happened in port or in a busy shipping area, or if a storage tank in or near a city were sabotaged?

Coal is the king of the fossil fuels. There is plenty of it in the ground. The United Nations says that there are more than 8,500 billion tons of coal less than about 4,000 feet down and in seams more than about a foot thick, and it has been estimated that over 6,500 billion tons more will probably be found. At present rates of consumption this would be enough to last for more than 5,000 years. As coal can be converted into both oil and gas and can be used as a feedstock for chemicals there seems at first sight to be little cause for concern about future energy supplies. However, the issue is not the amount of energy that is available in the world but how much of it we can put to use, and how fast we can do it; and this is just as true for coal as for everything else.

It is usually assumed that only about half of the coal that is found can be mined. Some experts say this estimate is too high, because increased mechanisation in mines has reduced yields in the past; others say it is too pessimistic because rising prices will make it economic to mine the more inaccessible coal, and that technologies could be much more efficient in future. The optimists also say that we may find ways of exploiting coal in seams thinner than a foot, and at greater depths than 4,000 feet. Several countries are carrying out research on turning coal into gas while it is still in the ground, and though there are still unsolved technical and environmental problems, this is sometimes advocated, for example, as a way of exploiting massive coal reserves lying more than 3,000 feet under the North Sea. However, even a cut of half, if we accept the usual assumption, does little to disturb a cosy view of the future. For even if we found no more than 8,500 billion tons we would still have coal enough for about 1,500 years, and the discovery of another 6,500 billion tons would keep us going at our present rate of consumption until well past the year AD 4500.

Nevertheless, this is far too simple a view. At the moment coal supplies only about a third of the world's energy. If it were to take over as oil and gas run out we would have to increase our present rate of production and consumption; and if we were to go on doubling our use of energy every fourteen years we would have to increase the production rate very fast indeed. This is not possible.

It can take between three and ten years to sink a new mine, and at the moment the industry is suffering from its neglect during the oil age. In Britain, for example, only 10 per cent of the coal comes from mines started since the First World War, and a high proportion of pits are being exhausted. By one estimate it would cost more than £57 billion just to construct the mines needed to double the world's output of coal by the end of the century. And that would mean that the industry was expanding at only about half the rate needed to keep pace with the general energy growth we are used to, and nothing like the rate required to enable coal to take over from oil and gas. Furthermore, rich countries are finding it increasingly difficult to find men to work in the pits, with all their discomforts and dangers, and there is an acute shortage of mining engineers. During the oil age we eliminated many of the ways of transporting and using coal. These would have to be revived and coal converted to oil or gas where appropriate, processes that would also take time and money to develop and install and may pose significant occupational health hazards.

Some of the difficulties of expanding coal production can be reduced by placing greater emphasis, where possible, on opencast, or strip, mining of seams near the surface. These mines can be prepared much more quickly and cheaply than deep ones. They avoid the dangers that go with underground work, from accidents to silicosis or 'black lung disease'. At least in the short term, this kind of mining offers the greatest potential for increasing coal production in the United States, where there are particularly big surface reserves. But American experience shows that it may well not be possible to expand this kind of mining quickly either, for environmental opposition to it has slowed down development of the coal industry. Strip mining devastates the land. Reclamation has often been ignored, and may not even be practicable in arid areas like the West where much of the nation's surface coal is situated.

Pollution presents another environmental problem in using coal. The sulphur dioxide, grit and smoke emitted through burning it has long been ruinous to health—they were, for example, the constituents of the great London smogs. Yet we can now burn coal much more cleanly, and new methods of doing this are being evolved. Fluidized bed combustion, a technology sadly neglected during the oil age, is one example of the new processes being developed. Tiny particles of coal are burned on a bubbling bed that behaves like boiling liquid. The plants are cheaper to build and run than conventional burners; they can burn extremely low-grade coal—thus stretching out reserves—and they can minimise pollution. Oil and gas made from coal will also be cleaner to burn.

Coal cannot be used to sustain the rapid growth and cheap energy of the oil age, but provided we cut back our growth rate and are prepared to pay higher prices, it does offer an important source of energy for centuries. We could thus have a bridge of coal to carry us from the oil age to the new sources of energy we develop.

Like other fossil fuels, coal is unevenly spread around the world, and its exploitation, like that of oil, will be primarily determined not by the needs of the world but by the interests of the countries that control the deposits. Three countries, Russia, the United States and China, account for just over half the world's production, and have about 90 per cent of its total reserves. This means that while many countries, such as Britain, India, Australia or Japan, have enough coal to provide themselves with a useful short-term bridge, any really major, long-term increase must be sustained by the three superpowers. They may not wish to do this. Russia, which has 60 per cent of world reserves, is one of the fortunate countries rich in energy and other resources; so she may have no great need to develop her coal rapidly. China's policy can only be guessed at. The United States may well need all the coal it can produce to satisfy its voracious appetite for energy, and may not be able to overcome environmental opposition. The rest of the world is faced with unpleasant alternatives if it tries to rely on coal to fuel a major increase in energy consumption. Either the superpowers will not produce the coal for export, and the fuel will not be available; or if they do so the rest of the world will become ever more dependent upon them. After their experience with oil, most nations have a great desire to be self-sufficient in energy supplies.

This desire, though it is not always entirely rational, is a powerful force in pushing governments towards the most widely canvassed of the alternatives to fossil fuels—nuclear power. The full fission programme, including the fast breeder reactors which produce more usable fuel than they burn, offers the promise of much greater self-sufficiency; but many nations are likely to be as dependent on imported nuclear technology as they would be on any of the fossil fuels.

Nuclear power is also promoted as offering continuing cheap and rapidly growing energy. This illusion is yet another example of scientific tunnel vision that denies the need for a basic change of attitude. Nuclear power is no more a panacea than was the Green Revolution or the pill. It brings with it, of course, a unique risk to national security—nuclear proliferation and terrorism—but also other hazards besides.

Chapter 10

Faustian Bargain?

The debate on whether or not we should commit ourselves to a full-scale programme of nuclear fission arouses a great deal of public concern and passion. Both sides have their scaremongers, but both also attract the commitment of hundreds of dedicated, sincere and able people. While one side includes the leaders of the atomic energy industry, the other includes atomic scientists of comparable distinction—among them pioneers of nuclear power. The argument ranges over highly complex technical data in several disciplines, but it ultimately boils down to issues of policy and priorities that can be, and must be, tackled by the public at large.

One side argues that our high-energy civilisation depends on nuclear power. A full programme, moving on to the fast breeder reactors, could, it is said, keep our use of energy growing and growing for centuries after the oil runs dry. Nuclear power, its supporters add, is already the cheapest known way of producing electricity. There are, they admit, unique safety problems, but these will be solved in time. Meanwhile the atomic industry has an excellent safety record. So these worries must not stand in the way of our using such a vast new source of energy. Failure to develop nuclear power will lead to greater dangers for society than the risks of doing so; for if we do not use it, they say, we will not be able to produce the energy that people need.

It is an understandable and sincere argument—particularly since it comes from a nuclear industry which was concerned with some of the safety problems long before they were widely publicised, and which is anxious to avoid another period of demoralisation like the one it suffered in the days of cheap oil. It is the argument accepted by the governments of nearly all rich countries. Between them they are prepared to spend thousands of millions of pounds on their programmes.

The opponents of nuclear power turn this argument on its head. The dangers of this new form of energy, they say, imperil both our civilisation and the future of the world. Such problems as the disposal of highly toxic wastes and the prevention of nuclear terrorism and proliferation may well be insoluble. Nobody knows about the long-term effects of accidental releases, or about the inevitable low doses of radiation. In such a situation it is extremely irresponsible to go ahead with a large programme of nuclear power, which in any case cannot achieve all that is claimed for it, and certainly not at the hoped-for speed. It would be much better, and much less disruptive in the end, to cut back our energy growth in the West, conserve fuel, expand coal production and use the breathing space this would provide to pay more attention to the clean sources of energy.

Not everyone fits neatly into one camp or the other, and the arguments themselves are merely summarised. Many who are unhappy about a rapid expansion of nuclear power would lend their support to a more cautious exploration of its potential. On the other hand, some eminent proponents of fission have grave worries. One of America's foremost nuclear scientists, Alvin Weinberg, concludes that accepting nuclear energy means striking a 'Faustian Bargain', by which we receive 'inexhaustible' power but have to ensure unprecedented vigilance and unparalleled social stability for ever.

Even when nuclear power stations are running normally there will be some release of radioactivity. This was one of the first big concerns of opponents of nuclear power, and it still raises public emotion. But it is something of a false issue.

True, it is normally accepted that there is no level of radiation which will not cause cancer and the genetic illnesses and malformations which will come out in our children or their descendants. True, too, we could expect dire results if ever we were exposed to the maximum level of man-made radiation recommended by the International Commission on Radiological Protection (ICRP) —the legal limit in force, for example, in Britain. The National Academy of Sciences has calculated that if radiation reached this level in the United States there would be thousands of extra cancer deaths annually, while after some generations thousands more babies would be born deformed or with genetic diseases every year. And other studies have produced far more horrific figures than these.

Yet these studies are not really relevant at this stage. The ICRP standard would allow a country's population to receive an annual average dose of 170 millirem (a millirem or 'mrem' is a thousandth of a rem, the basic measurement of the effect of radiation on a human being). However, at present both Britons and Americans receive only about 5 mrem a year from all manmade sources other than medical ones. Most of this comes from old atmospheric bomb tests, now discontinued, and only a small fraction of a single mrem results at present from the nuclear power industry. If we want to cut down on radiation we should concentrate on tackling unnecessary medical exposure (better techniques could halve the British average exposure of 19 mrem a year) rather than on emissions from nuclear power stations. Indeed, it seems that coal-fired stations can actually release more radioactivity in their normal operation than nuclear ones, and of course they emit other pollutants besides.

The health of people working in the nuclear industry provides rather more cause for concern. Naturally, they are liable to receive much more radiation than the general public. The doses they get will affect not only their own lives but also the future of the descendants of those of us who have nothing to do with the industry; for a relatively heavy genetic dose received by a few workers will—in time and through intermarriage—spread itself over the population.

Particular controversy surrounds the effects of plutonium. Although it is one of the most toxic of all substances, it is widely held to be essential to the long-term future of nuclear fission through its use in fast breeder reactors. The core of a fast breeder will contain several tons of plutonium; yet international standards lay down that no one should accumulate more than a quarter of a millionth of a gram of it in the lungs, or two-thirds of a millionth of a gram in the body as a whole.

We still do not know if even these miniscule doses are acceptable. Scientists argue over what the limits should be. The balance of opinion holds that the present standards are about right, but some experts have speculated that they may be too strict, while others say that they are many times too lax, and imply that proper standards would effectively rule out the use of plutonium altogether. Nevertheless, the effects of plutonium, and of radiation generally, have been researched much more fully than those of most other pollutants. Similarly, the nuclear industry has generally imposed much stricter precautions than industries dealing with dangerously toxic chemicals. Unfortunately, we have little evidence of how effective these measures have been in preventing death and disease. Cancer, the most likely cause of death following relatively low levels of radiation exposure, usually takes some twenty or thirty years to appear after the original damage is done. It can be caused by many other agents, and it is impossible to say positively that any particular case has been caused by radiation unless a really massive dose has been received. The claims sometimes made by nuclear advocates stating that no case of cancer has ever been positively attributed to plutonium should therefore be treated with great reservation.

Studies that compare the levels of death and disease among workers with those of the general public are clearly more reliable than such assertions, but they also have to be handled with care. For example, the National Radiological Protection Board, the British watchdog on radiation, published figures which, it claimed, showed that there was no significant difference between deaths among workers at Windscale and those in the general population. This conclusion was challenged on the basis of the Board's own data; but, more important, the data were incomplete. For they only covered men while they were employed at the nuclear complex. The Royal Commission on Environmental Pollution criticised the Board for failing to do 'a proper study' and said that the survey might have missed at least half the deaths from cancer by failing to follow up the people who had ceased employment. A much more comprehensive survey of workers at Hanford, the American equivalent of Windscale, came up with a gloomier verdict than that reached by the Board, suggesting that working in such a plant is up to twenty times more dangerous than has been supposed. But the methodology of this study has also been criticised.

In fact, data can be interpreted in widely differing ways in what is an immensely complex field. One nuclear critic, Amory Lovins, writes that 'some persons say that safety has not been proved, whilst others say that harm has not been proved. Both appear to be correct, and one must decide for oneself which position is ethically preferable.'

That may be fair comment but, at least at present, low-level radiation is the least of the problems arising from nuclear power. Many critics of nuclear power have even dropped the issue. Certainly we are in much less danger of radiation damage now than we were during the heyday of nuclear weapons testing in the atmosphere. Other pollutants present a more immediate threat, and are much less well regulated. Yet if nuclear power grows as rapidly as projected we will almost certainly be exposed to much greater radiation from civil processes by the end of the century; and that is a good reason for doing adequate research now.

Accidents and leaks greatly increase the radiation risks to workers. We know that there have been accidents, although the full facts are not always available. In 1973, for example, thirty-five Windscale workers were irradiated in one incident, and Anthony Tucker noted in the *Guardian*: 'Every establishment handling plutonium has had one or more accidental releases during the past decade.' The nuclear industry, for its part, can point out that no really catastrophic accident has occurred, and that the press often makes a major issue out of even the most insignificant leak. But the industry is prone to exaggeration too. Leading spokesmen in Britain, for example, like to compare the industry's safety record with the numbers of deaths in coal-mining and on North Sea oil rigs. This ignores the high death-rate from cancer among uranium miners—the United States Public Health Services has reckoned that between a tenth and a fifth of the men who have worked in American underground uranium mines will die because of lung cancer from radiation exposure. Yet such men do, after all, provide the nuclear industry with its raw material, just as the coal-miners and oilmen supply conventional power stations. A better comparison would be with normal power generation.* Furthermore,

*In fact, according to Michael Jacobsen, Head of the Statistics Bureau of the Institute of Occupational Medicine, a United States uranium miner is more likely to be killed, injured or get lung disease than a British coal miner; but since using coal is more labour-intensive, there are fewer deaths per unit of electricity.

neither coal-mining nor North Sea oil threatens the genetic future of the population.

Nuclear accidents can also blow radioactivity out of the station, and the reliability of reactors and other nuclear plants has become a question of intense public concern. We know most about the reliability of Light Water Reactors which make up the vast majority of the world's nuclear power stations. Since they were developed in America, they have been subjected to a rigorous independent examination unparalleled anywhere else. The United States has the most knowledgeable nuclear critics in the world, including men who once held important positions in the nuclear industry. She also has a remarkably open tradition of investigation and of public accountability, while nuclear matters in Britain, for example, are all too often covered in the secrecy which has traditionally obscured most pollution control. In France, which like Britain developed its own first generation of reactors and is pioneering the fast breeder, nuclear power station safety procedures are a state secret.

Contrary to popular suspicion, a nuclear power station (except in one instance mentioned later) cannot produce a nuclear explosion. Nevertheless, a U.S. Atomic Energy Commission study in the mid-1960s estimated that an accident could lead to 45,000 deaths, cause 17 billion dollars' worth of damage to property and contaminate an area the size of Pennsylvania. So it seemed reassuring in 1975 when the Nuclear Regulatory Commission (NRC), which succeeded the USAEC, produced a new report which reckoned that if a hundred reactors were in operation (there are sixty-three in the U.S.A. now) an accident big enough to kill ten people outright could be expected only every 30,000 years, and one big enough to kill 100 could only be expected every 100,000 years. The chances of being killed in this way, it announced, were no greater than those of being hit by a meteorite.

However, this kind of comparison is misleading, for such immediate deaths are not the main toll of nuclear accidents. Thus John Maddox points out that a reactor accident that would kill between 10 and 100 people outright would irradiate 'between 100,000 and a million people, among whom deaths would occur at intervals between ten and twenty years after the event'. Such delayed action is likely to multiply the death toll from an accident by a hundred times or more, and to this must be added the long legacy of genetic damage left by radiation. When such effects are taken into account the odds quoted in the NRC study shorten significantly. It estimates, for example, that an accident that would cause 100 cancer deaths a year over thirty years could be expected every 9000 years and one that would cause ten such fatalities a year could be expected every 900 years. This still does not seem a particularly great risk; but this is not the end of the story.

Expert criticism—apparently including some within the USAEC—tore holes in the report's methodology and conclusions. One authoritative study by a group of leading people chosen specially for their impartiality concluded that its estimates could be up to five hundred times too optimistic. Besides, the report specifically did not cover fast breeder reactors which are reckoned by many experts to be much more dangerous. It also excluded sabotage, nuclear terrorism and waste disposal, the major areas of concern over nuclear power. Moreover, the chances of human error, either in designing or operating plant, make meaningless any analysis that seeks to establish how frequently the equipment will go wrong.

The debate that followed the publication of a draft of this report was punctuated by a graphic example of this. An electrician and his mate lit a candle to look for a draught among the electrical cables beneath the control room at what was then the world's biggest nuclear power station, Browns Ferry, Alabama. The cables caught fire. All the emergency cooling systems on one of the power station's reactors failed. A major disaster was only prevented by an operator's quick thinking and improvisation, using pumps—not intended as safety equipment—to keep the reactor core cool.

Mishaps involving human error crop up with distressing frequency. Accidents have happened when a switch has been turned too soon, when a supervisor has said the wrong number by a slip of the tongue and when a fuel rod has been pulled out of the reactor core. At one station the control rods were inserted upside down, and the reactor was started up with the lid off the pressure vessel; another reactor was operated with a forgotten welding-rig sloshing around inside. A company insisted for years that it should build a nuclear power station just a few hundred yards from the San Andreas earthquake fault. And, under the pressure of a crisis, correctly reading controls have been overlooked and operating procedures ignored. Designers of nuclear plant seek to minimise the dangers by providing back-up safety systems, but they can neither foresee all eventualities, nor eliminate the human element. As a leading safety engineer said on resigning from the nuclear industry to join the opposition : 'Plants grow more complex. Safety hangs increasingly on the human error factor, and we can't eliminate it. Most of our operators have seen emergencies only on a simulator. The real thing can look quite different, and they may have just sixty terrified seconds to act.'

A colleague, who resigned with him, said that the Browns Ferry accident could be repeated at any time in most of America's plants. And that accident was the third occasion on which an American nuclear reactor came close to a core melt-down. One version of such an accident is sometimes called the 'China Syndrome'; in one minute the temperature of the reactor core could reach 3,000°F; the radioactive material would accumulate at the bottom of the pressure vessel and then melt its way through it, through the floor of the power station and head down into the earth in the general direction of the People's Republic. Nuclear critics say that the general public would inevitably get a huge dose of radiation. For many years the main defence against this happening in a Light Water Reactor, the Emergency Core Cooling System (ECCS), was never properly tested.

Confidence about preventing accidents is not heightened by the report of a USAEC task force that there had been 850 malfunctions or deficiencies in equipment related to safety in thirty Light Water Reactors in the United States between 1 January 1972 and 31 May 1973. In Britain the Royal Commission on Environmental Pollution said that they had doubts about 'whether the criteria adopted by the Nuclear Installations Inspectorate in establishing reactor safety are soundly based'. Meanwhile a specialist in nuclear safety at the International Atomic Energy Agency has warned that developing countries were being sold reactors that were less safe that those operating in the nations that supplied them.

Nevertheless, a major disaster is likely to be a very rare event. Unfortunately, what might seem relatively small accidents assume a new significance because of the particular dangers of nuclear power. Professor John T. Edsall of Harvard, a former President of the International Congress of Biochemistry, reckons that the escape of even one ten-thousandth of the radioactivity in a modern reactor 'would represent an unacceptable risk'. The results of accidents, as well as of sabotage, could be enormously reduced by building reactors underground. A committee of the European Parliament recommended this early in 1976, and President Jimmy Carter advocated it during his campaign for office.

By the end of the 1960s there had already been major reactor accidents in four countries, including most of the important reactor designs. Fortunately, there were very few deaths. That, and subsequent events, can lead to either a pessimistic or an optimistic conclusion. Perhaps we have been enormously lucky so far and the mishaps of the past may be worse in the future; or perhaps it is reassuring to know that though reactors have been sorely tested they have never yet unleashed a disaster.

Curiously enough, governments, the nuclear industry and insurance companies all seem to be among the pessimists. For whatever is said about the minute theoretical possibility of a catastrophic accident, they have combined to expect the worst in practice. In the mid-1950s it became clear in the United States that companies would not build nuclear plants for fear that they would be bankrupted by the claims following a major accident. A special Act was therefore passed by Congress in 1957 instructing companies to raise what cover they could from private insurance firms and providing additional coverage from the State. Companies were then excused from any liability beyond these sums. In the event the companies could raise only 60 million dollars from private insurance companies, and the State figure was limited to 500 million dollars. That same year a USAEC report estimated the possible damage from a major accident at 7000 million dollars; thus these limited sums scarcely represented a vote of confidence in the reliability of reactors. Similar provisions have been applied in other countries, including Britain. If the authorities really believe the latest, reassuring, study you would expect these provisions to be repealed. Private companies might be expected to give unlimited cover to such a supposedly good risk, and governments should see no need to limit cover so stringently. Furthermore, the nuclear industry might be expected to show enough faith in its own assurances to dispense with such special protection. Until that happens the public is entitled to be pessimistic too.

The difficulty of disposing of highly toxic nuclear waste is the most dismaying of the problems accompanying nuclear power, apart from nuclear proliferation and terrorism.

The wastes arise inevitably from the use of nuclear fuel, accumulating in the fuel rods as the power reactor is running. Reprocessing plants can separate them from the uranium and plutonium in the rods, so that these elements can be used again as fuel. But whether the wastes are separated out or not, they pose a particularly tricky pollution problem.

The real problem is not one of bulk. Spokesmen for the nuclear industry in Britain emphasise, for example, that by the end of the century the space needed to store all the waste separated out at Windscale would be about twice the size of a football pitch. This is little comfort, however, because of the extreme virulence of the poisons. Nuclear scientists calculate that a single nuclear power station of a typical size will produce annually as much radioactive waste as hundreds of Hiroshima sized bombs. Indeed, Professor John Holdren of the University of California has calculated that the release of just one ten-thousandth of only one of the radioactive wastes—strontium 90—in storage in the United States at the turn of the century would be enough to poison all the rivers and streams of the country to twice the permitted concentration.

Some of the wastes remain toxic for 600 to 700 years, and these are mixed with even longer-lived substances. Plutonium 239, some of which is not successfully separated out, has a half-life of 24,400 years. That is to say that even after a period ten times longer that has elapsed since the building of the Parthenon a bit of plutonium created today will still retain half its poison. If one grapefruit-sized lump is theoretically enough to kill four billion people today it will still be poisonous enough to kill two billion long past the year AD 26000. And in a quarter of a million years it will still be strong enough to kill nearly four million. Some of the other poisons in the mixture have much longer half-lives still. In all, the wastes need to be kept apart from all life for around a million years.

Until recently the problem was given relatively little attention, and, indeed, it is still sometimes presented as a relatively minor one that the industry has not yet had the time to solve. 'The lion of nuclear fission has been tamed: it remains to clear up what he leaves in his cage' was the theme of a lecture on the subject by one of the chiefs of the British industry.

At the moment we are storing the growing amount of left-overs while we decide what to do. They are kept in special steel tanks, shielded with concrete partly buried and cooled to prevent them boiling and thus cause widespread contamination. The nuclear industry stresses that this is perfectly adequate in the short term, and it is sometimes suggested that we should not hurry to find a permanent means of disposal since this could foreclose even better options in the future. Indeed, storage is sometimes presented as a solution in itself. Why not, said a senior official at the British National Radiological Protection Board, build a whole series of concrete buildings? They would have to be replaced every hundred years or so in order that the waste could be moved into new ones, and 'this would be tedious but not particularly difficult'. There was always a chance that some future generation might come up with a better answer. 'It is not a lot to ask that we should expect our descendants to look after this for us,' he said.

It does seem wrong, however, to bequeath the wastes to generations which have not shared in the benefits of the energy that produced them. We can have no idea of the type of societies that may succeed us over the next hundreds of thousands of years. They may know nothing of the perils of radioactivity. They may not even be able to read any records or instructions or warning signs that survive—after all, it took twentieth-century man fifty years to decipher the 3,500 year old Linear B script of the Knossos tablets.

Moreover, nothing in our past experience should give us much confidence that even people who knew what they were doing could look after anything for mere centuries without error or loss of concentration—or without the dangers that would be brought by war or sabotage. Indeed, there have been incidents that might make us doubt our ability to look after the poisons for a few years, let alone for generations. A series of leaks in tanks in the United States have released nearly half a million US gallons of high-level wastes since the early 1940s. About a quarter of this escaped in one incident in 1973, and lack of routine checking helped to ensure that this leak went undetected for forty-eight days. USAEC investigators later gave an assurance that the radioactivity would not eventually work down to the water table beneath the tanks.

Nuclear industries are working on ways of minimising the risk of this sort of incident by solidifying the wastes. The British industry is working on a way of binding them in glass. It is not expected to be ready for use until 1990, and as Nigel Hawkes wrote in the *Observer*, 'Waste solidification is no more than a better stop gap.' While such techniques can make both storage and permanent disposal more manageable, we still need an ultimate solution.

One suggestion, seriously put forward, was to fire the wastes into the sun by rocket. It sounds a neat idea until you contemplate the consequences of even a single rocket failing and plunging its cargo back to earth.

The more promising ideas are to place containers holding the wastes on the seabed, to bury them in the rock beneath it, or to sink them in what we believe to be 'stable geological formations' on land. The problem in all these is of making sure that the wastes will not get back to man, for any container holding them is bound to break up after only a small fraction of the time during which they are poisonous. Furthermore, this must be ensured for truly geological periods, during which there will be ice-ages, substantial erosion, massive earthquakes and changes in the shape of the earth as land once underneath the sea comes to the surface and other areas are inundated. The period during which the wastes should be kept isolated compares with the age of the polar ice-caps themselves.

Placing the waste on the seabed would be the cheapest option, but probably also the most hazardous. Man might accidentally bring them to the surface, through mining seabed nodules, for example. Glassified wastes are expected to dissolve totally within 3,500 years and might then find their way back to man through being concentrated in fish, or by sediments being thrown up on land. At present using the seabed in this way is forbidden by international treaty.

The other two options seem more attractive, though the magazine *Nature* has commented that this may only be so because little research has been done on them! Certainly when research has been carried out there have been some unpleasant surprises. Tests were made, for example, on a disused salt-mine in Kansas, and plans to bury wastes in it were approved. Later it was found to be—in the words of the Director of the Kansas State Geological

Survey—as full of holes 'as a piece of Swiss cheese'. Fortunately, no wastes had yet been put into it. The search for more reliable salt formations continues: the Soviet Union hierarchy, it appears, is also particularly interested in salt-mines. One grave disadvantage, even with the most impermeable salt formation, is that it represents a valuable resource, which a future generation might well unsuspectingly set out to exploit.

Meanwhile the Belgians and Italians are investigating clay, while Britain, Canada, Sweden and France are looking into hard rocks like granite. Already stiff local opposition is building up in many of the areas investigated as people rebel against any idea that waste might be buried near their homes. And land-based disposal has to be particularly careful to avoid contaminating ground water supplies that sooner or later might be used for drinking.

These difficulties could be overcome by burying the wastes in the rock under the deep ocean bed. Some say this is the preferable, if the most expensive, means of disposal, for it offers the most lines of defence against the poisons returning to man. Its feasibility will, of course, be influenced by the outcome of the negotiations over the Law of the Sea, and the authority set up to govern the oceanic abyss: but even if it is allowed, many uncertainties about the fate of wastes buried under the seabed have still to be settled.

As far as we know all conceivable ways of disposal have been canvassed, but so far no one has been able to establish that any one of them is satisfactory, and no nation has yet begun disposing of its wastes. This is causing considerable public disquiet—the General Accounting Office in the United States, for example, describes progress as 'negligible'. Nevertheless the industry insists that it has the situation in hand and that it will find the right answers in time. Many critics, on the other hand, are sceptical that a 'fail-safe' solution ever will be, or can be, found. Certainly, though a method of disposal that is politically acceptable may well be devised, we are unlikely ever to be sure that it will remain safe for all the wastes' poisonous lifetime.

One ingenious idea for reducing this uncertainty is to burn the longest-lived wastes in nuclear reactors in order to turn them into less durable ones. This would be extremely difficult technically, very expensive, and might expose people working on the process to danger. One authority who supported the idea said it would 'convert the waste management into a 1000 year problem instead of a million year one'. This may be a thousandfold improvement, but we still do not yet know how to isolate anything even for a millennium.

Meanwhile the debate over these highly toxic wastes obscures the fate of less dramatic, but still important ones—the dilute 'low-level' wastes arising from reprocessing that are routinely buried in the earth or dumped in the sea. Radioactive poisons can be concentrated up to thousands of times over in other forms of life and returned to man in his food. Drums that have been sunk in the deep ocean are already leaking plutonium. More serious, perhaps, plutonium routinely discharged from Windscale is turning up in plaice and herring. The wastes could also return to us through another route. Much of them ends up in sediments on the bottom of the sea. These could be brought to land again as the sea-level changes; more dramatically, they might be brought ashore by storms. Some authorities call for discharges of such wastes to be controlled as rigorously as the highly concentrated ones, but most conclude that there is no need for immediate action. However, we do need to do more research on the ways that these poisons may get back to us, and there is at least one incident on record to warn us not to be complacent about handling plutonium even in dilute 'low-level' wastes. Such wastes were poured into a trench at the Hanford reservation in Washington state. It was assumed that the soil would filter out the radioactivity; but—to the surprise of the USAEC—the soil also concentrated plutonium, creating the danger of a nuclear chain reaction, a 'mud vulcano' that could have showered the toxic element all over the area. The possibility that a similar volcano may actually have erupted is advanced as one explanation for a mysterious Russian nuclear catastrophe that seems to have killed hundreds of people and devastated a large area in the Urals.*

*Other important but less well known radioactive wastes include the hulks of nuclear reactors when they have finished active life; and the spoil heaps from uranium mining. These last, by themselves, it has been calculated, increase the normal radiation effects of nuclear energy so that they are comparable with the health damage done by coal-fired power stations, a comparison which otherwise seems favourable to nuclear power. Buildings in Grand Junction, Colorado, including schools and hospitals, have been constructed on this waste, exposing the inhabitants to radioactive poisons.

The effects of something going wrong with nuclear technology can be particularly serious and particularly long-lasting. It is an unforgiving technology that cannot brook major technical failures, or even natural disasters—'Acts of God,' says the Nobel Prize winner Hannes Alfvén, 'cannot be permitted'. Meanwhile the action of a few unthinking, or malicious, or unbalanced, or forgetful, or hurried, or tired, or momentarily absent-minded people could make nonsense of the finest technology, the most careful design, or the most reassuring estimate of the probabilities of accidents.

Our technical ability might well improve with expansion of the nuclear industry, but the problems of human fallibility would be bound to become greater. There would be more people to make mistakes, and as more and more people are recruited their standard of excellence would be likely to fall. If the good safety record continued it would be natural for people to become less vigilant. And is there not a risk, as one commentator has put it, that the dangers could rise through salesmen outrunning engineers and investment conquering caution? Judgements over the risks of nuclear power must be made not merely on the basis of technical figures and reports but through knowledge of human nature; not exclusively by atomic scientists but by all of us.

We need to weigh risks and benefits particularly carefully when considering what has long been envisaged as the next logical step for nuclear power—the large-scale reprocessing of spent fuel. The point of reprocessing is to recover plutonium, which can be mixed with uranium and used to produce more power. The plutonium can be put to work in the current generation of nuclear power stations, but would really come into its own with the development of fast breeder reactors.

Unfortunately, reprocessing magnifies the risks of nuclear power. It greatly increases the danger of nuclear proliferation, and is the key technology in making plutonium available to criminals or terrorists. Routine discharges of radioactivity from reprocessing plants, unlike those from nuclear power stations, do pose something of a problem; the gases released are much more dangerous, while the low-level wastes discharged to the sea from even the limited operation at Windscale are much greater than those from all other British nuclear installations put together. Reprocessing workers are also normally exposed to more danger than power station ones, and plants seem to have been particularly prone to accidents. The accident at Windscale in 1973 occurred when an unforeseen chemical reaction forced radioactive gas out through seals to contaminate the workers, while thirty-nine men were contaminated in fourteen separate incidents before the American plant at West Valley, New York, shut in 1972. Workers at the French reprocessing plant near Cherbourg went on a long strike over safety.

It has often been assumed that speedy reprocessing is an essential part of waste disposal. Certainly spent fuel from Britain's first generation of nuclear power stations cannot be stored under water for long before it corrodes, and the same may happen to the oxide fuel from her new ones after several years. But the oxide fuel used in most of the world's reactors, which is clad in a different material, can be stored for decades in this way, and even the British fuel can be safely kept in dry storage. Indeed spent fuel can probably be disposed of without being reprocessed at all, with the uranium and plutonium still locked up in the fuel rods with the wastes. Little work has been done on this because of the assumption that spent fuel would be reprocessed. But one highly authoritative study concluded in the spring of 1977 that reprocessing actually made waste problems *worse*, and that it would be safer, and possibly cheaper, to dispose of the fuel rods intact. This would also have the immense advantage of ensuring that the plutonium could not be used in bombs.

Besides being dangerous and not essential, reprocessing oxide fuel is difficult and expensive. Nations may find setting up a simple separation plant for bomb-making quite easy,* but running a large-scale operation on a commercial basis is a very different matter. The West Valley plant ran up big losses. General Electric built a plant with a different process, partly to try to reduce costs; but it could not be got to work and had to be abandoned as a 64 million dollar write-off. The Windscale plant closed after its accident in 1973. By 1977 not one large-scale commercial reprocessing plant for oxide fuel had been working anywhere in the Western world for some time.

*See Chapter 8. Unfortunately, too, the difficulties of reprocessing in large-scale plants do not seem to have discouraged nuclear threshold powers from wanting to buy them from France or Germany.

Several are now planned, but the economics of reprocessing, once thought to be favourable, are now looking increasingly doubtful. Both capital expenses and estimated running costs have soared. Many authorities believe that the cost of fuel produced by reprocessing will exceed its value, and so the operation will simply not be viable. 'Why', asked one analyst, 'take on proliferation, the worst environmental problems associated with nuclear power, and the only real terrorist problem, just to lose money?'

There is a reason, of course, why nuclear industries and the governments of most leading Western nations are eager to go ahead with reprocessing despite all these difficulties. While recycling plutonium may never make sense with present-day reactors, it could achieve enormous fuel savings with fast breeders. These reactors may seem like an industrial society's version of the philosopher's stone, for they can produce more usable fuel than they consume in turning uranium 238 (which cannot be used as a fuel) into plutonium (which can).* In this way, says the nuclear industry, fast breeders get at least fifty times as much energy out of uranium as present power stations. They therefore stretch uranium resources enormously, and offer countries much greater energy independence. The nuclear power industry promotes the new reactor strongly, and Mr Con Allday, Managing Director of British Nuclear Fuels Limited, the nationalised company that operates Windscale, has said, 'If we do not utilise the energy in plutonium then nuclear energy will not have been worthwhile.'

Unfortunately, the breeder intensifies the risks of nuclear power even further than does the reprocessing on which it depends. It brings its own dangers for nuclear proliferation and terrorism. Its spent fuel will be even more difficult to reprocess than the oxide

*Uranium 238, 99·3 per cent of natural uranium, will not sustain a chain reaction. It is the other 0·7 per cent, uranium 235, that can be used as a fuel. But when the uranium 235 is used in a reactor it will turn some of the uranium 238 into plutonium. This happens, as we have seen in Chapter 8, in any reactor, but in present power stations not enough plutonium is produced to compensate for the uranium 235 that is consumed. They are therefore sometimes called 'burner' reactors. Breeder reactors, however, are designed so that they can produce enough plutonium to more than replace the burned uranium 235. The plutonium can then be used again in the reactor instead of uranium 235, turning yet more uranium 238 into a powerful source of energy.

fuel from present-day reactors. A serious accident could have much more severe consequences if it took place in a fast breeder, and it may be more likely to happen.

The United Kingdom Atomic Energy Authority's own safety adviser has calculated that an accident in a fast breeder could be ten or a hundred times worse than one in a present-day reactor, and could conceivably cause up to 350,000 deaths and over 600,000 injuries. The two other near core melt-downs in the United States, apart from the Browns Ferry incident, both occurred in fast breeders, one in an experimental reactor, the other in a prototype near one of America's largest cities. Commenting on the second accident, an engineer of the firm that built the reactor said, 'We nearly lost Detroit'.

The nuclear industry believes that the fast breeders it is developing will prove stable in operation, though at least one of its experts states that, while they might possibly become safer than current power stations, they cannot yet be judged to be so. Some critics say that the reactor is inherently much more dangerous than the accident-prone Light Water Reactors. In fact it seems to have some features that would make it easier to handle than these, and others that will make it more difficult to control. The most emotive, if not the most likely, of the special hazards is that the fast breeder could conceivably produce a very small nuclear explosion.

The great advantage of the fast breeder is its power to stretch out fuel. Advocates of the reactor argue that we must employ this power as soon as possible, and therefore go in for large-scale reprocessing as a matter of necessity. Supplies of uranium are limited, runs the argument. Therefore, unless we have the fast breeder to use them more efficiently, they will run out. This contention relies on two assumptions—that uranium supplies are limited, and that nuclear power will grow fast enough to exhaust them. If either assumption is false the argument will not stand up.

Dire predictions of the scarcity of uranium are frequently made. But nobody knows how much uranium there is in the world; and nobody knows because until recently very few people have been looking. The uranium industry is only just emerging from a long and deep slump. Far from prospecting for new sources, companies were having to close mines down. Mr John Kostuik, Chairman of the Uranium Institute, told a symposium in London: 'Uranium is a relatively abundant mineral. However, it is generally accepted that only 15 per cent of the world's land surface has been well explored for uranium occurrences.'

Estimates showing a shortage of uranium can be misleading in another way; for they incorporate a cut-off figure and do not count uranium above a certain price. Yet, naturally, the more one is prepared to pay, the more uranium becomes economically available. Thus the 1974 World Energy Conference Survey of Energy Resources found that increasing the price by only 50 per cent, from 26 to 39 dollars per kilogram, quadrupled resources to about 4 million tons, and that at costs up to 200 dollars a kilogram the amounts of uranium available were in hundreds of millions of tons, and at costs of up to 500 dollars they were in thousands of millions of tons.

Of course, if you pay more for uranium you pay more for electricity, and uranium at 200 dollars a kilogram does not look particularly attractive at first sight. Nevertheless, an increase in the price of fuel has much less impact on the cost of generating electricity than it does in fossil fuel power stations. This is because the running expenses of nuclear power are comparatively low, and the cost of the electricity is determined much more by the high capital costs of building the nuclear plant in the first place. It has therefore been calculated, for example, that a fivefold increase in the price of uranium would only increase the cost of electricity generation by 30 per cent. And, by the same token, fast breeder reactors could not save us from increased electricity bills; for while their running costs are even lower than those of present-day reactors, their capital costs are very much higher. Indeed, by one estimate, fast breeders are unlikely to be able to compete with ordinary nuclear power stations until the price of uranium reaches between 220 and 440 dollars a kilogram. And that, of course, is about the price sufficient to unlock enormous reserves for conventional use.

Naturally, there are complicating factors. It takes time to find reserves and to start mines. The mining industry may now find it hard to expand fast enough to meet demand over the next ten years; but since even the most determined optimists do not expect the fast breeder to be in widespread use before the turn of the century it can do nothing to ease this pressure. There will probably come a stage at which it would take more energy to get the uranium out of the less concentrated ores than there would be in the finished fuel and there may also be other limitations on their exploitation. Uranium needs to be enriched before it can serve as fuel in most reactors, and the capacity of the plants that do this may prove to be a greater limitation than any absolute shortage of uranium, though the plants can be adjusted to process the fuel almost half as fast again as they do at present. Most serious, the mining and export policies of the countries that produce uranium may limit the amount of the material on the world market.

While these issues undoubtedly present problems for uranium supply, they do not add up to the open and shut case for uranium shortage that is so often presented. Furthermore, the second assumption—that nuclear power will grow rapidly—is even more questionable. The projections for nuclear growth submitted by the industrialised countries have been widely attacked as unrealistic and have in fact been scaled down drastically by most of the countries concerned. By one estimate we may actually have less than half the nuclear power capacity that they forecast for the end of the century.

Electricity demand need not, and will not, expand fast enough to require all the nuclear power stations to be built. In England, for example, it has grown much more slowly over the past decade than forecast, and in fact it has remained almost static for more than six years. Thanks to false expectations in the past, there is now a glut of power stations. The Central Electricity Board is shutting old ones down and expects to order new ones only slowly. Indeed it stopped new orders altogether, until forced by the Government to restart in order to save jobs in associated industries, and it may well not *need* to build any until well into the 1980s.

Even if the demand materialises, it may be impossible to build the reactors. For example, the Central Electricity Generating Board has said that 'it is questionable' whether the rate of growth forecast by the British Department of Energy could be achieved. It added: 'The programme beyond 1990 could not be carried out by the present resources of UK manufacturing industry.' We may not have the capital—estimated at 1,000 billion dollars for all rich countries between now and the end of the century—or the trained personnel. And already nuclear power programmes are getting bogged down by technical and design problems. Take Britain's experience. Her place in the van of nuclear technology slipped after she started building her Advanced Gas-Cooled Reactors (AGRs)—hailed by the Minister of Power in 1965 as 'the greatest breakthrough of all time.' Ten years and £1000m later not one watt of electricity had been produced, and indeed at the end of 1974 Britain's nuclear capacity was only about a third of the way to the target set in 1967. The AGRs eventually began coming on stream and were seen as successful, but meanwhile Britain had got into further difficulties. She had decided not to buy Light Water Reactors from the United States because of doubts about their safety, but then her industry ran into severe difficulty with its substitutes. Target dates were put back still further. Eventually the substitute was abandoned and the nuclear industry, the Government and the generating authorities became embroiled in an argument over whether to stick with the AGRs for the future or go back to the Light Water Reactors after all. 'Our record,' says Sir John Hill, Chairman of the UK Atomic Energy Authority, 'has got worse in spite of increasing ability and experience.'

John Maddox, while advocating nuclear power, has called its history one of 'comical misadventure' and 'spectacular engineering failures'. That seems harsh, for as he himself writes: 'The development of the steam engine in the nineteenth century took half a century. The exploitation of a technology every bit as novel is now planned in a mere decade.' He might have added that, unlike the technology of the steam engine, one bad slip in nuclear technology can mean not only death for thousands of people but thousands of delayed cancers, and a permanent legacy in genetic disease and disfigurement. It is hard to believe that we can safely implement a highly complex and potentially dangerous technology faster than we have ever managed to develop simpler and safer ones. Meanwhile, in the United States in 1975 there were twenty-five cancellations or deferments of nuclear power stations for every one that was ordered, and European governments have heavily cut back their construction plans. It really does not look as if those people who fear a uranium shortage need worry. Indeed, Sir John Hill seems to have conceded the point back in 1975, adding that the reason why we should speedily move on to the fast breeder was merely to keep down the price of fuel—an argument which, of course, is also of questionable validity.

A more sophisticated version of the uranium shortage argument holds that the fast breeder is valuable because it can give countries virtual self-sufficiency in nuclear energy. This argument has been particularly persuasive in nations that lack major uranium reserves. The ability of the breeder to stretch out uranium supplies seems to offer to protect them against OPEC-type action. Unfortunately, this case is undermined—and the simpler uranium shortage argument even further discredited—by the fact that it takes a very long time to mobilise the fast breeder's potential. For even if there are no serious technical hitches in the reactor's design—and these may well occur, because the engineering is extremely complex—there is a fundamental constraint on the speed at which it can be introduced.

The real fuel shortage may prove to be of fuel for the fast breeders themselves. The shortage will hold up their introduction even if the economic and technical difficulties of reprocessing are overcome. For though the fast breeder reactor does breed fuel, it does not do so particularly fast. It may take two or three decades for each reactor to produce the extra plutonium to enable a sister reactor to be started up. So at the beginning a fast breeder programme is heavily reliant on the plutonium produced by ordinary reactors. If such a programme is to be expanded at any speed it will have to be accompanied by a rapid expansion of conventional nuclear power stations to supply the necessary fuel. A recent analysis has examined the implications of this constraint. It concludes that at best a country cannot achieve virtual self-sufficiency through fast breeders in less than fifty years, and this involves a slow rate of growth both for the fast breeders and for nuclear power in general.

If countries want to speed up the rate of expansion—perhaps in a misguided pursuit of what they call 'independence'—they will have to build a large number of conventional nuclear plants, which will create a heavy demand for uranium. The country will then be stuck with a high proportion of conventional power stations in its nuclear system, and so will take much longer still to achieve near self-sufficiency. Indeed, if they keep up the high growth rate such independence will *never* be achieved.

On the other hand, if a country does settle for a slow expansion of the nuclear industry in order to achieve maximum independence as soon as possible it will make little difference to delay introducing the fast breeder for as long as thirty years, for the conventional nuclear power stations already in existence will be producing plutonium during this period, and will therefore build up sufficient stocks to allow the new reactors to proliferate quite quickly once they are brought in.

So the independence argument does not seem to justify an early introduction of the fast breeder, or a rapid growth in the reactors. Indeed, it may well not provide a good reason for having fast breeders at all. Even if a country manages to achieve the ideal programme, its breeders will be dependent on a relatively small number of reprocessing plants for their fuel. If one of these breaks down seriously or has an accident (and the past history of reprocessing is far from reassuring in this respect), then quite a large part of national energy supplies will be placed in jeopardy—and the same would happen if it was knocked out by saboteurs or in war. If a country is not able to build or operate sufficient, highly expensive, reprocessing plants to keep its fast breeders going it will be dependent on imports of fuel, just as it would be if it did not have these reactors. The dangers of nuclear proliferation and terrorism which accompany the spread of reprocessing and the fast breeder pose a far graver threat to any nation's security than lack of independence of fuel supplies. For though it is obviously advantageous to be as self-sufficient as possible, it is not exactly disastrous to have to purchase energy through international trade. Furthermore, if you really want to maximise self-sufficiency it may be better to pursue vigorous conservation and develop alternative sources of energy. Within the time needed for the fast breeder to have its full effect, it is likely that some renewable sources can be tapped on a large scale. These offer even greater promise of independence and have none of the undesirable side-effects of the plutonium economy.

It may still be argued that the breeder is worthwhile even though it cannot promise near-independence for a very long time, and even though uranium is not running out. Building breeders as quickly as fuel constraints allow will at least cut back the amount of uranium that has to be used, and therefore reduce imports and conserve supplies. And some nations without their own uranium reserves but with relatively well-advanced reprocessing plans feel that they would be wise to press ahead with fast breeders so that they could operate at least some nuclear power stations if drastic action by uranium exporting countries were to force them to cut back or close the rest of their nuclear industry.

However, a great deal of the energy savings can be achieved by choosing the most economical kind of conventional reactor, and still more can be saved by energy conservation. And if these nations are really worried about such dramatic restrictions of uranium they might be better advised to question the wisdom of proceeding with their plans for a large expansion of conventional reactors, while devoting very much more attention than they have done so far to implementing conservation and to developing alternative sources, for, as shown above, the overall contribution that fast breeders can make is not particularly great.

Any advantage gained by using fast breeders scarcely seems to justify the dangers associated with them. It seems that there are no really compelling reasons why we should embrace the plutonium economy, and many why we should try to do without it altogether.

President Carter's announcement in the spring of 1977 that he would seek to halt the development of plutonium for fuel in his country consisted of proposals to defer reprocessing and the recycling of plutonium through conventional reactors indefinitely, to scale down the research programme on fast breeder reactors, which had long enjoyed pride of place in government priorities, and to defer their introduction while other less dangerous models were investigated. These proposals did not satisfy opponents of nuclear power, or even go as far as many observers had expected, but they did represent the most considerable departure to date from the conventional view of nuclear expansion.

A few days before the announcement a weighty independent study had made similar recommendations. It cited proliferation as the most serious danger associated with nuclear power, and concluded that the economic benefits of both reprocessing and the fast breeder had been exaggerated, estimating that any net economic benefit from reprocessing during this century was 'questionable', and that fast breeders were not likely to prove competitive even in the first decades of the next one. The study carried particular authority as all the senior experts who prepared it (two of whom joined the Carter administration) had been specially chosen for not having previously taken up strong positions in the nuclear debate.

In Britain the year before, the Royal Commission on Environmental Pollution published the results of two years of study. In the words of its Chairman, Sir Brian Flowers, an atomic scientist of distinction, it had begun its work 'with an optimistic view of the science and technology of nuclear power in the normal course of events'. It finished up by saying:

> Our basic concern is that a major commitment to fission power and the plutonium economy should be postponed as long as possible, in the hope that it might be avoided altogether, by gaining the maximum time for the development of alternative approaches which will not involve its grave potential implications for mankind . . . . We should not rely for energy supply on a process that produces such a hazardous substance as plutonium unless there is no reasonable alternative.

It was just such concern as well as considerable public pressure, that forced the Government (at the last minute) to hold a mammoth and unprecedented public inquiry into the nuclear industry's plans to expand the reprocessing facilities at Windscale.

Reprocessing and the use of plutonium have, quite rightly, caused the greatest worries; but concern about nuclear power runs much deeper. The Royal Commission recommended that, whatever happened, there should be no commitment to a large programme of fission until a safe method of isolating nuclear wastes for the indefinite future had been demonstrated—a process expected to take at least ten years. In the spring of 1977 court decisions in West Germany stopped the construction of nuclear power plants on safety grounds.

Protest has been rising steadily in almost every country. In Sweden, where the Government instituted a programme of public education, national surveys showed about 80 per cent of the people against any further expansion of nuclear power on safety grounds, and a majority ready to accept a lower standard of living if necessary to reduce the use of energy. The Government decided to press ahead with nuclear fission nonetheless, and was defeated, after the party had been in power for over forty years, at elections in which nuclear energy was a central issue. At around the same time the Danish Government postponed *sine die* a bill giving it power to build the country's first nuclear power station, and an opinion poll showed for the first time that a majority of the people questioned were against the introduction of nuclear power. And people in the Basel area of Switzerland voted three to one in a referendum against plans to build nuclear power stations in the region.

In the United States in 1976, on the other hand, the citizens of seven states voted two to one against propositions to place stiff restrictions on the nuclear industry in their areas. However, the environmental opposition in that country, even if representing only a strong minority view, has been particularly effective in its fight against nuclear power. In Germany public protest has virtually halted a vast Government programme for nuclear expansion. Some protests there and elsewhere have been marred by a violent minority, repudiated by the rest of the anti-nuclear movement,—but it must be added that the authorities in several nations have been at least as violent. In France demonstrators have come up against riot police, explosive grenades and teargas. The French trade union representing most power workers has been at the forefront of the opposition, and other trades unions and four thousand scientists and technologists also called for a moratorium on expanding nuclear power from five to ten years. In the Netherlands, there has also been strong scientific and political opposition, and after debates on the subject the Government decided to postpone definite planning for three nuclear stations until after the next election. In Australia an official inquiry has urged caution over exploiting the country's enormous uranium reserves which could otherwise account for a large part of the world's supplies, and both the Labour Party and the trades union movement have called for a ban on it. In Spain, two hundred thousand people have marched against nuclear power, in Japan lawsuits and demonstrations have slowed progress dramatically, while in Italy local authorities have repeatedly refused to allow nuclear plants in their areas, arguing that they need schools and hospitals more. Delegates for embattled industries may have felt a bit wistful when a Soviet representative told a conference of 2,600 nuclear experts in Paris that public opinion in his country had 'fully accepted' the assurances given by the authorities over their nuclear power programme—but there seems to have been some sort of environmental opposition even in the USSR.

Almost everywhere the opposition is helping to slow down the expansion of nuclear energy. The more it grows, the less likely it is that nuclear fission will be successful in becoming the main energy source of the future. If, by some tragedy, there were to be a major accident, the public reaction might become overwhelming. In any case, the increasing alienation is a reason for countries to avoid becoming dependent on nuclear power.

In the final analysis, however, the debate over nuclear power rests on whether there are adequate alternatives. If there are not, we shall have to accept the hazards and trust to brilliant nuclear engineers to minimize them. Many believe that this is the real situation; many disagree. The first alternative proposed by nuclear critics is coal. There are also new sources to consider, and conservation.

Chapter 11

Sun, Moon, Earth ...

Suppose that we found that the world's oceans were filled, not with salt water, but with a fuel several hundred times as powerful as petrol. Developing fusion power could be the equivalent of making just such a discovery. Nuclear fusion would enable us to use deuterium, a form of hydrogen easily obtainable from seawater, and would therefore offer virtual freedom from resource limits. One per cent of the deuterium in the sea has the potential to supply more than half a million times as much energy as all the oil, gas and coal the earth has ever contained.

Unfortunately, the problem is the same as with almost every other form of energy; that of exploiting a theoretically abundant resource. The technical problems of fusion are almost as immense as its potential. It presents man with the Promethean challenge of creating on earth the process that takes place in the sun, which means kindling a fire of 100 million degrees Centigrade. Not surprisingly, the research has been extremely difficult and expensive. Two possible approaches have emerged from laboratory work, one creating a magnetic field to contain plasma at these high temperatures, the other using a laser or other high-energy beam to compress a pellet of fuel ten thousand times over. Formidable difficulties remain and each approach has yet to be proven. Even optimists do not expect that there will be a commercial fusion reactor in operation by the turn of the century; while the pessimists insist that it may never be possible to make one work. Even if the optimists are right, it looks as if fusion will be an immensely complex and expensive technology which will be hard to expand rapidly. We cannot expect it to make a significant contribution to world energy supplies for a long time to come.

Fusion, if it comes, will be much safer than nuclear fission, but it will not be entirely free of hazard. The most practicable means of fusion, on which both lines of research are concentrated, would use tritium, a radioactive poison that could be dangerous to workers and the public, though not nearly as vicious as some of the substances used in fission. It would give rise to some radioactive wastes, though on nowhere near the same scale. By adapting the process, it could be used to breed plutonium, and so there could be some risk for nuclear proliferation.

While research into such a process continues technology is being evolved to use the sun's energy here and now. Every year the equivalent of about 90,000 billion tons of coal lands on the earth's surface in the form of solar energy. If only 1 per cent of that energy could be tapped at about 5 per cent efficiency the whole of the world's population could achieve the same level of energy consumption as the United States. The fuel is free, clean and will be constantly available, whether we use it or not, for as long as life is possible upon earth. And although some nations—mostly poor ones—benefit very much more than others, all countries receive enough in theory to meet all their energy needs many times over. Even cloudy and densely populated Britain receives more than eighty times as much energy from the sun as there is in all the fuel that she burns. The problem, as usual, is not finding the energy but harnessing it.

We will never be able to exploit more than a tiny fraction of the solar energy that falls upon the earth, for obviously we cannot cover more than a minute proportion of the globe's surface with collectors, and there will be inevitable inefficiencies in conversion. The energy is so abundant that this does not matter; but there are two particular difficulties that do. Firstly, the diffuseness of solar energy requires relatively large collectors, which can be so expensive that they more than offset the advantage of free fuel. Secondly, solar energy varies from night to day, from season to season, and with the weather, while we usually need energy that is reliable and regular. Moreover, houses, for example, usually need more energy in the evening than in the heat of the day, and most temperate countries need much more energy in winter than in summer.

In one way, the diffuseness of solar energy can be treated as a benefit. Its wide spread means that it is distributed free. It can be tapped anywhere on a small scale, and this may very well be the best way to use it. The simplest and most practical method of doing this is to place collectors on the roof of a house to heat domestic water. They are already used widely in Japan, Israel and Australia, are becoming increasingly popular in the United States, and are even being taken up in Britain. The next step is to use solar energy for central heating as well as hot water.

Experimental solar houses were developed in the United States in the 1950s, and some have been working successfully for more than fifteen years in Denver, Colorado, and in Washington, D.C. They fell out of favour when oil was cheap in the 1960s, and only now are being developed again on both sides of the Atlantic. The designers of a solar house at Blyth, near Worksop, estimated that over a year the sun would provide 70 per cent of the family's hot water and between 30 and 40 per cent of their central heating. Another such house in Milton Keynes needs only half the conventional energy of the other houses on the estate, and the Building Research Establishment is building three houses, in which it plans to save two-thirds of the heating needed by conventional homes. Nine old people's homes on Merseyside are being built as solar houses.

Solar houses still have to move from the experimental stage to mass production. Between 200,000 and 300,000 may eventually be built in France each year if the Government-sponsored trial houses prove themselves. Some years ago a panel commissioned by the United States President's Office of Science and Technology called for a programme that would result in 85 per cent of all the country's buildings using solar energy by the year 2020. The United States Government was relatively unenthusiastic, but President Carter has placed new emphasis on this aspect of solar energy since coming to office.

Solar energy can already compete with electricity for heating in all the U.S.A. outside the state of Washington (where there is cheap hydro-electric power). This was recently underlined by an Energy Research and Development Administration (ERDA) report, which also gives reason to hope that it will be competitive with oil and gas as early as 1980. Solar technology is almost certain to improve and become relatively cheaper, while fuel prices are bound to rise. That also goes for Britain and other less favoured countries, where there is evidence that solar water heaters already prove less expensive than standard rate electricity.

In climates that warrant it, there is considerable potential for using solar energy for cooling by air conditioning. The sun's power is at its most abundant when it is most needed, and the combination of heating and cooling could obviously increase the economic attractiveness of solar installations.

These relatively simple ways of using solar energy match energy demands remarkably well, for a high proportion of all the energy used in industrial nations—and much the greater part of what is used in their households—goes to provide the low-grade heating which at least in theory could be met by these techniques. And air-conditioning means that the peak demand for many electricity grids in the United States, for example, is during the hottest weather. Meanwhile there is considerable potential for using troughs of mirrors focusing the sun's energy on to pipes to raise the intermediate temperature heat which makes up a third of American industry's requirements. This could also be used to drive turbines and to provide some electricity as a by-product.

Electricity is needed for a surprisingly small fraction of the tasks performed by energy, but it too is available from the sun. Again, it may be particularly useful to use the sun's free distribution system and tap the electricity where it is needed on a relatively small scale. Solar cells were used for this purpose in the American space programme, but their costs were also astronomical. However, their prices have been falling dramatically, and many experts are confident that this can continue in the same way as did the costs of transistors and pocket calculators. Japan is aiming to reduce the cells a hundredfold before long, and, researchers in Britain and the United States already claim to have made the breakthrough to economic competitiveness. In the past solar cells have absorbed more energy in their production than they have been able to produce during their working lives, but the energy costs seem to be falling as rapidly as their financial ones.

Solar cells tap an inexhaustible source of power. They produce no pollution, and no wastes. They contain no moving parts, and need very little maintenance. They could be integrated with solar heating and cooling systems to provide household needs, or grouped in appropriate numbers for whatever scale of task is required. If they can be made viable they offer the most attractive way of obtaining electricity from the sun.

Another approach goes back to Archimedes, the mathematician, who is said to have enlisted the aid of the sun against the Roman fleet that besieged Syracuse during the Second Punic War. We are told that he set fire to the ships when they were within bowshot of the city walls by using mirrors to reflect and concentrate the sun's rays. Two of the best-known advocates of solar power stations, Aden and Marjorie Meinel, reckon that he probably used 4,300 gold and bronze shields on wooden towers to reflect the sun. They estimate that this would have raised a temperature of 1,550 degrees Fahrenheit, more than enough to set fire to the dark sails within a few seconds.

During the 1950s and 1960s Dr Felix Trombe was working in the Pyrenees on essentially the same idea. By 1970 he had produced a huge solar furnace. Sixty-three mirrors, each about three times the height of a man, reflected the sun's rays onto another mirror which concentrated them on the furnace. Temperatures of up to 4,000 degrees Centigrade have been achieved in this way. Now France, the United States and the U.S.S.R. are working on a similar concept. In these 'power towers' a boiler mounted on top of a tower receives the sun's rays focused from banks of mirrors around its base. In January 1977 a prototype power station began feeding electricity into the French national grid, and both France and the United States plan to have larger commercial models in the 1980s. At present, however, they do not look economically competitive. The Americans reckon that the arrays of mirrors would have to cost no more than advertising hoardings, which are made of much simpler materials and do not need sophisticated steering mechanisms to keep them tracking the sun! Other developers are using the principle of troughs of mirrors and pipes to try to generate electricity on a large scale from 'solar farms', but since these produce it less efficiently than power towers, they look uninviting unless they are simultaneously used to provide heat. However, as the costs of conventional fuels continue to go up, the economic prospects of solar electric power stations should improve.

Such stations require a great deal of land, intense sunlight and stable weather in order to overcome the problems of diffuseness and variability. The United Kingdom section of the International

Solar Energy Society doubts whether they, unlike solar cells, will ever be viable in Britain. Desert areas not more than 35° North or South of the equator are the most attractive sites. By one estimate an area one hundredth of the Sahara could provide all the world's energy needs, even if the systems only achieved the very low rate of 5 per cent efficiency. By another, 115 square miles of desert in Arizona and California could provide three times the U.S.A.'s 1974 electricity demands. Unfortunately, transmitting electricity from such areas to distant centres of population like Western Europe and the eastern United States may be very expensive, even if it is feasible, so we are unlikely to decide to power most industrial societies from the deserts. Rather, energy intensive industries may eventually be attracted to sunny poor countries.

Two kinds of solar power stations that would not be dependent on stable, sunny weather are being pursued. One, promoted by NASA, the US space agency, seems zany. A monster satellite, equipped with two panels of solar cells, each many square miles in extent, would hover above one point of the earth, collect the sun's rays, and beam the electricity in microwaves to receivers on the ground. It would receive sunlight twenty-four hours a day for most of the year. Indeed, it would receive ten times the solar radiation of a station on earth because it would be above the filtering effect of the atmosphere. Among its many drawbacks, however, is the enormous amount of energy that would be needed for the rockets to assemble the satellite piece by piece in space—surely enough to kill the project. Moreover, many proponents of solar energy are frankly alarmed at the thought that the microwave might prove to be a death ray if it wandered from its course.

Another plan is to use the sea as a free collector of the sun's energy by generating power from the difference in temperature between the warm water near the surface and the cooler water deeper down. The United States hopes to have a prototype power station operating by the early 1980s, leading to a plant that could conceivably supply all the electricity needs of 50,000 people in 1985. The capital cost of such stations will be high, so a great deal will depend on whether they can withstand storms, corrosion, wear and tear and fouling by marine life, and so operate for long enough to justify the initial outlay. More worrying, some authorities fear that a large number of these plants could have profoundly disturbing effects on the life of the ocean, and on the climatic system of the world. Supporters of the technology say that these fears are groundless, but no more than small numbers should be deployed until they have proved their case. As we still know very little about the natural processes involved, it may be a long time before they are in a position to do so.

The attraction of these two ideas is that they exploit a constant source. The more variable the energy, the more storage it needs—and this is the biggest obstacle of all to solar power. Enough solar energy can be trapped by a house in Britain to satisfy its yearly heating needs; but lack of long-term storage makes this irrelevant. No way has yet been developed to storing the surplus energy provided in summer for heating the house in winter; although the short-term storage that we do use allows the sun to make a significant contribution to heating in spring and autumn as well as in the summer. Experiments are under way to try to store the heat chemically, and other ideas are being tried out, but until there is a breakthrough 'solar houses' in cool climates will have to rely on another source of energy besides the sun.

Storing electricity is equally difficult. There are several theoretical ways of doing it, but the only really practicable one at present is by using conventional batteries. They are bulky and expensive. In the unreliable climate of Britain, for example, these disadvantages would make the use of solar cells out of the question, despite the forecast reduction in their costs, unless new forms of batteries or other methods of storage were also developed.

Electrical industries get round the problem of variability by the grid system, starting up power stations to meet extra demand and shutting them off when they are no longer needed. But solar power, whether generated by scattered panels of cells or by solar stations, is unlikely to be popular with utilities, for they would have to provide back-up capacity to meet the demand on cloudy days when all the solar systems ceased operating at once. However, a possible solution is being developed by a utility in New Mexico which plans to combine 'power towers' with gas-fired plant. The sun would run the generators when it was out, and gas would take over when it failed to shine. No storage would be needed.

Besides, utilities have an interest in developing large-scale electrical storage systems, not least because nuclear power stations cannot be started up and shut down as easily as conventional ones. Indeed if nuclear electricity is to take up the load as gas and oil run out, as is planned, some form of storage will *have* to be developed. Unless it is—the Nobel prizewinner, Sir Martin Ryle, calculates—Britain will have to build three times as many power stations as would be needed to meet her average demand in order to provide enough energy on the few days of the year when it is most needed, an enormously expensive, and probably prohibitive undertaking. If some form of storing their energy for about a week were developed, less than half as much generating capacity would need to be built; but then, he points out, some renewable energy sources would also come into their own—and would, indeed, prove far cheaper than nuclear power.

Sir Martin believes that this energy would best be stored as low temperature heat on a fairly small scale near where it is going to be used. Several ways of doing this may well be feasible for a week, although not for longer periods. If storing electricity is preferred, one way of doing so, given suitable terrain, is to use surplus power to pump water uphill to a reservoir and then let the water run back through a hydro-electric power system when the energy is needed. This, of course, could be used to store energy for weeks or months rather than days, as could other forms of power storage being devised.

In Germany a unit for storing electricity by pressurising air is being built, while the Japanese are pursuing a particularly promising approach for solar energy, using electricity generated by the sun to split water and make hydrogen. This is excellent fuel in itself. It can be stored and transported, and it leaves no pollutants or wastes when it burns. Japan has plans to replace her electricity grid with hydrogen pipelines by 1999, and her scientists have developed a convenient way of running cars on the fuel. Furthermore, they are working on ways of using the sun's light to make hydrogen directly from water, without the need for electricity, and claim that this will make the fuel available at about the price of today's power.

Some supporters of solar energy say that the best long-term solution may be to use a storage system that nature already provides. As plants grow they convert and store the sun's energy; indeed, this was how the world's stocks of fossil fuels was first formed.

However, on average plants only manage to make use of 0·1 per cent of the solar power they receive, and far too much land and energy would be required to exploit them. But the proponents of the idea point out that some plants achieve efficiencies ten to thirty times greater, and that such crops could be grown on marginal or waste ground, or even in the sea, so as not to compete with normal agriculture. Brazil has launched a 500 million dollar programme with an initial target of providing a fifth of her motor fuel from fermenting cane sugar and manioc by 1985, and the Nobel-Prize-winner Melvin Calvin is enthusiastic about Euphorbia bushes, which grow on arid land and produce a sap similar to petroleum. It is true, too, that most of the world's people already use firewood as their main fuel, and sensible reafforestation schemes could help to preserve the land as well as produce a continuing supply of energy. Generally speaking, however, growing plants for fuel is only a promising proposition in hot developing countries with plenty of land and manpower available.

It is only realistic to acknowledge the technical problems in harnessing solar energy; but they should not stop us either from seeing the potential of using the sun's power, or from undertaking the research and development work needed to realise it. Serious work on solar energy and the other 'natural' sources is only just beginning. Had anything like the sums that have been poured into nuclear power been devoted to them we would almost certainly be immeasurably further ahead. Solar energy may already be proving its feasibility in poor countries; and while it offers no hope of helping rich countries to continue their recent *growth* in energy use, it can still make a substantial contribution to meeting energy needs. Even the British Government reckons that solar power could eventually provide the equivalent of 20 per cent of the country's present energy demand; while in 1975 ERDA estimated that by 2020 the sun could produce the equivalent of two-thirds of the United States' enormous present energy consumption.

The United States figures include a relatively small contribution from wind power, which at first sight looks one of the least promising of the alternative sources of energy. There is, of course, no lack of wind energy. The World Metereological Organisation calculates, for example, that 20 million megawatts of electricity, more than thirteen times the capacity of all the world's power stations, is theoretically available at the choicest sites on land, and considerable amounts could also be harnessed by windmills at sea. Again the question arises, however—can it be exploited on the right scale?

Small windmills certainly have a role in remote rural areas and as part of the intermediate technology that is needed in the poor world. While this has been conceded for some time, wind power has seemed a dubious source of energy for industrialised societies. However, some hard-headed surveys have recently been coming up with surprisingly optimistic estimates. One study, carried out for ERDA, predicted that wind could be making ten times the contribution contained in the solar energy figures quoted above. It reckoned that, as early as 1995, wind power could be meeting a fifth of the national electricity demand. Other studies suggest that Sweden coud achieve the same contribution from windpower by 1990, and that in time more than a fifth of Britain's present electricity supplies could also be provided in this way. On a local scale it is also useful for producing low grade heat.

Storage again presents a problem. The wind seems to be even more unreliable than solar energy. However, it will often compensate for lack of sunshine by blowing most strongly at times and places little favoured by the sun. In Britain, for example, it is strongest when the energy is most needed, during the winter. It is likely to be windy somewhere in each country almost every day and, moreover, there are sites where the wind is very steady.

The flat lands of Denmark, for example, are one of the windiest areas of Europe. The longest calm period ever recorded there is seven days. It now appears that electricity from windmills may be cheaper than supplies from nuclear power, and that if it could be stored for only twenty-four hours Danish windmills could provide power as reliable as nuclear reactors. Advocates of the system say that wind could provide Denmark with half its energy.

Denmark and Sweden, moreover, are considering linking up windpower and hydro-electricity. Existing Swedish hydro-electric stations would provide energy to both countries on calm days, while on windy ones electricity would be generated from Danish and Swedish windmills that would both take over from the hydropower and pump extra water back into the reservoirs. This combination could make sense elsewhere. Meanwhile another ingenious solution has been proposed in Britain. Dr Peter Musgrove of Reading University suggests building windmills in the shallow, windy areas of the southern North Sea. At present the country's major natural gas fields are in this area, and as they are exhausted they could be filled with compressed air produced by surplus windpower and kept ready to be used to drive the turbines when the wind stopped blowing. Winds are steadier at sea, and one other way of exploiting this would be for such mills, or ones floating in deeper water, to produce hydrogen from seawater.

Power generated by the wind could also be fed into electricity grids. The grids are flexible enough to accommodate it, so long as they do not become dominated by nuclear power, though the utilities are likely to be less so. The utilities have good reasons to be unenthusiastic about windpower as well as solar electricity, but national energy needs may mean that using the grid is in the public interest all the same.

Windmills have been used for thousands of years, but little work has been done to develop them recently. However, several prototypes of giant mills are now being built, and new designs are being devised. One of the more exotic is the 'tornado machine' now being developed on a U.S. Government grant. A tall tower would let wind in at the base and make it swirl up through 'sails' inside them, thus, it is suggested, generating as much electricity as a small conventional power station.

There is fierce debate about the economics of windpower; some experts insist that it can already compete with conventional sources of energy; others are equally emphatic that it still has some way to go. The prototypes and new designs now being built and tested should provide us with some firm evidence, though, of course, this is another field where mass production should reduce capital costs while the free fuel becomes more and more of an advantage as the costs of conventional fuels rise. Most plans envisage groups of large machines on particularly windy sites. This makes some sense, as the amount of power generated increases dramatically with both the size of the windmill and the speed of the wind; if the diameter of the blade is doubled the power output is quadrupled, while a doubling of windspeed increases power eightfold. On the other hand, small machines might be more economical, for they may benefit more from mass production, they can operate in much lower winds, and it may be possible to site them closer to electricity consumers and so reduce transmission costs. We should know a great deal more about windpower's potential in a few years. Meanwhile, despite first impressions, it cannot be written off as an insignificant source of energy; indeed it may well prove to be one of our most promising options in the medium term, particularly since windmills can be constructed more quickly than most other ways of generating electricity.

By contrast, hydro-electric power is a well-tried method of generating electricity, and although its potential is limited—the 1974 World Energy Conference estimated that at most it could meet a sixth of the world's present energy needs—most of the available resources are in poor countries. China, Africa, Latin America and South-East Asia are particularly favoured. Unfortunately, without substantial aid the capital cost needed for big dams is well beyond the means of most poor countries; and even when the money is available the sudden rush of power from a big dam (it can triple or quadruple a country's energy supplies at a stroke) cannot be easily distributed to the people who need it, and it may lead to the establishment of energy intensive industries to mop it up, hindering balanced development. Often, too, the dams have unforeseen side effects, while collapse through engineering failure or sabotage could possibly cause comparable deaths to a major accident in a nuclear power station and knock out a large proportion of a poor country's energy supply. Furthermore, silt builds up in the lake behind the walls, eventually drying up the whole scheme so that, while the river will go on running forever, many installations may not have a life expectancy of much more than a hundred years.

Fortunately, exploitation of the power of the rivers does not depend entirely on big dams; small schemes not only avoid many of these drawbacks but also increase the resources available from hydro-electric power, for they are usually ignored in official estimates of potential. By 1975 China had some 60,000 small hydro-stations in operation. Though their capacity is small, they have contributed greatly to bringing electricity to the Chinese countryside. Apparently they produce most of the power for three-quarters of China's communes and half her production brigades. They were built quickly by labour intensive methods, and also provide irrigation and flood control which may prove even more important than their electricity. Other ways of using water power on a small scale include axial flow turbines, which can generate electricity without dams, providing power from relatively slow-running rivers. More than fifty sets of these turbines are already in use or under construction on French rivers.

Wave power is the 'natural' source of energy given the highest priority by the generally unenthusiastic British Government. The north-west coast of Britain is pounded by particularly energetic waves which are at their strongest in winter, when Britain most needs the energy. The Government says that about half of Britain's present electricity supplies could be provided from a six-hundred-mile stretch of ocean. Dr Stephen Salter, who has developed a pear-shaped hull that rocks with the waves, is much more optimistic. He believes that arrays of them, the size of modern super-tankers, could satisfy the equivalent of all of Britain's present electrical demands from only three hundred miles of sea. He sees no reason why the whole of Europe's supplies should not eventually be met from the Atlantic rollers, and believes that, despite some difficulties, wave power could be entering large-scale use in the 1990s. Another system is being developed by Sir Christopher Cockerell, inventor of the hovercraft. In the spring of 1976 the British Government launched a million-pound investigation into these two systems, and two others. It found the results so encouraging that it more than doubled the spending before half the time set for the inquiry had elapsed. Japan is also pursuing wave power energetically.

The winds, falling water and the waves are all part of the massive system of forces set in motion by the solar radiation that enters the atmosphere. The tides, powered by the moon as well as the sun, present another challenge for harnessing the self-renewing energy of the oceans. The Central Electricity Generating Board estimates that the Severn Estuary could provide 10 per cent of the country's electricity needs, though it says that the cost of tapping the energy, £3–£4 million, would render it for the present uncompetitive with other sources of power. A relatively small tidal energy station is already operating in France, and the United States and the U.S.S.R. are also making studies. Although certain sites can yield enormous amounts of energy, tidal power is limited to relatively few places around the globe. The 1974 World Energy Conference estimated that there might be a potential world capacity of 64,000 megawatts— rather more than all the electrical power stations in England and Wales.

Another source of energy lies, literally, at our feet. The top six miles or so of the earth's crust contain ten thousand times as much heat as could be produced by burning all the reserves of fossil fuels so far discovered. Geothermal heat continually flows from the core of the earth to the surface. Here again there is no shortage of energy, but a problem in how to exploit a theoretically bountiful resource.

By the time the heat reaches the earth's surface it is normally so diffuse that you would need to collect all the heat emerging from an area the size of ten football pitches in order to power a single electric kettle. So to exploit geothermal energy effectively you either have to find unusual conditions or bore particularly deep into the earth. Indeed, you may have to do both.

Dry, superheated steam, trapped in rock, provides the simplest way of generating electricity from the earth. One such source has been powering turbines at Larderello, Italy, since the beginning of the century. Another is working in California. Both are about a quarter of the size of the biggest conventional power stations being built. Unfortunately, these reservoirs of steam are relatively rare; only about a dozen have been found so far, but then exploration has scarcely begun. Sites that produce both steam and hot water are much more common, although harder to exploit. They generate electricity in New Zealand and Mexico. There are also places where the pressure of water is so great that its sheer force, rather than its heat, might be used for generating power.

But, of course, hot water can be used for heating rather than electricity, and this opens up more possibilities for the use of geothermal energy. Water hot enough for heating can be found more often than the water and steam at the temperatures above 200 degrees Centigrade that are needed to generate electricity. While the really hot kettles in the earth are confined to areas of comparatively recent volcanic and geological activity, the cooler ones can be found in more placid areas. So two thousand houses near Paris are heated from the earth as well as most homes in

Iceland,* and geothermal heat is used extensively in Hungary as well as in New Zealand. Such reservoirs appear to be very widespread, though once again little exploration has been done.

All these reservoirs depend on there being water or steam in the earth to absorb the geothermal heat before being extracted. The potential of geothermal energy could be greatly increased if ways were found of tapping the heat in dry rocks. We have not yet developed the technology to do this; a great deal depends upon a pilot scheme under way at Los Alamos, New Mexico. This has already shown that it is possible to drill deep into granite and fracture it with water pressure, and then inject water down one borehole, let it pass through dry rocks, heat it up, and bring it back to the surface through a second well. In theory this method could be used almost anywhere on earth; in practice, of course, it will depend on geological conditions. Volcanic areas would be the most favourable; but it looks as if hot water, and possibly electricity, could be produced economically even in a country such as Britain.

Some geothermal schemes will cause pollution, and there is some concern that injecting water could cause earthquakes. Most schemes will deplete their rock, water or steam reservoirs of heat in time. The small amount of geothermal electricity production that has already taken place cost less than power from nuclear or fossil fuel plants. Admittedly this production was from prime sites, but prospects should be improving all the time. Indeed, seventeen developing countries are planning or building geothermal electricity plants.

Little work has been done to find out the geothermal potential of the earth. The conventional view has been that the resources are significant only in a few local places. However, Dr Joseph Barnea, Director of the Resources and Transport Division of the UN Department of Economic and Social Affairs, has said that 'geothermal energy has a vast potential on a global basis and can be developed in many countries of the world. In fifty years it will be recognised as an energy resource of even greater significance than petroleum.' Other United Nations experts support him, though unquestionably the significance of geothermal power will differ

*France plans to expand her use of geothermal hot water to heat half a million homes by 1990.

from country to country. One authoritative United States report estimated a few years ago that with vigorous research and development the U.S.A. could by the year 2000 be producing more electricity than its entire present production from all sources. United Nations earth scientists have found enough geothermal resources in Ethiopia to satisfy the whole of Africa's demand at the end of the century.

The optimists may be theoretically right, but it is hard to see how geothermal energy could be developed on such a scale in so short a time. There are technical difficulties in the exploitation of hot water from the earth which will almost certainly delay its expansion; the potential of dry rock techniques is still undeveloped; and the less favoured countries are unlikely to find the geothermal resources to make up more than a small fraction of their needs.

Surprisingly perhaps, the refuse in our dustbins is another source of energy. Each household in Britain throws out almost a ton of rubbish each year, and the eighteen million tons of domestic garbage is joined by about twice as much from industry. It can be burned as it is to provide central heating or to generate electricity, and several cities in Britain and America already do this. It can also be turned into oil or gas. America's dustbins produce a particularly 'rich' blend of garbage, rich enough to provide a barrel of oil with three-quarters of the fuel value of ordinary oil for every ton of rubbish. The British Government is developing an elaborate mechanical sorting scheme in the North-East of England which will separate valuable waste for recycling and turn plastic and useless paper into a fuel pellet to be mixed with coal in furnaces. Fluidized bed combustion may be particularly useful for burning rubbish.*

Until now burning rubbish has mainly been seen as a convenient means of disposal. More recently people have come to see it as a new source of energy. In fact it is really a form of energy conservation; for energy has been burnt to produce almost everything that goes into the dustbin. By using the rubbish as fuel again, some—but never anything like all—of that energy can be reclaimed. Eliminating the unnecessary packaging that produces much of the household waste in the first place would be a better way of saving energy.

*See Chapter 9.

Agricultural wastes offer more potential. A U.S. Government study concluded that even a moderate development programme could provide more energy by the end of the century than is expected from the nation's nuclear power programme. In smaller, more densely populated countries like Britain there is clearly much less scope, but substantial energy savings are possible, at least in theory. If surplus straw was turned into fuel instead of being burned off, if fertilisers were not wasted, and if animal and crop wastes were turned into methane gas, British agriculture might need only half the conventional energy it uses at present.

The last of these processes can be particularly valuable in developing countries. Animal, human and vegetable wastes can all be used to produce 'biogas', so called because the gas is not pure methane. The gas can provide energy for cooking, generating electricity, pumping water, even for driving farm machinery and light industry. The production of gas removes hardly any of the nutrients from the wastes which can then be spread on the land as fertiliser. It is a remarkable example of how an appropriate technology can help to provide the best of both worlds. At present millions of poor people get their energy only at the cost of impoverishing the land, by burning dung or wood. On the other hand, a big artificial fertiliser plant produces nutrients for the land, but only by consuming enough energy to meet the needs of several hundred villages. But a village biogas plant, if handled and maintained with care, can both meet the community's energy needs and more than double the amount of fertiliser that it puts on the land. At the same time such plants provide a safe means of sewage disposal, are non-polluting, and can provide up to a hundred times more jobs than either modern fertilising factories or an energy supply based on oil or electricity. India pioneered biogas plants. The Chinese say they have more than 4 million of them, and they are in wide use in Taiwan and in both North and South Korea.

The Sudanese Government and NASA have joined forces to try out another way of producing biogas. They hope to reap benefits from a weed which everyone has been trying to exterminate. Water hyacinths, one of the most prolific plants in the world, clog up rivers, ditches and irrigation canals in more than fifty countries. If harvested and encouraged to rot they seem to be equally prolific in producing gas. What is more, they will purify water of both sewage and highly toxic industrial pollutants. NASA wants to use them to recycle water in space stations. Before long they may be doing the job of sewage and industrial treatment plants in the warmer countries of the earth, and producing energy at the same time.

Eventually we may exploit even more exotic ways of producing energy from wastes by using the sun's power to grow organisms upon them. There have already been promising results from growing algae on sewage and fungus on waste paper, for the growth can be turned into food, into fuel or even into a feedstock for chemicals.

The prospects of getting fuel from wastes are very much the same as those from the 'alternative' energy sources in general. They have some immediate uses in rich countries; but they cannot provide anything like enough energy fast enough to allow us to continue to double our consumption every fourteen years. However in poor countries some of the processes already developed could make an immediate impact. And further research and development could bring enormous advances and make some of them major sources of energy throughout the world, certainly by the next century. A strategy of developing a mix of these alternatives, combining the advantages provided by the various sources at different times of the year and at different locations, is needed urgently.

Chapter 12

... *And People Power*

'The process is the policy', remarked Maurice Strong, the 'father' of the United Nations Environment Programme, and now President of Petrocanada. Nowhere is this more true than in the formulation of energy strategy. New sources take so long to be developed that energy policy may be determined, whether by omission or commission, long before any formal decision is announced.

Research and development is particularly important. Everything turns upon it. Neglect in this area in the past is a major reason why the use of alternative sources is so little advanced, and why we still have only a vague idea of what their ultimate potential may be. Until recently the research and development that was put into new sources of energy was devoted almost exclusively to nuclear power. The United States spent 63 per cent of its 1974 research and development on nuclear energy, only 4 per cent on other new sources; and other developed countries showed an ever greater imbalance.

So it is not surprising that nuclear power is presented as the only new source of energy capable of meeting a major part of our needs in the next quarter of a century. Indeed, this increasingly becomes a self-fulfilling prophecy, for the longer nuclear energy continues to appropriate almost all the available research funds, the more it becomes the only new option open to us. Nor is the imbalance merely financial. If all the effort goes into a single new source, that is where the brightest scientists will tend to make their careers. The monopoly of specialist talent that results has an even more lasting effect than the monopoly of resources. It is a short-sighted policy, for if the gamble fails there is no other new source to fall back on; and it seems particularly foolhardy when the source on which we are staking our future is nuclear power, which faces such exceptional difficulties, and which arouses such strong public reactions.

A few countries, however, like the United States and Japan, have dramatically increased their spending on natural sources. Government funding for solar energy in the United States soared from 13 million dollars in 1974 to over 300 million in 1977, and there is also a major programme in geothermal power. Japan is allocating large sums to be spent over the last quarter of this century—more than $3\frac{1}{2}$ billion dollars for geothermal power, and more than 3 billion for both solar energy and the development of hydrogen as a fuel. These national plans may not satisfy proponents of such sources in those countries; but they do provide an example to the rest of the world through showing up the inadequacy of what is being done elsewhere. In the spring of 1977, for example, Britain was spending only about 4 million dollars a year on all natural sources put together, while considering spending more than three *billion* dollars on a prototype commercial fast breeder.*

Of course, a heavy bias towards spending on nuclear power is irrelevant to the needs of the Third World. The OECD is no opponent of nuclear power; nor is it opposed to rich countries exporting their know-how to poor ones for cash; but it reports, 'Nuclear power is ill-suited to developing countries because of its complexity and high cost and the need for highly qualified personnel.'

Nuclear energy, like many other Western energy production technologies, is highly capital intensive. The report goes on,

> Even if these technologies could be transferred on a large scale—which is unlikely because of bottlenecks in the production of energy equipment in the OECD countries—it could in the final outcome go against the interest of developing countries. Instead of stimulating the use of local resources, for example, it would merely replace the Third World's present dependence on the Middle East for oil or capital by a far more permanent dependence on the developed countries for technological capability.

*In 1976–7 France, however, budgeted 15 million dollars for solar energy alone as part of a general programme on natural sources; and West Germany budgeted about $12 million.

Besides, nuclear power has to be generated in big, expensive power stations. It can only be used to produce electricity, which then has to be distributed through a grid system. It is beyond the means of most poor nations to install an adequate grid or to extend one far into the country. At best, nuclear power would tend to produce power only for the cities, and would do nothing to aid the rural development which should be the priority throughout the Third World.

So nuclear energy fails almost every test in the new strategy for development. It would be likely to increase the dependence of poor countries upon rich ones. It is capital intensive, and so creates few jobs. It does nothing for rural development, and can only aggravate some of the worst effects of the Trickle-down strategy.

Some of these strictures apply equally to certain applications of the 'natural' energy sources. Fusion power and solar satellites would be inappropriate; and in most cases big 'power tower' solar electric stations, big dams, huge tidal energy schemes and similar concepts would be out of place. But most of the natural sources, unlike nuclear power, are flexible. They are not confined to big installations, but can be tapped on a small enough scale to benefit local communities, the countryside and small towns. The technology needed to do this can be made cheap enough, and need not involve complex processes. Above all, these are resources—the sun, wind and falling water, for example—that many poor countries enjoy in plenty. The OECD report, which so roundly dismissed nuclear power, concludes that it is through using these resources rather than more conventional ones 'that a number of countries might achieve relative independence in energy and technology'. What is more, their use could encourage rural development, more employment and decentralisation.

The biogas plants provide one good example, and there are others. Heat from solar panels can be valuable even in warm countries; hot water improves hygiene, and the energy collected by panels has also been used to drive pumps. Solar cookers and solar stills are being developed. A small solar power station, it has been calculated, could provide all the energy needed for cooking, lighting and pumping irrigation water in an Indian village—and would use up less land than is needed to feed the animals that are now used for pumping water alone. Cheap solar cells could have a considerable impact on small communities. Windmills can be particularly useful for pumping water, processing crops and powering small industries. Geothermal power, so it is said, is not dependent on economies of scale, and so can be harnessed in small amounts where it is available. Water power is also valuable on a small scale. Where climate and terrain permit, a village may be best served by a mixture of these techniques. Appropriate technology can also ensure that poor people get as much value as possible out of the little fuel they can afford; simple improvements in the design of wood-burning cooking stoves can increase their efficiency four-fold.

Poor people have access to so little energy that providing quite small amounts of it can greatly improve living standards; but laying on additional supplies to a village does not automatically reduce poverty, any more than does supplying the new seeds of the Green Revolution. Social conditions are crucial. If a source of energy is put into the hands of the rich man of the village, for example, disparities may only increase. In the hands of a genuine co-operative it will have much greater benefits for the whole community. Despite the need for this caveat, such decentralised ways of providing energy present the only real hope of meeting the basic needs of most of the poor. How else, for example, are proper energy supplies going to reach the 600,000 Indian villages that lack them? That is not to say that they should be the *only* form of energy in developing countries. The needs of some cities and industries will demand more intensive, centralised systems; before too long, if they can be properly developed, renewable sources of energy may be the best option for these systems as well. Gerald Leach writes that the poor countries have only three broad alternatives, 'to remain in fuel poverty, to buy traditional fuels at crippling prices, or to develop indigenous income sources such as solar energy'.

In some ways poor countries will find it easier than rich ones to make the most of alternative energy. Besides possessing many of the sources in abundance and most of their people in the countryside, they are not yet totally committed to rich world patterns of energy use that demand centralised systems and can only be changed with difficulty. Unfortunately Third World governments, enmeshed in the Trickle-down theory and enamoured of grandiose projects, have done their best so far to emulate developed societies —and rich world aid for energy has overwhelmingly been provided for the same purpose—even though oil and gas are running out and nuclear power cannot expand fast enough to meet their needs. Between 60 per cent and 80 per cent of their energy investments have typically been devoted to the electrical systems that cannot reach the mass of the people. So the money desperately needed for energy in the villages has been squandered.

Supported by most rich-country governments, the atomic salesmen will continue to travel the globe with their totally inappropriate wares; and the more nuclear programmes are slowed down at home, the more they will be anxious to sell abroad. Poor countries will be told that alternative sources are old-fashioned or second-best, even though they may be the only way of providing modern energy to most poor people. Some countries may be persuaded by the salesmen (and by the subsidies offered by rich-country governments), some may hope to have the chance to build nuclear weapons, and some may simply remain more interested in developing pockets of affluence in the cities than in meeting the basic needs of the poor. Only Papua–New Guinea responded to a call to decline the atomic option made by a group of eminent people at the 1976 UN 'Habitat' Conference in Vancouver. Nevertheless, the salesmen may yet be disappointed. Nuclear power is so inappropriate to developing countries that even the International Atomic Energy Authority, which is dedicated to promoting it, is having drastically to cut back its expectations.

Meanwhile, the energy establishments in most rich countries argue that a major programme of nuclear power is not only appropriate for industrialised economies, but vital for their prosperity.* By and large, governments and their advisers expect that the use of energy will, and should, go on growing at much the same rate as it has

*Some nuclear advocates, while accepting that atomic power is inappropriate for poor countries, argue that developed nations should expand their nuclear industries so as to release oil for developing nations. It sounds an appealing argument, but it has little validity. If we are really concerned about energy for poor countries we should concentrate much more on developing the renewable sources. It makes little sense for poor countries to base their societies upon oil when oil is running out; while the renewable sources also promise to be a much better economic bargain for them. But if the West were to expand nuclear power full-out it would have little cash or attention to spare for alternative energy sources.

done in recent decades. None of the fossil fuels, of course, can sustain that kind of growth, and none of the renewable or 'natural' sources of energy can be exploited quickly enough to take their place; some of them, indeed, can never be more than supplementary sources. So what is left but nuclear power?

Unfortunately for this viewpoint nuclear power will not be able to expand fast enough either; and if further confirmation is needed that it cannot satisfy a continuing growth of five per cent a year in the world's use of energy one calculation should provide it. Even if we assume that by the beginning of the next century we were able to burn twice as much oil, gas and coal as we do at the moment (which may not be a wise assumption considering the closeness of oil and gas to extinction) we would have to build about one big nuclear power station a day between now and then to sustain the growth rate.

So, despite fond expectations, recent rates of energy growth simply cannot be perpetuated. Indeed attempts to continue past trends are likely to lead to economic disaster. For since fuel production could not long go on keeping up with this kind of expansion in consumption, energy would soon become scarce and enormously expensive. The effect would dwarf that of the 1973 OPEC price rises.

Fortunately there is good reason to suppose that the growth rate will naturally slow down, if it is not artificially stimulated. The fall in population growth in rich countries is bound to have an effect. The number of households is also likely to increase much less rapidly. Since 1900 the average number of people in Britain's dwellings has declined from 5 to 2·75, and so there has been a much greater increase in the number of homes than in the population as a whole. Household size can scarcely halve again and the growth of dwellings is, indeed, expected to be much slower in future. This is important, for households are a basic unit of demand, not only for heating and lighting, but also for private cars, electrical appliances, and goods from furniture to floorcloths which take energy to produce. Similarly as more and more existing houses achieve central heating, washing machines, fridges and television sets a saturation point is approaching. The same sort of thing may happen in road transport which accounted for one-third of the increase in British fuel use between 1960 and 1973. There are limits both to levels of car ownership and to the number of miles each vehicle is likely to cover each day, and the nearer we get to them the more the rate of growth of petrol consumption is likely to decline. Again, if, as many predict, much of the future expansion in the economy will be in such areas as services, electronics, communications and other industries less energy-intensive than those that have fuelled our growth in the past, this will also have a significant effect. And the fact that energy prices will certainly continue to rise, instead of declining in real terms as they did for a long time before 1973, should in itself have an impact on trends.

At any rate, once one accepts that the use of energy in the rich world cannot, and will not, grow at the same sort of rates as in the past, the renewable sources of energy begin to look more promising. It is possible to construct scenarios which could take advantage of the remaining oil and gas, the bridge of coal, and the growing use of the new sources, thereby avoiding major dependence on nuclear power.

The natural slowing of increases in fuel consumption may make conventional expectations ludicrous, but it cannot be enough in itself to make these new scenarios practicable or to avoid a future energy crisis. Deliberate measures to reduce growth must also be taken. But in reacting from the fantasy of the official projections it is important not to become equally unrealistic. For example, it is theoretically possible to stop energy growth altogether, and if this were to be done then we could immediately convert to a policy of developing only the natural sources of energy. Josef Kates, Chairman of the Science Council of Canada, for instance, says that investigations have shown that if the country stopped its energy growth it could meet all its needs from 'natural' sources within fifty years, gradually phasing out fossil fuels and ignoring nuclear power. Dr Peter Chapman, Director of the Energy Research Group at the Open University, has shown that Britain could—again in theory—immediately convert to a zero growth policy based on solar heating, use of agricultural waste and more efficient use of existing energy sources; and she could still produce the rising standard of domestic comfort she would gain from an all-out, and probably impracticable, expansion of coal, nuclear power and oil production. Professor Bent Sorensen of the Niels Bohr Institute at the University of Copenhagen has worked out a programme, using technology that is already available, whereby Denmark could convert to major dependence on solar and wind energy and eliminate both nuclear fission and fusion, while at the same time reaching a higher standard of living. However, an immediate halt to energy growth would just not be acceptable in any society, nor would it be any more practical than an immediate stop to the economic growth to which it has been linked. There are social as well as technical barriers to a rapid change of direction. After outlining his low-growth policy Dr Chapman himself commented, 'It is the perfect recipe for reproducing the Great Depression of the 1930s.'

Fortunately the choice is not merely between the perils presented by stopping growth altogether on the one hand and by continuing past policies on the other. On the contrary energy conservation allows us to moderate growth rates, both in the short and long term, to everybody's benefit. So much energy is wasted in rich countries that we can deliberately achieve a much slower rate of growth with little or no damage to rising prosperity or comfort. This allows us to make considerable changes in the short term, and the long-term advantages are overwhelming. By taking energy conservation seriously we can keep our options open. We can stretch out our use of fossil fuels and delay the point at which we may exceed the climatic limit on energy consumption; we shall have time to develop the natural sources of energy, or if this is possible, safe nuclear power; indeed, the gradual transition made possible by conservation could allow us eventually to opt for zero energy growth without unpleasant economic consequences. But we shall have to tap the greatest, and most neglected, energy resource of all—the will and imagination of consumers of fuel.

Until 1973 there had been scarcely any research on how to make better use of energy. It was the soaring cost of oil, and the world's belated shock at discovering its dependence on it, that suddenly made energy conservation fashionable.

It is important to see conservation in perspective, however, and not as an end in itself. Conservation means ending waste. After all, if our aim were purely to *save* energy our best policy would be to close down industry, turn out the lights, and shiver without heating. The industrial recession of the mid-1970s has led to a lower use of energy because industry is moving at a slower pace, but the resulting saving of energy is scarcely a reason for staying in a slump. Similarly, poor families who have insufficient energy to keep themselves warm, need like poor countries to *increase* their consumption. No energy conservation strategy should ignore this.*

Although some reductions have been made recently, all rich countries could do a very great deal more. Some have a particularly large amount of slack to take up. Each American uses about twice as much energy as the equally wealthy Swede or German. Britain uses about twice as much energy per unit of GNP as France.

Great amounts of energy can be saved without any reduction in the standard of living. A multimillion dollar Ford Foundation study concluded in 1974 that energy conservation could enable the United States to meet demand for a decade without increasing her use of nuclear power, oil shales, off-shore oil, or even, strip-mined coal where reclamation is not feasible. This could be done by four measures that seem moderate enough: the construction of buildings with appalling heat wastage should be stopped; all new cars should be required to achieve twenty-five miles per US gallon by 1985; research into energy conservation and its application should be encouraged; and energy prices should be allowed to rise. Combined with intensive propaganda, the report concluded, these measures could cut the growth in energy consumption by more than half, to 1·9 per cent a year. After ten years, if the country so chose, more stringent conservation measures could be taken to move the country towards zero energy growth in the 1990s without serious effects on the economy, and with only a very small reduction in the growth of the gross national product.

When the report first came out its conclusions were vigorously attacked by orthodox opinion and by the energy industries, and it was pointedly ignored by Government. Recently, however, it has been attracting increasingly distinguished support. President Carter now proposes to cut the growth rate to under 2 per cent, though only from 1985, and a major study prepared by the leading nuclear advocate Alvin Weinberg concluded that the slow growth in the use of energy could permit a thirty-year halt on new atomic power stations from that date.

*There need be no conflict between the importance of eliminating waste and of meeting the needs of the poor. Insulating their houses, for example, both saves waste and reduces the bills they have to pay to keep warm.

Studies in Sweden and the Netherlands have come to broadly similar conclusions. In fact the Swedish Parliament has approved an energy policy with conservation goals that parallel those suggested in the study—a reduction in the growth rate from four and a half per cent to two per cent a year, leading to zero energy growth in the 1990s. Meanwhile the British Department of Energy's own adviser on conservation told the Royal Commission on Environmental Pollution that the rate of growth that the Department was using to support its proposals for the expansion of nuclear power could be cut in half. On that basis the Royal Commission calculated that an alternative strategy could be devised in which a substantial amount of energy could be generated by renewable sources, the fast breeder reactor could be avoided, and the country could *still* enjoy the same level of comfort and prosperity as under the Department's plans. Other experts have come up with similar calculations. Indeed the Department of Energy later cut its projections of energy consumption for the year 2000—forecasts that were repeatedly used by nuclear proponents to justify an early committment to the plutonium economy—by 30 per cent.

More immediately the House of Commons Select Committee on Science and Technology concluded that so much energy is wasted in Britain that energy consumption could actually be *reduced* by 15 per cent in three years 'without sacrificing output, employment, or living standards' at an annual saving on the fuel bill of a billion pounds. And some important studies suggest that cuts in energy-use are also possible over the long-term, so that in the next century rich countries could actually be using less than they do now without paying any economic penalty. If these projections were to come about a large scale expansion of nuclear power would be all the more unnecessary and a transition to a civilisation powered largely by alternative sources all the more feasible.

Some 40 per cent of Britain's fuel is burnt to heat buildings and their water supplies. The Building Research Establishment says that a third of this can be saved merely by adopting straightforward conservation practices like insulating roofs, walls and water tanks, reducing draughts and installing double-glazing. In fact this may be an underestimate of the potential for savings—one major study suggests, for example, that cost-effective measures could reduce the use of fuel for heating the nation's homes by some 60 per cent. Homes account for easily the most of the energy demand of all buildings. At the time of the 1973 oil price rises, however, well over two-thirds of Britain's houses had no roof insulation at all, and only a few hundred were insulated to standards mandatory in Sweden and Denmark. Partly because of this, the cost of domestic heating each square yard of building in Sweden was then less than half what it is in Britain—despite a colder climate and higher heating standards. Although there has been much exhortation since then, an enormous amount remains to be done in practice. The Government announced in 1977, for example, that two-thirds of local authority housing still had little or no roof insulation.

Further savings can be made by slight changes in life-style. Over the last decades the temperatures at which people feel comfortable in winter have been rising in both Britain and the United States. S. David Freeman, Director of the Ford Foundation's Energy Policy Project and now one of President Carter's advisers, says that heating and air conditioning has become so extreme that, 'by most sensible standards the interior of the typical American building is too hot in the winter and too cold in summer'. Some estimates suggest that a reduction of only three degrees Fahrenheit in all American houses, offices and shops would save 12 per cent of the fuel oil and 14 per cent of the natural gas consumed in a typical winter. Meanwhile, a United Kingdom Government programme that put heating control systems into three hundred offices, shops, hotels and public buildings achieved savings of between 30 and 50 per cent.

More energy still could be saved by the use of heat pumps. These can draw heat 'uphill' from a cooler area to a warmer one. If you put your hand behind a refrigerator you can feel the heat being discharged from the cool interior of the appliance. Similarly, pumps could draw warmth from cold outside air to heat a house. More than a million are already installed in homes in the United States. Only a few homes have them in Britain for there have been several difficulties among them the development of designs better suited to the climate, since the American models are also used for cooling houses in summer and therefore work best in reverse. Heat pumps can provide three times the heat that could be gained from the fuel used to power them, cutting consumption by two-thirds, and in sunny countries can be linked to solar power. Meanwhile other technical innovations can apparently cut electricity consumption in lighting and electrical appliances to at least half the present levels at little extra cost.

In the longer term even more could be saved by designing our buildings sensibly. Traditionally societies planned their buildings to keep them cool in summer and warm in winter with the minimum use of energy. The 1000-year-old pueblo in Acoma, New Mexico, and the cave dwellings of Mesa Verde in Colorado, are both built to make sophisticated use of the sun's power, while igloos are so well insulated that families are kept warm in Arctic temperatures merely by the heat from their own bodies and from a small fire. Modern buildings that need intensive heating in winter, cooling in summer, and lighting by day and by night—commonplace in cities all over the world—are, in this respect, more out of date than cave dwellings.* In New York, offices built in the last half of the 1960s have been found to use twice as much energy per square foot of floor space as those constructed fifteen years before. So designing buildings more carefully can save a great deal of energy, and if better design is combined with good insulation remarkable cuts in fuel consumption can be achieved. The potential of new buildings must not deflect attention from the urgent job of insulating old ones (after all most of the houses, for example, that will be standing in rich countries in the year 2000 have already been built), but it is well worth bringing to realisation.

Meanwhile, several studies suggest, the amount of fuel used by cookers, electric lighting and appliances can be cut by a third—maybe even by a half—at little extra cost.

Transport absorbs a fair share of the energy consumed in rich countries, ranging from a tenth in the Netherlands to a quarter in the U.S.A. Most of this is used by road vehicles, and almost all of it is oil. About half the developed countries have introduced speed limits on roads, and these have been variously estimated to save between 3 and 5 per cent of fuel. Careful driving and tuning of engines can cut consumption by 10 to 15 per cent. In the longer

*Glass-walled office-blocks are particularly inappropriate. Heat passes quickly through glass, chilling buildings in winter and making them far too warm in summer. And yet the interiors are so big that even the daylight from the glass walls cannot reach them, and so lighting is constantly needed.

term there is more promise in improving the efficiency of cars. On average United States cars achieve only about sixteen miles to the gallon. If they were only to achieve the average efficiency of cars in the rest of the world 80 million tons of oil could be saved a year—twice the amount used for all purposes by the fifth of the world's population that lives in China. The governments of the United States and Canada are in fact now forcing manufacturers to increase the efficiency of their new cars but this is only a beginning. Fuel economy could also be greatly increased even in less profligate rich countries; British consumption, for example, could be cut by 40 to 50 per cent through technical improvements, according to the Government's Advisory Council on Energy Conservation. Similarily new technology in aircraft, which use a large share of the remaining fuel burnt by transport, could more than halve their appetite. Fortunately the greatest consumers of energy can be improved most speedily; for the average lifetime of a car is some ten years, relatively short compared to the 20 to 25 years expected from an aircraft, the 25 to 30 years of a ship or the 30 to 40 years of a railway locomotive.

Meanwhile, energy-saving means of transport must be made more attractive to the traveller. A train travels 390 passenger miles for every U.S. gallon of petrol or equivalent source of energy. A suburban bus travels 250 passenger miles per gallon. A small car with four passengers manages 100 passenger miles, with two people this sinks to about 60, while most cars only manage 33. A Boeing 747 manages 30, and a supersonic plane 10. It is possible to design cities in ways which greatly reduce the energy used in transport. It is also important to try to cut out unnecessary freight journeys, and where possible to use more economic ways of moving it. The one-fifth of American freight that goes by road uses more energy than the four-fifths carried by rail, water and pipeline.

Enormous savings, therefore, are possible in buildings and transport. Indeed one British study shows that techniques available now, or due to become so in the next few years, could cut total consumption in these sectors to three-fifths of its present level by the year 2025, despite enormous increases in the nation's comfort and prosperity. As these sectors account for most of the country's fuel, such a reduction would have a dramatic effect on total national energy demand.

Almost all the rest of the energy is used in industry. In Britain, at least, it appears that ten per cent of it could be saved merely by better housekeeping. In the longer term new processes and re-equipment might save another quarter of it. One process in the cement industry, for example, uses 40 per cent less fuel than one it might replace. A giant chemical firm reports that large scale new plant for fibres production now consumes only three-fifths as much fuel as plant built a few years ago. The steel industry in Britain has reduced its fuel consumption over the last 15 years, and it has been estimated that the energy used to produce each ton of steel could be cut by a further quarter here and abroad over the next 20 years. Recycling some materials can also save large amounts of energy. But industrialists will only install expensive new equipment when they need to do so, and in many industries energy may not constitute a large enough part of their costs to make them speed up the process without government encouragement.

The most wasteful industry of all, however, is an energy industry, electricity supply. In Britain it throws away more than a fifth of all the fuel burnt in the country, fuel worth one billion pounds in 1974–5. In the United States the same industry throws out the equivalent of three million barrels of oil every day—double the imports received from the Middle East on the eve of the Yom Kippur war. In both countries the electricity industry wastes twice as much energy as it produces. This happens because there are physical limits to the amount of electricity that can be made from raw fuel—whether coal, gas, oil or uranium. The theoretical limit is about 60 per cent. In fact the best that has been produced in the most modern power stations is about 35 per cent—and this represents an enormous technological achievement. Only about one-third of the raw fuel is converted into electricity and sent out to consumers. The other two-thirds are turned into heat which is normally cast to the winds through cooling towers and chimneys or sluiced out to rivers and the sea. Enormous savings in energy could be made if a large part of this heat were used either for space-heating or process steam in industry. The heat would have to be taken out of the electricity generating process sooner, at a point when it was still hot enough to do the job. This would reduce the amount of electricity gained from the fuel, but it would vastly increase the amount of useful *energy* available.

When power stations produce both electricity and useful heat in this way their efficiency can soar from a maximum of about 35 per cent to around 80 per cent. A power station of this efficiency provides 98 per cent of the demand for heat in the city of Vasteras, west of Stockholm.* In all, Sweden generates over a third of all her electricity from other than hydro-electric stations by this process, saves some 600,000 tons of oil a year, and is said to balance its national budget by doing so.

The Russians claim to provide about one-third of the nation's demand for heat from power stations. They say that in 1973 this practice, and the use of other district heating schemes, saved them 78 million tons of fuel—15 per cent of all the fuel needed for heating in the Soviet Union.

In Germany the Government is making large investments in such schemes and has been studying the feasibility of a national heat grid which, it is estimated, could meet 94 per cent of the nation's demand for space and water heating. Austria, Denmark, Finland, France, Italy, Hungary, Czechoslovakia and Poland all have large-scale production of heat from power stations. The United States is reported to have given it 'little consideration' until recently, but the government is now developing pilot schemes. The British power industry has no large-scale schemes at all. There are difficulties involved, but the achievements of so many other countries show what can be done.

Nor need this process be confined to power stations. Industries which have to raise their own steam can use it to produce electricity simultaneously, thus meeting their needs for heat and power from the same fuel and feeding surplus electricity into the national grid. Already more than one-eighth of Germany's electricity is generated in this way. A U.S. Government study suggests that as much as 40 per cent of the nation's present electricity supplies could be provided by these means by 1985, and studies at Imperial College, London, put the potential contribution in Britain as high as 80 per cent. If only a fraction of these estimates could be achieved enormous amounts of fuel would be saved, and the building of most new power stations, at huge capital cost, could be avoided. Yet such schemes are obstructed by electricity utilities in both

*As this means that the city needs virtually only one tall chimney, it has the lowest air pollution of any in Sweden.

Britain and the U.S.A., for they offer to pay very low prices for the extra power put into the grid and insist on high charges for contracts to supply back-up electricity when the industrial units have to be shut down for maintenance or repair. As recently as the 1950s, 17 per cent of United States electrical generating capacity was associated with industrial process heat. By 1974 the proportion had dropped to 4 per cent.

Conservation has many advantages besides saving fuel. Releasing energy by conservation almost always costs very much less than producing it—and provides more employment. It normally saves imports, and therefore helps a nation's balance of payments. As less fuel is burned, so there is less pollution to endanger individual health or the world system.

There is also a moral case. At present the United States wastes more fossil fuel than is used by two-thirds of the world. Saving only a twentieth of the fuel used in Western Europe would release enough energy to power half of Africa. By saving this fuel we do not automatically guarantee that poor countries will be able to use it; but if we waste it we do ensure that it can never be available to meet the needs of the poor.

Unfortunately, despite the lip service paid to it by rich country governments, energy conservation still gets a low priority in practice. By and large governments have hoped that the rising cost of energy would be sufficient to encourage people to save. This plays its part—certainly the countries where energy has been cheapest in the past are the most wasteful today—but it is not enough. Energy prices do not reflect coming scarcity adequately, since they are partly based on the costs of sinking mines and wells and building power stations many years ago, not on those of the much more expensive installations and inaccessible supplies that will be needed to replace them. Furthermore, buying energy takes up too little of personal and industrial budgets for this level of price rise to have a major effect on demand quickly enough. Indeed, the OECD recently had to admit that increasing prices had had much less impact on consumers than it had anticipated.

Most governments apply much more enthusiasm and commitment in attempting to expand energy supplies than they do in trying to restrain demand, through conservation. President Carter's administration became a noticeable exception in the spring of 1977, but his programme was soon being dismembered by Congress. So why are our rulers reluctant to take conservation seriously?

One reason advanced is that it is hard for governments to control conservation. Decisions to exploit new resources, it is argued, can be taken by a relatively small body of people, while conservation depends on millions of small decisions taken by ordinary people all over the country. But there are many measures that governments can take to encourage conservation, from setting new insulation standards to taxing energy or adjusting tariffs to encourage economy, to aiding people to insulate their homes.* Furthermore, though a few people can take the decision to mine or generate more energy, the decision to *use* it also depends on millions of decisions by ordinary people. Why should it be assumed that people can take, or can be persuaded to take, decisions to use more energy but not to save it? And if persuasion fails, neither governments nor people should be scared of legislation—after all statutory powers were used in Britain to implement The Clean Air Act and the conversion of appliances to North Sea gas—so long as it does not compromise basic liberties.

Another possible explanation is more straightforward. Energy industries, like all industries, depend on growth. They therefore cannot be expected to be particularly enthusiastic about conservation, despite their occasional protestations to the contrary. They and other industries which would benefit from unrestrained energy growth form a powerful lobby—as the United States found in the summer of 1977—while there is no group with comparable muscle pressing for conservation. Similarly the industries can put much more money behind research into exploiting energy than is devoted to finding ways of saving it. In the interests of their country, however, governments and legislators will just have to reduce the industries' expansionist dreams and plan for serious conservation. If supply *is* expanded, and then the people do not use it, the industry will be in a far worse mess than if it had planned for

*If prices are to be raised, then some positive help must be given to poor people to insulate their homes and protect them in other ways from the effect of rising fuel costs. Since research shows that poor people's homes are the worst insulated, this could be a particularly valuable measure.

conservation—as the troubles of the British electricity industry testify.

Small-scale exploitation of renewable sources of energy also comes up against both of these obstacles. Governments may well feel that individual decisions to install them constitute too haphazard an element in energy strategy, while the big energy industries would lose custom. And all renewable sources, and some forms of energy conservation, are dogged by another institutional difficulty; for present accounting practices can show them to be 'uneconomic'. There is a relatively high capital cost in, for example, building a solar or tidal power station, converting to combined heat and power schemes or installing energy saving technology, but there are little or no running costs, for the fuel is free, or it has been saved. Conventional energy sources are balanced rather differently; the original capital cost is usually lower, but there are significant running costs over the years. The accounting practices used by the British Treasury, for instance, favour the lower capital cost and high running charges to the once-and-for-all big initial outlay. On this basis we are told that implementing conservation is 'uneconomic' or that renewable sources of energy are 'not competitive'. Such statements should not be taken at their face value but examined in the light of the accounting bias. The big initial capital outlay may be the most economic course in an inflationary world. As the value of money goes down, so does the real cost of the interest on the initial outlay. And as the price of conventional fuels goes up—as it surely will—the savings provided by conservation or free renewable fuels escalate. Conventional practices, moreover, take into account neither the depletion of resources nor environmental costs. Both fossil fuels and nuclear power burn up fuel and therefore make it inevitable that, sooner or later, there will be a shortage, and prices will have to rise to cope with it. Both pollute, and so take a toll on health and in the world's system that comes back to us in other costs—in, for example, the expense of building hospitals or the consequences of lower crop yields.

Furthermore, some forms of energy conservation are 'economic' even when measured by these distorting practices. The capital cost of insulating houses, for example, is cheaper than building the amount of extra generating capacity that would be required to provide the electric heat that would otherwise be wasted. In sunnier countries than Britain solar heating can be similarly competitive on its capital cost alone. However, the householders who would install insulation or solar panels cannot obtain capital at the low interest rates available to big energy industries. So, as well as rejecting inappropriate accounting systems, governments should also provide incentive or other help to mitigate the impact of high capital costs which might put householders off installing systems even though these would more than pay for themselves over the medium- to long-term. The California State Energy Commission expects 170,000 homes to have solar heating by 1980, compared to twenty-five in 1975, thanks to tax credits provided to householders who install it.

Oddly, nuclear power seems to escape the condemnation of being uneconomic although it too has relatively high capital costs and relatively low running expenses. Indeed, these provide the basis for frequent, but misleading, claims that it is a particularly cheap form of electricity. It is often said, for example, that Britain's present nuclear reactors produce much the cheapest electricity in the country. So they do, but this is only what you would expect—the high capital costs were paid years ago, and nuclear power has not had to cope with the rising prices of fossil fuels. Whether it will be the cheapest in future is a much more open question which has to be based on *today's and tomorrow's* capital costs. It is particularly hard to come to a verdict, because nuclear power has hidden costs, subsidised by the tax-payer. One is its special insurance provisions. Another is the fact that enriching uranium and reprocessing spent fuel has been carried out in plants built originally by governments for weapons production.

Already it looks as if nuclear power costs much the same as coal-based electricity in the United States, and the greater unreliability of atomic power stations may make it a good deal more expensive in practice. Conventional nuclear energy is by no means prohibitively costly, but neither is it really particularly cheap. Except in the Third World, where nuclear power does seem to be uncompetitive, cost does not provide a compelling argument either for or against building more of the present generation of reactors.

Fast breeder reactors, of course, look like being much more expensive. The proposed Severn tidal energy scheme would provide nearly four times the electrical capacity of Britain's first fast breeder for roughly twice the cost; while if the money proposed for building the breeder were instead devoted to insulation, it would be at least three times as effective. Of course, there is a difference: the fast breeder (or so the atomic industry hopes) would be the first of many, while there are very few sites like the Severn, and homes can only be insulated once. But the normal measurements of economics,—often used to condemn alternatives, including tidal energy and conservation—do seem to have been waived in this case, at least for a while.

When policy makers consider the energy question they usually look first at what resources are available and then evaluate the contribution they can make to demand. To a certain extent this is inevitable, particularly in an energy-scarce age, but valuable perspectives can be gained from looking at the issue the other way round. We need to spend more time studying precisely what energy is needed, and which sources fulfil these needs best.

About half the total energy demand in Britain and many other European countries, and about a third of it in the United States, is for low-temperature heat. Some 86 per cent of all the energy that enters British homes, and three-quarters of what enters American dwellings, is used for this purpose. This can be provided by a wide variety of fuels. It can be obtained from coal, gas, and oil, and more suitably, wherever possible, from solar energy, waste heat from power stations and geothermal sources.

Heat, of course, can also be obtained from electricity; but electricity is a particularly valuable fuel, for it can do jobs much more efficiently than any other form of energy. It drives lifts, provides lighting, works machinery both at home and in industry, operates telephones and television. Important as these and other electrical jobs are, however, they do not make up much of national energy demands. In the United States, for example, electricity is only *needed* for about 8 per cent of all energy-use.

Of course, electricity is used much more widely; in particular it is used to provide the low-grade heat that can be won from a variety of other sources, and higher temperature heat that can also be provided by any fossil fuel. This is extremely wasteful, for the electricity produced in power stations is only one-third of the energy in the original fuel. Because of this, and because electricity suffers losses in transmission, it is senseless to use it where the original fuel would be perfectly satisfactory. Thus while electricity is three times more efficient than oil in working power machines, oil is three times more efficient in net energy terms for heating. To use electricity for central heating or fires is as stupid in energy terms as using oil to drive a Hoover or food-mixer.* Yet one-third of all the electricity produced in Britain is for heating. To make it, the equivalent of more than fifteen million tons of oil is thrown away each year as waste heat. This means that more energy is used up to provide electricity for heating than is used in heating direct from any other source. Most of this heating is used in homes. In the 1960s the use of electricity for central heating doubled every two and a half years. Because of this the amount of fuel burnt to provide our homes with heat has increased by about 50 per cent since the end of the war, while the amount of heat we have actually used has remained the same. During the decade before the 1973 Yom Kippur war Britain's use of electricity, for both appropriate and inappropriate purposes, went up by more than 50 per cent. In America it was doubling every decade, in Japan it was doubling in less than five years.

Governments show no sign of breaking their electrical obsession. They plan electricity, generated in big power plants, to take over more and more of their countries' energy supplies until it dominates them entirely. This is partly because nuclear power can only produce energy by these means; but it may be no coincidence that many of the alternative technologies that attract most official enthusiasm are proposals for providing electricity on a large scale, like wavepower, solar power towers and fusion.

Clearly the determining factor in our choice of energy strategy must be the sources that are available. All the same, we may not need to concentrate so much on centralised electricity production. Combined heat and power stations serving communities the size of small towns, and, where practicable, small-scale applications of natural energy resources have many advantages. Much of their

*When it is used in this way the sequence goes like this. We burn primary fuel, whether it be nuclear or fossil, to produce twice as much heat as electricity. We then throw the heat away. We next take the electricity and send it down a wire where it loses more energy in transmission. When it gets to the other end of the wire we turn it back into heat—the very thing we produced and rejected in such abundance in the first place.

energy is heat, which is *what* is needed. They provide it *where* it is needed, potentially cutting the transmission and distribution costs estimated to account for half of American electricity bills. And they can more easily provide it *when* it is needed; for while big units need to be planned years in advance, many small ones can be built quite rapidly to meet needs as they arise, and thus the need for the kinds of forecasts that have led to the present troubles of the British electricity industry can be minimised. Economies of mass production could replace economies of scale; the vulnerability of nations to strikes, sabotage, or even breakdown, at key facilities could be greatly reduced; and the greater autonomy that such small units could provide seems more attractive than the increasing centralisation that is bound to result from the big all-electric programme.

Attractive though it may seem, however, a network of small facilities cannot be the sole means of providing a nation's energy needs, even if the necessary technology all proves itself; but nor should a preoccupation with grandiose plans be allowed to crowd it out. The essence of energy strategy at this stage must be to maintain diversity as far as is possible, both in the sources developed and in the way they are exploited. We do not yet know enough to close any realistic options, and, besides, conditions vary widely from country to country and region to region. For this reason I believe that the nuclear option should be kept open, through much more cautious development in rich countries; although there is no case for reprocessing or the fast breeder, and a major commitment to the atom should be avoided if there is any realistic alternative. The danger, however, is that the opposite will happen; that a premature espousal of nuclear energy will close the door to safe and better ways of supplying our needs.

There is therefore no neat formula for sorting out the world's energy situation; but there are guidelines within which there is a range of options. The use of energy in the rich world can no longer increase at the accustomed rate; on the other hand, it needs to accelerate in the poor world. There is enough energy to sustain a sensible use for the foreseeable future. Nuclear energy carries unique hazards, and should not be developed too fast; it is inappropriate to poor countries, while 'natural' sources suit their needs well. In rich countries, energy conservation can provide a breathing space. Energy sources should be matched to need where possible, and the trend towards increased use of electricity for inappropriate reasons should be checked. For all these reasons it makes sense to move towards a low growth in the use of energy in the rich world, but this must be done gradually so as to avoid economic disruption.

Whatever policies we adopt will take time to become effective. In the meantime countries are still going to be dependent on the momentum of past strategies. Those which, unlike Britain, are not lucky enough to become self-sufficient in oil will depend on OPEC for many years ahead. Ironically, however, if Britain does not use North Sea oil to wean herself away from dependence on the liquid, she will become even more dependent on the oil-exporting countries within a decade or two when her own supplies run out.

Chapter 13

Strange Diseases

Jitsuko Tanaka was a particularly lively and mischievous child. Many children might envy her. Her home stood only a few yards from the sea in the west of Japan. She was always out of the house, playing on the shore, shouting and laughing.

Today Jitsuko has grown into a strikingly beautiful girl in her early twenties. But no one would envy her now. She is neither lively nor noisy. She cannot walk. She cannot talk. She sits endlessly at home, rocking to and fro, slowly twisting her fingers. She would not feel anything, apparently, even if she fell into a fire.

Her transformation springs from what the people of her area, Minamata, once called *kibyo*—'the strange illness'. It broke out in the early summer of 1953, about the time when the British expedition reached the peak of Everest and seemed to proclaim a new victory in man's much-heralded conquest of nature.

As the Japanese fishermen got ready for the best catches of the season, a cat leaped wildly into the air. It dashed through the streets, ran screeching down to the shore, dived into the sea and drowned. Soon cats were going mad all over the area. Then crows began to fall from the sky. They would drop until they almost hit the ground, recover themselves just in time, flutter up into the sky, and fall again. The ancients would have had no difficulty in recognising the portent of tragedy to come. Three years later it became clear that *kibyo* was spreading among people too.

Jitsuko was not alone. Her elder sister Shizuko, who used to play with her on the shore, was taken to hospital in convulsive agony. Her pain was so great that her mother had to carry her back and forth in the corridors every night so that her screams would not keep others awake. She did this until Shizuko died.

Others live on. There is Tsuginori Hamamoto, who saw his father go to bed one night a sturdy, self-confident fisherman, and wake the next morning crazy, unable to stand, walk or dress himself. Now Tsuginori himself is permanently crippled with the disease. He says, 'Being born a human being, but not being able to live as a human being is the most painful thing to me.'

As the disease spread, it changed its name to Minamata disease. But it was not confined to that area. There was another major outbreak in the inland town of Niigata. Up to now, forty children have been born with the disease. By 1974 more than a hundred Japanese had died of it, eight hundred more had been officially recognised as living victims, and two thousand five hundred had applied for recognition; and even this may be only the tip of the iceberg. In the most heavily contaminated area of Minamata nearly a third of the children born between 1956 and 1959 suffer from mental deficiency, against a national average of one in ten. At least a quarter of the people in roughly the same area show some symptoms of the disease. By some estimates as many as ten thousand people may have been affected.

Charlie and Sally Hirst live on the other side of the world. They are a quiet, homely couple in what we call the prime of life. They and their two children have made their home in a small row of terraced cottages perched on the fellside above the Yorkshire town of Hebden Bridge. They both know, however, that they are going to die of another incurable disease.

'My husband was the first to know that he had got it'. Mrs. Hirst told me: 'Before I realised what I was suffering from I used to worry a terrible lot about him. But when I found that I had it, it was just the end of the world to me.

'When there are two of you, one is going to be left behind knowing that he is going to die in the same way. I'm hoping I go before my husband.'

Mrs Hirst told me that three of her relatives also have the disease. Indeed, she is surrounded by fellow victims. One of them, Mrs Kasha Polanis, an immigrant from Poland, describes the wasting effect of the disease: 'Sick. Sick. Tired and sick. Short breath. Pain in chest. Pain under mine arm. Mine hand, night time, I don't know where to put them. I put them behind head, I put them straight, and pain me. Muscle of mine is go. Flesh is go. Just bone and skin of me.' For his part, Charlie Hirst becomes breathless from the effort of merely lifting his hands to his face to shave.

The specialist looking after these people estimates that over seventy people have died of this and related diseases in and around the Yorkshire town, and two hundred and sixty have contracted them, and that another two hundred are doomed but do not yet know it. Meanwhile at least a hundred and twenty people have died in Plymouth, and there are many other concentrations of tragedy in Britain and other countries of the developed world.

The tragedies of Minamata and at Hebden Bridge both resulted from pollution caused by a local firm. Both forms of pollution had long been known to have devastating effects on people.

Organic mercury, the thief of life at Minamata, is an old enemy. As long ago as 1866 two laboratory technicians at St Bartholomew's Hospital in London died after handling it. Since the 1930s it was used in various forms for seed dressings, and there were several cases of death and disablement of workers who handled them, sometimes at much lower levels than were then thought to be safe. One expert writes that research published before 1940 made it clear that two forms of organic mercury were so dangerous that they should never be manufactured again. He adds, 'The warning remains unheeded and the grim record of deaths occurring in many countries is a sad monument to the greed and stupidity of men.'

However, the Minamata factory was discharging mainly *inorganic* mercury, which, though poisonous enough to justify great caution,* is nothing like as toxic as the organic forms of the metal. How was it, then, that the less poisonous form of mercury in the firm's effluent turned up as a much more poisonous one in the bodies of the victims of the strange disease? The answer appeared only years later when researchers found that inorganic forms of mercury (and indeed the quicksilver metal itself) could be turned into the organic ones by bacteria in underwater mud. The inorganic mercury in the effluent at Minamata had been transformed by the bacteria and then passed up the food chain through fish to the

*A century ago hatters used inorganic mercury in dressing beaver hats. In time they would go mad—as mad, we say, as hatters.

crows, cats and men who ate the food from the sea.* Until this discovery was made it had been generally assumed that inorganic forms remained inorganic when discharged into rivers and the sea, and so they had been allowed to flow out from factories all over the globe in the blind belief that they would do little harm. The world suddenly found that it had a completely unexpected problem, for the poison that had already been released proved extremely persistent. The Swedish Government banned all fishing from eighty lakes, and advised its people to eat no more than one meal a week of fish from coastal or other inland waters. More recently cats have died and men developed symptoms of poisoning on Canadian Indian reservations beside a river seriously polluted by mercury; one of the principal researchers into the Japanese tragedies described the situation as 'exactly like that of Minamata before the mass outbreak of the disease'. Yet despite these shocks and other warnings, about half the world's production of mercury is thought even now to reach the oceans every year from industrial sources.

Asbestos was the cause of the tragedy at Hebden Bridge. Fire-resistant and virtually indestructible, yet so fine and pliable that it can be spun and woven like cloth, it is no wonder that it came to be called 'the magic mineral'. Its production rose from a hundred tons worldwide in 1878 to four million tons in 1972.

Knowledge of its killing power was available from very early in this expansion. In 1890 a factory for weaving asbestos opened in Normandy. Within five years fifty of its employees had died. Similar results were found in London, and governments were optimistic that safety would soon follow. Twenty years later the International Labour Organisation was still urging that the asbestos industry should expand no further until it was made safe. But it went on growing.

*The food chain is like those pictures you sometimes see where a small fish is about to be swallowed by a bigger fish, which is about to be swallowed by an even bigger one. It describes the 'eating order' for example, from the smallest plankton to man. At each stage mercury, and other poisons, accumulate in the body of the prey and are transferred to the flesh of the hunter. As each hunter eats many prey he builds up far greater concentrations in his body than were present in those of any of his victims. Fish can concentrate organic mercury to more than ten thousand times its level in the water around them.

After almost another twenty years had gone by a British Government survey established that more than a quarter of asbestos workers—and over 80 per cent of those who had worked in the industry for more than two decades*—had symptoms of asbestosis: the suffocating, incurable disease from which the Hirsts suffer. Dr Merewether, then the Chief Medical Inspector of Factories, concluded that the asbestos industry would be safe within ten years, and regulations which were supposed to clean it up were agreed between the Government and industry. But new dangers soon emerged, and were met by much the same tardiness over research and regulation.

Indeed, the pattern has been remarkably constant; first the danger is noted; then there is a long interval before there has been enough research for it to be considered probable among the experts; and then there is a similar delay before it is thought to have been proven. The distinction is important, for governments have often been reluctant to act against a pollutant even when its danger has been proved, and are much less likely to do so at any earlier stage.

In the mid-1930s cases of lung cancer among asbestosis victims were reported from London and South Carolina, but it was not until the late 1940s that Dr Merewether and his colleagues published a report showing that 14 per cent of the people who had asbestosis died of lung cancer. The proportion increased over the next years, but it was not until 1955 (twenty years after the first cases were reported) that it was considered 'proved' that asbestos caused the disease—though apparently the mineral only produces a massive number of extra lung cancers among workers who also smoke.

There was much the same delay over mesothelioma, an untreatable cancer of the chest wall, cases of which were coming to light and being linked with asbestos in the early 1940s. 'There was an interval of about fifteen years before this association was generally thought probable and another ten before it was widely recognised in all countries', wrote Dr J. C. Gilson, when head of the Medical Research Council's Pneumoconiosis Unit; and he went on,

> It now looks as though history may be repeating itself. Clinical reports and surveys suggest that other cancers may also

*Asbestosis usually occurs after a latency period which is often as long as twenty years.

be linked with asbestos—gastrointestinal, ovarian and possibly leukaemias and lymphomas. The excess risk is, however, not yet certain enough to be rated as more than 'probable'.

Dr Gilson laments the fact that 'no continuing research effort' followed the British Government's first survey. 'Had this been done', he says, 'better controls would almost certainly have been introduced earlier'.

In fact controls have lagged even further behind than research, and sometimes they have not been enforced. The Hirsts were born at about the time the first regulations were being brought in, when Dr Merewether was saying that the industry would be safe from asbestosis within ten years. And, indeed, if these regulations had been thoroughly implemented the prediction would have come true—for they demanded that no asbestos dust whatsoever should be allowed to escape into the working environment and that breathing apparatus should be provided for people doing jobs where dust was unavoidable. The Factory Inspectorate say that this stringent regime was unworkable and unenforceable, although they now admit, with hindsight, that they were not tough enough with industry.

The Hirsts and fellow victims at Hebden Bridge worked at a factory run by the Cape Asbestos Company. Its management were never prosecuted—and only seem to have been sent one letter warning them that they might be taken to court—during its entire thirty years of operation. An investigation by the Ombudsman shows that for most of that time, during two decades in which many of the victims must have been contracting their diseases, the Inspectorate concluded that the safety performance of the factory was as good as, if not better than the average in the British asbestos industry as a whole. When the watchdogs did become concerned, the Ombudsman says, the local staff were not decisive or determined enough, the Factory Inspectorate as a whole was insufficiently persistent and co-ordinated, and the responsible government department failed to pay enough attention to statistics that would have shown the mounting toll of disease in the area.

Following this and similar tragedies, the Factory Inspectorate appear to have become much tougher. New regulations, brought in in 1969, laid down a standard for the amount of asbestos permitted in the air, and this standard has been adopted as a model by countries all over the world. Unfortunately, the regulations are concerned only with asbestosis,* despite the fact that the links between asbestos, lung cancer and mesothelioma were 'proved' many years before they were introduced. By 1969 lung cancer was killing more than 60 per cent of asbestosis sufferers.

In fact there is grave doubt whether the present standard sufficiently protects workers even against asbestosis. John Finklea, director of the U.S. Government's National Institute for Occupational Safety and Health (NIOSH), says that it does not, and recent research supports him. The Committee on whose recommendation the standard was first set up confessed that its findings were based on 'scanty' evidence, a sad reflection on the state of research almost a hundred years after it first became clear that asbestos workers were dying. Indeed, one of the two men who provided this evidence told me in the summer of 1976 that it was 'not adequate for the purpose'. He added: 'The authority with which it has been accepted around the world has worried some of us.' It was primarily based on just one set of figures from one survey carried out by one asbestos company among its workers. Further research at the same factory has increasingly brought the validity of even this evidence in question. One follow-up study suggests that between five and ten per cent of those who worked for a lifetime in dust levels permitted under the standard will die of asbestosis or cancer.

Mr R. M. Wagg, Senior Chemical Inspector of the Health and Safety Executive, which now incorporates the British Factory Inspectorate, says, 'Only if there is no asbestos dust in the atmosphere is there no danger or no risk at all.' Other authorities agree, and pressure is building up for the dust to be almost entirely excluded from the working environment. In Britain, where some hundred thousand people work with asbestos, the Trades Union Congress has asked for the standard to be cut to a tenth of its present level, as a strictly interim measure pending the banning of

*By putting a more stringent limit on the most dangerous form of asbestos—crocidolite or 'blue' asbestos—the standard effectively stopped any work with it in Britain. This would be likely to have some effect on cancer, because as well as being the most dangerous form of the mineral for causing asbestosis, it is also the form most commonly associated with mesothelioma.

asbestos altogether. In America, where several million workers have been exposed to the dust, NIOSH has recommended that the standard should be reduced twenty times over to 'the least detectable level'. Sweden is phasing out the use of asbestos altogether and the European Parliament has called on all EEC states to do the same.

Wives and children of asbestos workers have also contracted asbestosis and cancer when the men of the house brought home the dust on their clothes. A survey at one U.S. plant shows that a third of the members of families of workers and former workers have some level of asbestosis. Recently alarm has been rising over dangers to the general public. Eleven cases of mesothelioma have been found among people who lived within a mile of an asbestos factory in London, and more have been found in similar circumstances in Hamburg. Other cases of mesothelioma resulting from environmental rather than occupational exposure to asbestos have been found in Britain, Israel and South Africa—and Sir Richard Doll, Britain's most eminent epidemiologist, told a Royal Society meeting that some of the deaths from mesothelioma in Britain each year could presumably be attributed to low concentrations of asbestos particles found everywhere in city air.

This evidence does not add up to proof that the levels to which the public are normally exposed are hazardous, though it is likely that there is no safe level of exposure, it seems that some people will inevitably be at risk. But it does serve to heighten anxiety about standards in factories since the public and workers' families are normally exposed to far lower concentrations than the workers themselves. It also draws attention to the widespread and often unnecessary use of asbestos in our lives.

Asbestos is used in over three thousand ways, from insulating buildings to filtering drinks. It is widely used in household do-it-yourself products. As long ago as 1968 a British Government committee expressed particular concern about these household materials, and recommended that they should be marked with a warning that they contained asbestos and guidelines on how to use them safely. It was not until 1976, however, that the recommendation was carried out; the asbestos industry, according to the Government Department involved, had hitherto suggested that this proposal would not be practicable. No sooner was this marking scheme announced than another disturbing story came to light. Blue dust blowing about the corridors and homes in a London block of flats was found to be the deadliest of all forms of asbestos, one effectively excluded from further use in Britain because of its extreme danger.* One resident said that she had been sweeping the dust off her floor for five years; the tenants association said that they had been complaining about the dust for eighteen months without knowing what it was.

Asbestos is so widespread that a high proportion of city dwellers have its dust in their lungs. This does not mean that many of us will necessarily develop diseases caused by the mineral; some people can absorb the dust without any apparent ill-effects, others may develop disease after even tiny exposures to the fibres. Since this can take twenty years or more to develop, and since the main public exposure is quite recent, it may be some time before we know the full effect of asbestos on the health of the general public.

The asbestos and organic mercury stories contain factors which have to be borne in mind with almost all forms of pollution. They show that the effects of pollution have a habit of surprising us. Sometimes this is because a pollutant is neglected or thought unimportant, as was the case with organic mercury. Often it is because the effects can take a long time to become evident, as happens with asbestosis and cancer. In either case a disaster may build up over the years before we pay attention—by which time it may be too late. In the extreme cases of Minamata and Hebden Bridge many people were affected in a limited area, and the diseases were unusual enough to provoke attention. But this is not always so. The early symptoms of other pollution diseases can be as ordinary as headaches and stomach upsets, and so pass unremarked. Then there are so many other causes of a fatal disease like lung cancer, and the victims resulting from pollution may be so scattered about the country that the contribution of a pollutant may never be noticed.

Even when a danger is seen and attempts are made to deal with it, we may still be surprised because we do not understand the natural processes around us, as the story of inorganic mercury

*See page 258.

shows. We may also be surprised because we do not understand how one pollutant can cause many diseases, or may be misled because one disease masks another. For example, asbestosis may kill off potential victims of lung cancer before the cancer can get a hold; as conditions in the industry improve people live long enough to contract the asbestos-induced cancer, and the proportion of cancer deaths rises. Tackling asbestosis alone, as regulations attempted to do, is therefore no answer.

Sometimes we may see the effects of a pollution-induced disease but find it hard to identify the cause. In making scientific and medical tests you will generally only find something if you have specifically set out to look for it and it alone. The team investigating the strange disease at Minamata had to test for poison after poison before they found mercury.

Sometimes a 'solution' may itself cause a problem. In Britain attempts to reduce sulphur dioxide (one of the main constituents of the great smogs) led to the building of power stations with high chimneys so that the gas would be more widely dispersed. But some of the gas is blown over the North Sea to Scandinavia, where it is joined by the contributions of other European nations. As a result rain falls as dilute sulphuric acid, harming the soil, entering drinking water and poisoning lakes.

All this means that despite nearly a decade of intense concern we still know very little about pollution. The stories of mercury and asbestos also illustrate our tendency to assume the best; to be complacent simply because we know so little of the effects of pollutants. And that is a dangerous approach in a world where, for example, a single mistake or accident can have incalculable long-term effects on a whole community.

On July 10 1976, a cloud of vapour spread over homes in the North Italian town of Seveso after an explosion in a nearby chemical plant. It contained a small amount of TCDD—one of the most poisonous chemicals known—which settled on the area, contaminating it with persistent toxicity. Pets and small animals died and people became ill, but it was not until two weeks after the event that serious action was taken and more than seven hundred residents were evacuated. The most seriously affected land and buildings were sealed off, while the authorities decided what to do. More than a year later they had still not begun to destroy the poison, which is scarcely surprising since the main methods for doing so put forward by the world's scientific community all risked spreading the danger even further. Meanwhile the chemical and cases of poisoning were turning up in the city of Milan more than ten miles away.

We know even less about the effects of the poison on health than we do about how to get rid of it. Despite several, much smaller, incidents in factories since the Second World War the long-term consequences of TCDD are almost completely uncharted. Experiments on some animals have suggested that it may be one of the most powerful agents yet discovered for inducing birth defects, but, fortunately, so far only a few of the babies born in the area since the incident have been malformed. There is some evidence that it may be mutagenic—causing malformations in succeeding generations—and a suspicion that it might cause cancer. Certainly no antidote is known. The people who lived in the most contaminated area for two weeks before being evacuated, those who continued to live nearby, the hundreds of thousands of people in the region as a whole—and their descendents—are just going to have to wait and see what happens to them.

The aftermath of the episode has been filled with recrimination. The owners of the factory did not provide enough information early enough, it is said; the authorities vacillated; both underestimated the danger. A year after the event the varying degrees of responsibility still had to be decided in court. But a member of the consultants brought in to advise the firm on cleaning up, while not criticising the Italian authorities, drew a wider moral. 'The system as it existed in July 1976 was not capable of dealing with such an accident of modern technology,' he said. 'This is a problem we are going to have to face time and time again throughout the world.' Meanwhile a government attempt to assess the size of the problem in Britain concluded that some 300 factories presented a major accident risk to the public, and between 2,000 and 3,000 were hazardous.

At the same time the people of Michigan were beginning to learn of the human effects of another mishap, one which started less dramatically than the accident at Seveso, but which looks like having much wider consequences. During an American paper shortage in 1972–3 the Michigan Chemical Company ran out of the red bags in which it packed a fire-retardent, Firemaster. So it put it in the brown bags normally used for a similarly-named additive for cattle feed, Nutrimaster. With an awful inevitability the two were confused, and in October 1973 2,000 lbs of the fire-retardent were mixed into food for cattle.

That, at least, was what was discovered later, for nothing was noticed until a mysterious plague began developing in cattle all over the state. Milk yields went down, cattle developed strange deformities and died, there were fewer calves and many of them were born dead or half size. Agricultural officials could not work out what was wrong, and the cause was only found by accident, when a farmer took samples of milk, feed, and dead cows to a university for analysis. By mistake a technician failed to turn off a machine analysing one of the samples when he went for his lunch break, and when he came back he found an unusual peak late on the graph—one that would not have emerged during the usual period of operation. By chance again, another researcher at the same laboratory was able to recognise that peak, because four years before he had happened to do a similar analysis of samples of polybrominated biphenyls (PBBs), chemicals used in the fire-retardent, which he had asked to examine after seeing them advertised by the Michigan Chemical Company. Concerned researchers then knew what to look for, and the mystery began to be unravelled. But by then it was too late. The PBBs had worked their way into the meat and dairy products eaten in the state and virtually every one of the nine million people of Michigan has the chemical lodged in their tissues.

Eventually, after public pressure, the state government initiated a major investigation into the effects of the chemicals on health. A study of farmers and those who had eaten their produce, found that about a sixth had gastrointestinal troubles, a quarter had swollen painful joints and more than a third had neurological disorders (including memory-loss so bad that one man had to leave his job because he could no longer remember the way to his work, and a farmer found that he kept misplacing his tools—including his tractor!). In each case the levels were many times more than those among farmers from Wisconsin, who had not been exposed to the PBBs. A bigger study of the general population of the state is to follow, but, whatever it reveals the people of

Michigan, like those of Seveso are just going to have to wait for long-term effects to show, for once again they are completely unknown.

It is quite possible, moreover, that the Michigan disaster is only part of the story of PBBs. It arises from the misuse of some 2,000 lbs of the chemicals. But over the years some 12 million lbs were produced, and who is to say that their normal use does not also present some hazard? The Environment Protection Agency, which has announced plans to ban them as fire-retardents, has already found traces of them in people living near one factory that uses them.

In fact the main toll of pollution almost certainly comes not from spectacular tragedies where something has evidently gone wrong, but from the 'normal' routine exposure to substances that have become part of our everyday lives.

Chapter 14

Chemical Reactions

After heart disease, cancer is the biggest killer in the Western world. Perhaps it is the most feared because it does its work so slowly.

Specialists now generally agree that some 70 to 90 per cent of cancers are caused by environmental factors; that, broadly speaking, they are brought on by the way we live. They have found that the incidence of all major types of cancer varies enormously—sometimes by several hundred times—between different countries and communities, and that when people migrate they soon adopt the pattern of cancers common in their new environment.

At a time when little progress is being made towards cures, this discovery means that, in principle at least, we could prevent most of our cancers by changing the way we live. It also means that, through changing our lives in other ways, we can increase the incidence of the disease.

If we knew enough about the precise causes of cancer we could at least try to avoid them. However, only about one-tenth of cancer research funds is devoted to this purpose. We have made a few discoveries and we have found some clues; but the rest is conjecture and contested ground.

Some cancers result from social habits. Cigarette-smoking accounts for a large fraction of cancer cases; heavy drinking of alcohol appears to cause others. Further tumours may well result from our affluent diet. Dr John Higginson, Director of the International Agency for Research on Cancer, reckons that men living in rich countries could avoid nearly half their environmental cancers if they did not smoke, drink to excess, over-eat or grow fat.

Much the same, of course, could be said about heart disease; indeed, the major killers of the rich world often symbolise our way of life as eloquently as the plagues brought on by poverty testify to the plight of the poor.

Some specialists would lay even more emphasis on diet, looking for causes of cancer in specific foodstuffs. Others believe that pollution is more important, among both industrial workers and the general public. Some occupational causes of cancer are known. Most of them, like asbestos, have only come to light as a result of a cluster of deaths in a particular industry. Often they have been overlooked for a long time, and often there have been long delays even after a chemical has been identified as dangerous.

By 1970, 450 cases of bladder cancer had come to light in the British rubber industry, many too late for effective treatment. Two of the victims took both their employers and a major chemical manufacturer to law, alleging that they had suffered precisely because of such a delay. The courts held that the chemical company knew by 1943, long before the men started work, that a substance it made posed a cancer risk to workers in the industry. But it was not until six years afterwards that it had warned the men's employers of the hazard, or withdrawn the chemical from sale. For its part, the rubber factory failed to screen its workers early enough, despite a recommendation from the manufacturer that it should do so and despite the fact that 'early diagnosis of this insidious disease is most important'.

Every year almost twelve million tons of vinyl chloride, one of the key chemicals in the giant plastics industry, are produced. It is used in producing PVC, the common plastic. Because it is so cheap it was also used 'indiscriminately' as an aerosol propellant in products like hair sprays and insecticides. Then early in 1974 an American company reported that three of its workers had died from a rare form of liver cancer. After some research it was established that vinyl chloride was the cause. Investigation around the world brought more and more cases to light.

Yet Russian studies had discovered liver damage in PVC workers as long ago as 1949, and one American company, finding that vinyl chloride was dangerous in animal tests, had cut its exposure limits to 50 parts per million in 1961. Its competitors did not follow the lead, and at the beginning of 1974 workers in the U.S.A.

and in several other countries were still working in atmospheres that contained up to ten times this amount of vinyl chloride—the official standard. Within a year public pressure and rising death records had forced the United States limit down five hundred times over, to one part per million.

Pollution causes cancer among the general public, but we know little of the details or dimensions of the danger. Both smokers and non-smokers are more likely to contract lung cancer if they live in urban areas than if they live in the countryside, and this is generally ascribed to air pollution. Recently the U.S. National Cancer Institute published an atlas of maps showing the incidence of death from different types of cancer in every county in the United States. At present detailed investigations aimed at finding the reasons for the variations have only just begun, but significant parallels already seem to be emerging. Deaths from bladder, liver and lung cancers are particularly high in the counties where chemical industries are concentrated; more nasal, lung and skin cancers are found around petroleum refineries; and increased lung cancer is also prevalent near copper, lead and zinc smelting works. The numbers of women affected suggest that excess cancers in these counties cannot just be ascribed to occupational hazards, but that environmental pollution is implicated as well.

There are other instances of more widespread exposure to chemicals suspected of causing cancer. For example, almost all of us who live in industrialised countries have polychlorinated biphenyls (PCBs) lodged in our tissues. This useful group of chemicals found in a wide variety of industrial applications, turning up in products as diverse as electrical goods and pesticides. Then, when they had become almost universal and had been concentrated in the food chain, the world learned that they might cause cancer and other diseases in animals. Other common substances under suspicion include trichlorethylene, the widespread industrial degreasing agent, which has also been used to decaffeinate coffee; chloroform, a common constituent of medicines; nitrosamines, which are formed by cooking bacon, may develop in the stomach from substances in drinking water and cured meats, and are themselves widely found in urban air, soil and water; benzopyrenes, a common constituent of smoke, also widespread in city air; and many kinds of hair dye.

None of these are established indisputedly as causes of cancer in the general public. Most of them have only been identified as carcinogens from animal tests, but we would be wise to take them seriously, rather than repeat the mistake made with oestrogen, given to menopausal women. Its dangers were long overlooked, and it is now suspected to be responsible for much of the recent increase in womb cancer in the U.S.A. It has also been linked with breast cancer and other serious illnesses.

Naturally, cancer is not the only worrying effect of pollution. Most cancer-causing agents also seem to affect gene structure, so that children or succeeding generations could be born malformed or with an incurable disease. Chemicals capable of causing cancer can have other effects too. Vinyl chloride, for example, has been linked with acro-osteolysis (a crippling disease which can result in deformity in a worker's hands), with abnormalities in the lungs and spleen, with interference with blood circulation, with aching bones, with sexual impotence, and with the occurrence of still-born or mutilated babies.

Meanwhile evidence is emerging that levels of lead not high enough to cause conventional lead poisoning may bring about permanent mental retardation to children in Britain and America. One study suggests that the level at which this occurs is around the same as that found in 30 per cent of the children of New York, another suggests that the amount of lead in the tap-water of more than one and a half million British households may be dangerous to unborn babies. One of the researchers on a third study says that the evidence suggests not that lead turns all children into morons but that it makes a bright child less bright, an average one dull, and a dull one subnormal. The issue is still in dispute, but it would be ironic if we were doing the same thing to our children as malnutrition accomplishes in the poor world.*†

Pollutant after pollutant can be mentioned. The production of cadmium, is doubling every decade and the toxic metal is building up in both crops and people. In Britain alone because of noise in

*Lead may be associated with other afflictions, including some cancers, and in impairing the body's defences against disease. Some researchers even believe that low levels of lead may produce hyperactivity—leading to vandalism, assault, and football hooliganism—though this remains a fringe view. view.

†See Chapter 2.

the places where they work six hundred thousand people are reported to be progressively losing their hearing.

Above all, we know that different pollutants react together. A few, we are finding, seem to neutralise each other; others magnify each other to produce far more devastating results than would be calculated from the sum of their individual effects. For example, asbestos and cigarette smoking react together, so that a smoking asbestos worker is about ninety times more likely to die of lung cancer than someone of the same age who neither smokes nor works with asbestos.* Smoking also reacts with alcohol. Sulphur dioxide and ozone (another pollutant of city air despite its beneficial reputation) may together affect our lungs far more than either of them would do alone. Even non-toxic substances can become dangerous when combined with another 'harmless' chemical, while the effect of pollutants working in pairs is only the simplest form of this 'synergism'. We know that they can work in threes, and there is theoretically no limit to the numbers that can act in combination.

Indeed, many scientists think that the effect of many relatively weak carcinogens working together may be one of the main causes of cancer. This might, for example, help to account for the increased cancer rates in cities, and for evidence of a higher risk in places where minute amounts of several suspect chemicals have been found in drinking water.

Far from winning the battle against cancer, we are increasing our chances of getting it or other pollution-induced diseases by introducing new and largely untested chemicals into our environment at an alarming rate. There are already estimated to be some 600,000 different chemicals in daily use. The U.S. National Cancer Institute says that only about 6,000 or 7,000 of the chemicals in large-scale commercial use have been tested in any form. About 1,000 of these have been shown to cause cancer in animals—although only thirty have been 'proved' to cause human cancer. Every year several thousand new chemicals enter significant use.†

*Smoking by itself is estimated only to increase the likelihood by ten- to fifty-fold depending on the heaviness of smoking among other factors.

†This is a conservative estimate. Dr John Higginson, Director of the International Agency for Research on Cancer, reckons that 6,000 new substances receive significant human exposure every year, with no less than

Most are introduced in ignorance of their long-term effects either singly or in conjunction with other chemicals. Even if we are beginning to discover some of the potential effects of pollution on man, we still have no real idea of what may happen to the world.

Drifting across the Pacific on the power of the Humboldt current soon after the Second World War, Dr Thor Heyerdahl could look over the side of *Kon-Tiki* to the clean surface of the ocean. When he sailed again in *Ra I* and *Ra II* just over twenty years later he found the Atlantic visibly polluted from coast to coast. 'How', he asked 'can such a change have taken place in a matter of two decades, when the ocean has taken care of natural and man-made pollution for thousands and millions of years?'

His experience, like the story of the Antarctic penguins and Arctic polar bears found with DDT in their bodies, has passed into pollution tradition as an illustration of the basic truth that pollutants travel freely about the world. More recently the west coast of Ireland has been found to have levels of ozone (a largely city-formed pollutant) similar to those of central London—and, indeed both sites seem to receive a good deal of it from continental Europe.

The effects of pollution on the world's systems are almost unknown. We do not even know how much pollution we are releasing. We know that some of many of the pollutants are absorbed by natural processes, but we do not know how much, or what effects the absorption itself may have on the world's systems.

Some of the more catastrophic predictions of doom have been discredited. The world is not about to run out of oxygen, nor are the oceans on the point of death. A greater respect for the resilience of the earth is developing among environmentalists, just as a greater awareness of its fragility is growing among the public as a whole. Both are necessary to achieve a balanced view. It is unlikely, if not impossible, that we will destroy life on earth through pollution, though we are likely to cause many people to die if we persist with it. It is less likely that we shall destroy the world than that we

---

200,000 new substances being produced. The United Nations Environment programme says that 10,000 are produced annually in quantities between half a ton and 1,000 tons.

shall make it a less easy place to live. There is little cause for despair, but a good deal of evidence to justify caution and concern.

Thor Heyerdahl notes that the various kinds of pollution he saw, including opaque greyish-green ocean water looking like the harbour water at the end of city sewers, 'must inevitably reduce light-penetration and hence photosynthesis by phytoplankton on which virtually all other life in the ocean depends'. Pollution of estuaries and inshore waters is particularly hazardous, for it is thought that half of all commercially important fish are dependent on them during at least some stage of their life.

The ozone which roams so freely causes millions of dollars worth of damage to United States crops, and may even cause trouble in Britain. Other common pollutants in the air can also be very damaging to life.

We know very little about how pollution interferes with some of the most basic life-cycles of the planet. Jeremy Swift, of Sussex University, reports: 'The dangers here are frightening. The American Chemical Society, a very unalarmist organisation, claims that if man were to destroy any of at least half a dozen types of bacteria involved in the nitrogen cycle life on earth would end.'

Big oil spills in the wrong part of the ocean could, it is maintained, melt the arctic ice-cap, and so inundate coastal areas, drowning most of the world's capital cities and dramatically changing the world's climate. Some scientists predict that it might happen if drops of oil carried by the ocean currents built up on the underside of the ice. Since ice melts on the top and freezes on the bottom, the layer of oil would gradually rise, darkening the surface of the ice and absorbing much more of the sun's heat. The process, once begun, is likely to be irreversible. It is not fanciful to predict the possibility of oil spills in the Arctic. The area is thought to contain large untapped oil reserves.

There is a layer of ozone from about 55,000 feet to 100,000 feet above the earth's surface. At this level ozone is not a hazardous pollutant but a life-saver. It filters out most of the harmful ultra-violet radiation of the sun. Life on land probably did not begin until this layer developed. Recently there has been concern that man's activities might impair it, leading to an increase in skin cancer on earth, serious damage to crops and climatic changes.

Supersonic aircraft fly close to the bottom of the ozone layer and their exhausts include pollutants that can be expected to react with the ozone and deplete the shielding layer. Concern over this was one of the major factors in the successful campaign to stop the development of an American supersonic aircraft. It has also been one of the reasons for opposition to Concorde. Recently, however, a series of weighty scientific surveys have concluded that the number of Concordes or Russian Tupolev 144s ever likely to fly would have only an infinitesimal effect on the ozone layer. But they recommend that research is now undertaken to make the engines of any future supersonic aircraft cleaner.

There is more concern about a threat that is almost certainly sitting on our shelves at home—the propellant gases of many aerosols. Half a million tons of 'fluorocarbons' are pushed into the air every year as the power behind instant freshness and spray-on sex appeal. They appear to be indestructible in the lower part of the atmosphere, and the theory is that they drift slowly up to the ozone layer where, by a series of complex reactions, they release chlorine which attacks the ozone. The layer would take many decades to recover and, if present rates of consumption continue, there could be tens of thousands of extra (but mainly non-fatal) cases of skin cancer each year in the United States alone. Almost every link in the theory has been challenged, and our knowledge is certainly limited. It has to be based on laboratory experiments, since we do not have sensitive enough techniques to measure exactly what is going on in the layer. After much controversy and some confusion, however, a major investigation by the United States National Academy of Sciences recently upheld the theory. It also supported concern that a build-up of fluorocarbon could reinforce any 'greenhouse effect' caused by the burning of fossil fuels; its chairman estimated that by the end of the century the gases might be adding as much as 40 per cent to the effect of carbon dioxide.

The study concluded that there was no immediate cause for panic. It suggested that research should continue until 1978 in the hope of clearing up uncertainties about what happens in the ozone layer before there were regulations to restrict the use of the chemicals. The United States' Food and Drug Administration, which has authority over four-fifths of the products packaged in aerosol cans, took a sterner view. Following the National Academy of Science study, it announced that it intended to phase out the use of 'fluorocarbons' and later the Consumer Product Safety Commission and the Environmental Protection Agency joined it in ruling that no aerosol cans containing the chemicals should be sold after April 1979, except for essential medical uses.

The Food and Drugs Administration could present its decision as a straightforward one. 'It's a simple case of negligible benefit measured against possible catastrophic risk, both for individuals and our society', said Dr Alexander Schmidt, one of its Commissioners. But as he spoke scientists were becoming more and more concerned about another, more difficult threat to the ozone layer. Nitrogen fertilisers, it is suggested, add to the release of nitrous oxides at the surface of the earth, which in turn change into nitric oxides, the most important of the natural enemies of ozone. Some scientists were predicting that increasing use of the fertilisers to feed the world's growing population would reduce the layer more effectively even than the gases from aerosol cans. If they are right we may have to choose between hunger or cancer—an illustration of some of the difficult political decisions involved in pollution control.

The political decisions reach into what might be thought the most technical of subjects, the testing of chemicals. The small amount of research that has been done so far is an indication of our priorities, and so is the type of research.

The traditional way of discovering substances dangerous to man is through body-counting. We still rely on it far too much, finding out about a hazard only when people have died as a result. It is obviously unacceptable to the main thrust of research. The human cost is too great. The final death roll can be very long, for cancer and many other pollution-induced diseases appear only twenty years or more after the initial damage is done. Even if our monitoring is good enough to pick up the first group of people to be affected, there will be many deaths to come; for a whole generation of others will have been exposed to the hazard, while the damage done to the initial victims has yet to evidence itself.

Body-counting is also a remarkably haphazard business, though this is easily obscured by the fact that it is the only sure way of proving danger to man. It may establish hazard with certainty for some chemicals; but it will miss many others. It is best suited for picking up the causes of rare diseases common among a small concentrated group of people, like liver cancer among vinyl chloride workers. Even then it may be reliant on the thoroughness and concern of local or company doctors, and most other causes of disease will be very much harder to spot.

The people exposed to a chemical may be spread thinly over whole continents rather than concentrated in a few places; they may be a few workers in thousands of factories who handle a degreasing agent, for example. Their deaths, even from rare conditions, may never be linked. On the other hand, the disease caused by the chemical may be so common that the deaths do not stand out, even if they are fairly concentrated. As likely as not, the deaths may *both* be scattered *and* be from common diseases.

There are other difficulties. Because of the long latency period of cancers and other diseases, the victim may have changed jobs many times since his fatal exposure. If he is already dead only his last job may be recorded. If he is interviewed when still alive, he may not remember his working experience in enough detail. He may have caught his disease from one brief period working with a particular chemical which he no longer recalls. Just as likely, he may have been exposed to many potentially dangerous substances during his working life.

The body-counting method is even more unsatisfactory outside the workplace. The wider the population at risk, the less sharp the difference between the people in danger and those who are not, the harder the task becomes. The method is at its poorest in identifying the effects of relatively weak carcinogens or other dangerous chemicals to which virtually everyone is exposed, and is adequately taking into account the reaction between chemicals, but these may be precisely the areas that present the biggest pollution problem.

Of course, the method has a vital role where exposures have already occurred and should not be abandoned, but it should be used only as a backstop. Employers should be made to keep comprehensive records of their workforces, and the chemicals to which they, and the people living near their factories, are exposed. Doctors should be warned to keep alert for such dangers, and adequate national records should be kept. There should also be enough studies like the American cancer atlas to help identify trouble-spots. But research must concentrate as far as possible on identifying dangers before they show up in people.

Animal tests are useful, but expensive and time-consuming. For example, to test a single chemical for cancer in a single animal at a single exposure may take three years and cost about 100,000 dollars. There is an acute shortage of laboratories and of experts able, and willing, to do the job. Despite the hundreds of thousands of chemicals in daily use, and the thousands entering large-scale use annually, all the world's cancer research laboratories put together can test no more than 400 substances in a year.

However, scientists are discovering cheap and quick systems of testing, including ones using bacteria, that can pick out chemicals likely to cause trouble. This gives hope of at least a coarse screen to isolate potentially dangerous chemicals for more detailed examination, but it is not a complete answer either. The systems being developed only provide screens for carcinogens and mutagens, and even some of these will inevitably slip through.

The earlier a substance is tested the better. It will then have done less damage to people or the environment, and will be less integrated into the economy. Testing substances before they go on the market is obviously best of all, particularly if there is a rapid method of screening so that potentially beneficial chemicals which pass the test are not held up for long. Several countries now have laws requiring this; most notably, the United States' Toxic Substances Control Act, passed in the autumn of 1976.

The Act only became law after five years of argument, and despite intense opposition from the Republican administration. Even when it was finally passed little money was authorised for its implementation. This gives some idea of the political steam that can build up even over the issue of testing. The decision over what to do when tests suggest a substance is dangerous is even more difficult.

Naturally, this decision will be easiest when the chemical has not yet reached the market. But even then there will be a powerful commercial interest in the substance, and there may be a potential benefit to society to be weighed against the risk. When a material is already in large-scale use, with production runs and consumers committed to it, the decision will be much harder. But tests and decisions on the chemicals already in use will also be needed; for even if no more dangerous chemicals were ever to be released we would still be left with the causes of a large proportion of our cancers and other diseases, and with potential perils to the world system.

The first decision to take when regulating pollutants is how evidence of danger is to be assessed. One obstacle to effective controls, early enough, has been the demand for 'proof'. It sounds a reasonable enough demand on first hearing, but it can all too easily serve as a smokescreen.

There is rarely complete scientific 'proof'. For example, it is not *proved* that smoking can cause lung cancer, although this is now generally accepted. It might be that a general acceptance could be regarded as 'proof' for practical purposes; but this too takes time to achieve. There may be little research. There are almost bound to be disagreements between scientists. Moreover, the industry that produces a pollutant will often employ many of the best qualified scientists in the field and pay for the research. It is easy for an industry to use such research to muddy the waters and make general acceptance harder.

Furthermore, obtaining 'proof' of effects on human beings means relying on epidemiological data, with all its limitations, and this is often ethically unacceptable. For while it is unexceptional, indeed praiseworthy, to carry out retrospective studies on the effects of *past* exposures on people, it is an entirely different matter to set out to use people as guinea-pigs. Yet those who say that a chemical should not be regulated until there is evidence or proof that it is hazardous to humans are advocating that we use people in this way. Where we do not have retrospective epidemiological studies, reliable tests that show hazards to animals must be accepted as proof enough, for, despite their critics, and some shortcomings, they are relevant to human experience. Meanwhile we must stop using limited knowledge as an excuse for doing nothing and regulate precisely because we do *not* know, on the basis of reasonable doubt.

Once we have decided whether a chemical poses a hazard, we next have to decide what to do. It is, of course, unnecessary to call for *all* pollutants to be eliminated. Some are absorbed into the environment without danger; all are diluted in it. Some seem to be safe beneath certain concentrations; others, like carcinogens, are assumed to cause some hazard however much they are diluted. Where there is danger to people, a value judgement has to be made; for example, when setting pollution standards for factories and exposure levels for those who work within them. Since the only way to eliminate hazardous pollutants entirely is to shut down the process, a decision has to be taken as to the level at which the cost of reducing pollution (in terms of loss of jobs, wealth, and useful services to society) outweighs the benefits from further reducing danger to health. The need for these judgements is perhaps seen most starkly in the decisions that have to be taken on whether to ban uses of dangerous chemicals altogether.

Obviously, if the hazardous chemical is an irreplaceable cure for an otherwise fatal disease it should be allowed. Equally obviously, from the ethical point of view (though less so in practice) a hair dye, cosmetic, junk food flavouring or other substance that provides negligible benefit to society should be banned if found to be dangerous as should hazardous substances for which there are safe and practicable substitutes.

Many substances offer a less clear-cut choice, but the same kind of judgements can help to a certain extent. Consider the threat to the ozone layer. The possible danger from fertilisers strengthens the argument for banning 'fluorocarbons'. If the relatively frivolous threat is removed, the danger from the fertiliser may be acceptable.*

Asbestos might seem to provide another difficult decision. There is no way of counting the people who owe their lives to its fire resistance or its use in brakes. Some say that it saved more lives in the Battle of Jutland alone than it has taken since. In fact, asbestos, which has over three thousand uses besides life-saving, proves the point for at least a form of regulation. Had some control based on its true social costs been available from the outset, its unnecessary and even frivolous use could have been curtailed, and there would have been less exposure. Such regulations could have been enforced more easily on an infant industry than on the giant we have today. Interestingly enough, now that the full social costs *are* becoming known, and partly enforced, asbestos is being used less. The two largest makers of asbestos insulation in Britain have

*In making such a calculation, however, the amount of extra food produced by additional use of fertiliser would have to be weighed against the amount that could be lost through reducing the ozone's protection from ultra-violet rays.

changed over to different materials. The mineral is even being replaced for fire-resistance and some brakes. Tests by the London Fire Brigade on the ability of different kinds of gloves to protect firemen from hot objects were found 'clearly to show that asbestos is inferior to all materials tested'.

In the end each society has to decide what level of risk it will accept. Sweden, which is building up a thorough system of testing and monitoring, takes a strict line. In 1973 she legislated that mere suspicion of a hazard is enough to warrant prohibition or restriction of chemicals. America prescribes that no chemical that has been shown to cause cancer in man or animal shall be allowed as a food additive.

Authorities in other countries, such as Britain, reject this kind of approach. They argue that it is impractical, can cause scares, and can keep potentially life-saving drugs from being marketed. There is room for argument. British authorities can claim that lives would have been saved if some drugs had been permitted earlier in America; in return averted tragedies can be pointed out. These arguments seem to cancel each other out, with the promise of rapid screening probably giving the advantage to the strict approach. Food additives usually offer far smaller benefits than drugs, and here too the balance seems to be in favour of strictness. Yet the American dilemma, where rules against cancer hazards threatened to ban artificial sweetners and so force people to embrace the health risks associated with sugar, shows that regulations must also be sophisticated enough to allow for relative risks.

Scares can be tragic. Nine women seem to have been frightened into having abortions after some spray adhesives were banned in the U.S.A. on the grounds that they could cause birth defects. A few months later the suspicion was discovered to be ill-founded and the ban was lifted. Two scientists who examined the story concluded: 'The consequences of the episode illustrate the need to distinguish suspicion of toxicity from evidence for toxicity.'

But while scares and premature bans cause anxiety and inflict commercial damage, they only rarely cost lives. On the other hand, the consequences of complacency may well be fatal. Again there is no easy answer, but it is probably better to err on the side of caution.

A conscious bias for caution may also be desirable because there are strong biases in the other direction. An administrator faced with a decision may often have to weigh obvious short-term damage against possible long-term consequences. An industry can clearly show the cost that a ban would occasion it; the administrator can only guess at the magnitude of the health risk. There may be no real risk at all; and even if damage is done it is likely to become apparent only many years later, the source may never be traced, and the administrator never held accountable for his mistaken decision.

The same sort of pressures apply in setting pollution standards and exposure levels for factories. This makes it tempting to advocate imposing absolute standards to which industry must adhere. Ideally, however, a more flexible system is better, for then authorities can make firms lower their emissions as improvements become possible without having to go through the cumbersome procedure of formally changing the standards. The trouble is that flexibility is open to abuse, and that systems which merely require people to use the best practicable means depend heavily on how the word 'practicable' is interpreted. The best system is probably a mixture of the two; stringent absolute standards which must not be exceeded, and a requirement to use the best practicable means to reduce pollution as far below them as is economically and technically possible.

But whatever the system, the people who are most at risk should be fully involved. And, however this is arranged, there must also be sufficient public information. Up to now, as often as not, people have not been told enough. Indeed until recently in Britain it was a statutory offence to give workers or the public any information about the hazards they faced from individual firms.* And Mr Peter Thacher, Deputy Director of the United Nations Environment Programme, says that government laboratories all over the world keep two sets of figures for mercury in fish—the real ones, which they would not release, and a lower set 'for public consumption'.

Information should, of course, be checked. There is an obvious need for independent monitoring of the reliability of tests; on the one hand tests done by industry may take on too optimistic a view; on the other many substances have been declared dangerous—and

*See Chapter 17.

some even been banned—on unreliable evidence. And a sceptical eye also needs to be kept on industry's contentions of what it is practical for it to do. Dr Tokue Shibata, Director of the Tokyo Metropolitan Research Institute, told me: 'We set up a target for car emission control. The industry said; "It's impossible." So we said: "The emissions are harmful. So long as you do not stop this kind of pollution you must stop automobile production." Suddenly an excellent new invention comes up!'

The political decisions should also take account of a deeper ethical question. The fate of many victims of pollution diseases, the failure of research, the tardiness of regulation, the complacency of lack of knowledge have surely sprung from a philosophy of maximizing economic growth at all costs. Japan is the rich country that has perhaps embraced this philosophy most enthusiastically. But as Dr Shibata said, 'Ours was a terrible success, for there was horrible environmental disruption.' Besides Minamata and Niigata, besides frightening outbreaks of cadmium and chromium poisoning, recent figures show over 45,000 victims of disease induced by air pollution. Japan provides only the most prominent example of a philosophy that has been practised almost universally. Is the price we pay in pollution just another indication that continued all-out blinkered economic growth is not in the best interests of even the rich world? Is it an argument for a new economic order?

It is no contradiction to argue for rapid development for the poor. Their environmental threats are those of poverty, poor housing, inadequate food, bad water, limited access to education or health care. Concentrating resources on their development may actually reduce the threat from pollution. To give one instance, any peril posed by nitrogen fertiliser reinforces the argument presented for using a higher proportion of it in poor countries, where it produces more food. And they could develop in ways which avoid many of our mistakes.

In recent years there have been notable achievements in the revolution towards care for the environment in rich countries, such as the gradual cleaning of filthy British and American rivers, the improvement in air pollution in Japan, and the meetings of Mediterranean states on controlling pollution of their common sea arranged by the United Nations Environment Programme

(UNEP). But poor countries are coming to realise that it would be less costly to avoid creating the pollution in the first place.

Not long ago Brazil was the most vociferous exponent of the view that poor countries could not afford to be bothered about pollution, that their task was to concentrate entirely on growth. Recently there has been an abrupt change of policy. In the wake of a series of nasty pollution incidents,* Brazil was making a reappraisal similar to that which took place in industrialised countries at the beginning of this decade. The public was up in protest, and the Government were hurriedly drafting tough pollution legislation. Top officials freely admitted that they had been mistaken, and that it would have been far less costly to have decided to avoid pollution as part of their development strategy in the first place.

The point is borne out by Robert McNamara, who told the Stockholm Conference in 1972 that the World Bank had found that the environmental hazards of each new project it had started could be reduced either at no cost or at a cost so moderate that those borrowing money were quite happy to borrow a little more. A major United Nations study headed by the Nobel prize-winner Wassily Leontief concluded that world generation of pollutants would more than quadruple by the year 2000, and that vast expenditure would be needed to clean them up. But, the study went on, all this extra pollution could be avoided and the world could actually be made cleaner, if only 1·2 per cent of the projected world output was devoted to pollution control. While such a growth in pollution would endanger economic growth, the measures taken to control it would yield substantial economic benefits.

The countries that border the Gulf of Guinea, recognising that pollution will hinder their development, have already asked UNEP to help them agree a convention to avoid soiling the sea on which they depend. The growing acceptance, at least in principle, of the benefits of a 'basic needs' strategy is also important. For that kind of strategy, concentrating on rural development rather than big cities, on appropriate technologies rather than those merely copied from the West, on the small entrepreneur rather than the industrial tycoon, protects and enhances the environment while being the most effective means of development.

*For the effects in São Paulo see Chapter 16.

Chapter 15

Change of Habitat

Until a few years ago there was little to disturb the people of the small town of Petaluma in California. Their community grew at an orderly pace until it reached 24,000 inhabitants. Then the population jumped by 6,000 in two years. Frightened by this glimpse of gigantism and contrary to the Californian tradition of rapid growth, the people said, 'That's enough.' They decided to ration new building. Not surprisingly, the building industry was alarmed. It said that the rationing was unconstitutional and took the citizens of Petaluma to court. The court agreed, but the people appealed, and in 1975 the Federal appeals court sided with the town. The building industry replied by saying that it would take the case to the Supreme Court.

The people of Petaluma may win their battle, but they are going to be on the losing side in a *world* war. Nothing seems likely to stop the rapid growth of towns and cities around the globe, and in the next twenty-five years, for the first time in his history, man will have become an urban rather than a rural species.*

Even at the beginning of this century, despite the Industrial Revolution, 85 per cent of the people of the world were still rural. The world had changed further by 1960, but still two out of every three of us were country-dwellers. By the end of the century, however, slightly more people are expected to live in towns and cities than outside them. And we are told that by the year 2025, 80 per cent of humanity will be urban. These figures portray an even greater scale of change than may at first be apparent: they

*For the purpose of this chapter an urban area is defined as a settlement of more than 20,000 people.

suggest that by the end of the century there will be more people living in urban areas than there were alive on the globe in 1960. During this century the world's people will have almost quadrupled; but the population of towns and cities will have multiplied about thirteen times over.

'One has the obscure feeling', writes Barbara Ward, 'that only the distant billennia of geological time can provide any adequate concept of the scale of upheaval. The Indian sub-continent detaching itself from Antarctica and sweeping across the Indian Ocean to its violent collision with Asia's land mass along the Himalayas, the sea pouring in to change the Caribbean or the South China Seas into a chain of islands, the grinding of continental plates against each other, heaving up the Andes and leaving volcanic chains where Asia and Europe collide—these surely are the images that are appropriate to the scale of the twentieth century urban deluge.

'We are in the full tide of this great sweep. Its final consequences lie ahead. But already the ground shakes. We should hear, if we were listening, the mutter of the approaching storm.'

At first sight her analogy may seem exaggerated. But it is hard to think of a better one to convey both the physical change that the urbanisation of man is etching on the face of the planet and the shocks that the process is bringing about.

Not long ago, she reminds us, the city of a million people was a rare phenomenon. As the century began there were only eleven of them, and six of them were in Europe. By the mid-century the total had grown to 75. Now there are 191. In 1985 there are likely to be 273, in the year 2000, 414. Developing countries, the nations with the least resources to cope with the change, are experiencing the most rapid growth. They had only 24 cities with one million people in 1950. Now they have 101. By 1985 they may have 147, by the year 2000, 276.

Developments, of course, have not stopped with the 'million cities'. There are now two 'super-conurbations', each of more than twelve and a half million people, larger in themselves than the present population of most nations. The United Nations predicts that by 1985 these two, Tokyo and New York, will be joined by Mexico City, São Paulo, Shanghai, Los Angeles and Bombay—with Calcutta, Peking, Osaka, Buenos Aires and Rio de Janeiro not far behind. The major growth, once again, will be in the Third World.

Meanwhile, Tokyo may have led the way into a new class altogether, the city of 25 million, to be followed, and probably overtaken, by Mexico City and São Paulo before the century is out.

The shocks of the abrupt change of habitat are already being felt. The varied and interlinked crises that have been the subject of this book are all made more acute by the growth of the cities. The decisions taken about them and their expansion will largely determine whether the crises are solved or whether they run out of control.

The prospects for food production in the poor countries of the world depend very much on rural development. But the bias of most developing countries' economic policies is towards the 'formal sector' in the cities, and this has been directly responsible for the neglect of the countryside; for shortfalls in food production; and for the migration of the younger and more energetic people from the land.

It is the towns and cities that make by far the greatest demands for energy. It is here that the battle for conservation will be won or lost; and the choice of energy strategy will be largely determined by urban pressures. Indeed, the planning of towns and cities can have particular effects on energy consumption, quite apart from the general demand. Buildings can be designed either to conserve energy or to gobble it up; a community's layout and means of transport pose similar choices.

Pollution is largely a problem of the cities, and always has been. Shelley wrote:

> 'Hell is a city much like London,—
> A populous and smoky city.'

The smogs of the capital swirl through John Evelyn's diary and Charles Dickens' novels. Britain has since solved that problem through the Clean Air Acts, but the world's cities still pour out the greatest insults to man and to the biosphere.

Cities, for example, are overwhelmingly responsible for polluting the estuaries and inshore waters that are so important for marine life.* If you fall into the Hudson river at New York, it is said,

*See Chapter 14.

you will not drown but dissolve, and the Statue of Liberty stands with her feet in sewage. Cities from Los Angeles to Tokyo, from São Paulo to Sydney, have become symbols of air pollution; in January 1975 the situation became so serious in Madrid that citizens were advised to breathe only through their noses in heavily contaminated areas, to take no physical exercise and to speak only at home. Meanwhile air pollution in Athens is turning to acid and destroying the marbles of the Acropolis. Over the last twenty-five years it has done more to ravage that great monument to the birth of the city than the wind and weather of twenty-five centuries. The friezes of the Parthenon and the Temple of the Wingless Victory are being eaten away; the serene faces of the caryatids of the Erechtheum have been so ravaged that the statues have been covered with an ugly corrugated iron roof for temporary protection, and may have to be moved to a museum and replaced by replicas.

It is not just stone bodies that are in danger, however. The venomous mix of environmental carcinogens is at its most potent in the conurbations. Cancer has become the major cause of death even in some of the big cities of the poor world.

The cities have likewise become the symbol of the sense of alienation and malaise in the rich world. New York has long vied with Calcutta for the reputation of the world's greatest urban disaster. Half a million people in New York, one in every fifteen or so of its citizens, may have some kind of venereal disease. There may be 150,000 active drug addicts. There are, on average, four murders, eleven rapes, 213 muggings and 112 serious assaults every day. Of course, part of New York's troubles arise because it has always been a refuge for the poorest and most destitute people, as well as a playground for the richest and most ambitious; but it is far from being a special case. Its crime rate ranks only eighth among America's twelve biggest cities; and even in Britain the inner cities have treble the crime rate of the rest of the country.

Research in New York, therefore, has implications for cities all over the developed world. It indicates that the big-city environment brings on nervous tension and chronic mental illness.

It is too simple to blame such social ills wholly on the environment, but it does seem clear that crime and mental illness decrease where there is a sense of community, of privacy and of belonging. All over the rich world the people living in huge areas of cities have been deprived of these fundamental human rights, most notably through the anonymous, lonely high-rise blocks that perch their inhabitants in isolation from the city and play areas. Indeed, Mr Richard Seifert, the architect of ten thousand British high-rise homes, ended by denouncing them as socially evil.

The failure to eliminate poverty in the rich world is most obvious in its cities. While the poor minority in rich countries is much better off than most people in the Third World, its condition is made all the more bitter by the general affluence. Poverty exists in rich countries by choice, not necessity. There are the resources to eliminate it; it survives only by a failure in society's will. The situation is made all the more desperate and explosive by the rapid growth of ghettos of the poor. On both sides of the Atlantic the city centres themselves are becoming reserves for the destitute.

Since the early 1950s the number of people living in New York has remained much the same. But 1,800,000 middle-class whites—nearly a quarter of the population—have left for better homes in the suburbs. The space they left has been filled by almost exactly the same number of poor Puerto Ricans and Blacks. Today one in seven of the people of the city receive some form of public assistance. During the 1950s and 1960s the number of people living in Boston shrank from more than 800,000 to 600,000—but the Black population expanded from 20,000 to 120,000. At the end of the process one in five of the citizens was living on welfare. Detroit and Baltimore have much the same story to tell. Detroit inspired the famous analogy: 'a fat white doughnut with a black hole in the middle.'

While the doughnut grew in the United States, planners in Britain were telling themselves, and anyone else who cared to listen, that this was a peculiarly American problem. Suddenly, and belatedly, they realised that the same was happening to their own cities. In recent decades the populations of London, Manchester, Liverpool and other cities have dropped by hundreds of thousands. Now, more than three-quarters of all the inhabitants of the country's inner cities live in areas of concentrated poverty, few amenities and vandalised and overcrowded housing. A quarter of the families of the whole of London, for example, now live below the poverty line, while there are twice as many homeless people in the city as when Engels wrote about the problem. Vast areas of the inner cities are derelict, and 'deprived areas' have erupted not just in the traditionally poor conurbations of the North, but in such genteel resorts as Exeter, Brighton, and Hove. In the autumn of 1976 the Government reversed its policies and announced that the country's development resources would now be directed towards the inner cities. Politicians who differed on almost everything else agreed that unless there was urgent action Britain's urban crisis would rival that of the United States. Although little cash was forthcoming over the next year or so, for his part Mr Peter Shore, the Minister for the Environment, admitted that the plight of the inner cities was the biggest complex of economic, social and physical problems that we face.

Employment, as is now being officially realised, has long been the heart of the problem. In the last ten years Inner London has lost a third of its industrial employment; Glasgow saw a hundred thousand jobs disappear between 1964 and 1974; New York lost a quarter of a million manufacturing jobs in the first three years of the decade. Some of the British jobs have been lured away to new towns and greenfield sites by special incentives. Most of them, however, have just disappeared, mainly, as Mr Shore admits, because of bad planning practices. Zoning has sought to segregate homes from work. Factories and workshops have been swept away in redevelopment schemes, never to reopen, and others have been forbidden to expand. Often office buildings—and proliferating local government bureaucracies—have taken their place, but these provide little employment for those who had previously worked in industry. As a result, one-third of the people on inner city estates in places as diverse as Liverpool and Nottingham are unemployed.

The poor are further penalised by lack of transport. When oil was cheap, more and more right of way was given to the private car. Jobs, leisure facilities, even shopping centres became scattered all over cities with seemingly little thought of how they were to be reached by public transport. The scatter is now so wide that it is almost impossible to make effective links, even if public transport is revived after a long period of decline. The poor, the old, the disabled and the infirm have been increasingly denied mobility.

Deprived of jobs, trapped by inadequate transport, the poor

grow increasingly isolated from the prosperous suburbs. People have always moved out of the city centre when they can afford it. But now the poor are stuck. Conditions in the centre deteriorate. More relatively prosperous people—including skilled workers—move out, and thus the ghetto deepens. As firms disappear and the wealthier citizens move, city revenue often declines while the need for spending at the centre increases. New York's brinkmanship with bankruptcy has some of its origins in the swelling of the doughnut, and European cities from London to Düsseldorf to Turin have also been plunged into financial difficulties as the poor move in and the richer move out.

The social cost may be far greater than the financial one. At the beginning of this decade an American Government report issued this warning about Detroit: 'Between the unsafe, deteriorating central city on the one hand and the network of safe, prosperous areas and unsettled corridors on the other, there will be, not unnaturally, intensifying hatred and deepening division.' When David Lane, a former Home Office Minister, became Chairman of the Commission for Racial Equality, he said, 'We are becoming two nations—the middle-class in the suburbs and the poor of all races in the inner cities', and other authorities, including Mr Shore, have commented on the mounting bitterness that is likely to result from this.

The forecasts are already coming true. People in New York are now remembering the great black-out of 1965 almost with nostalgia. The power failure, one November evening, seemed to bring out the best in people. With a bit of grumbling, and a lot of amiability, the citizens helped each other through. There were only about 100 arrests and none for looting. There was no serious rioting.

On July 13 1977, there was another great black-out. Within minutes looting had begun: the ghettos boiled over, shop grills were torn down, windows smashed, and stores stripped. In at least one spot there was organised sniper fire to keep the police at bay. By the morning whole shopping areas looked like war zones, and still the pillaging continued. More than 3,500 people were arrested for looting, yet the rioters carried their booty through the streets in full daylight, some seeming glad of the chance to justify themselves to TV reporters. One young woman shouted over the air, 'The way I look at it, God put out the lights for one night so we could take the opportunity to make good for all the things we are missing.'

Responsible organisations maintained that it was poverty—and the provocation of the full display of swollen wealth just a walk away from the ghettos—that was at the root of the looting. But it only served to deepen the divisions in the city. So sharp are the unmarked boundaries between different areas, there as elsewhere, that middle-class people knew nothing of the anarchy (which took place mainly in poor areas) until they heard the radio news the next morning, even though it was sometimes happening as little as half a mile away from where they lived. And when they heard they felt deep revulsion for fellow citizens who, as they saw it, had completely different values from them.

That night of violence brought an emerging picture into focus. For long the people of the hopeless, spreading ghettos have been putting their own city to sack—and to the torch. Arson is endemic; in parts of the city, it is believed, most fires are started deliberately. For long, too, the polarisation of classes has been growing. Even many former liberals, even many of the city's traditionally tolerant Jews, look on the inhabitants of the ghettos with horror and hatred. And where, as in the United States or Britain, the poverty and wealth are grossly imbalanced between people of different colours, an added dimension is given to the division, discrimination and bitterness.

In New York unemployment among blacks is more than twice as great as for the city as a whole, itself double the national average. In Britain immigrant unemployment is twice the national rate and joblessness among young coloured workers has been growing three and a half times as fast as among the population as a whole. In parts of London and Birmingham more than half the young West Indians may be unemployed. With young immigrants feeling, justly, that they suffer from discrimination, with hopelessness and alienation growing, with fear and prejudice developing in both communities, with demonstration and counter-demonstration by extreme organisations breaking out on the streets, the inner cities on the mainland of Britain are becoming uneasily like Belfast and Derry in the 1950s and 1960s.

The inner cities are the main crisis points in rich countries. Yet despite all their problems, the main impact of man's change of habitat, the real crunchpoint of the developing human crisis, is in the poor world. In the last half of this century the urban population of the rich world will more than double—while that of poor countries will grow eightfold. Only about half their new citizens are born into urban life; the others choose to migrate to it. They pour in, refugees from the neglected countryside, cheap fuel for the industrial engine that cannot take them. There are no houses waiting for them; no water supplies, no sewerage, no schools—and no welcome, for they are resented by the wealthier citizens, and ignored, at best, by the authorities. They arrive on the outskirts of the city and camp, illegally, on what vacant ground they can find. They throw up flimsy shelters, makeshift hovels built of whatever they can get their hands on—sticks, fronds, cardboard, tar-paper, rushes, straw, petrol tins, maybe even some corrugated iron. These shanty-towns sprawl around the cities and grow and grow and grow.

In the Argentine they are dubbed *villas miserias*, which speaks for itself. In Chile they are *callampas*—'mushroom cities'. In Turkey they call them *gecekundu*—meaning that they are built between sunset and sunrise in a single night. In Brazil they have a number of names, including the most famous of them all—the *favelas* of Rio. And in return their people, the *favelados*, have their own eloquent name for those who are better off; they call them *asphaltos*, the people who live on the asphalt.

Let one old man, one of the most revered leaders of the favelados, tell part of his own story.

> I was born in the sugar cane country, north-east of Rio de Janeiro in a small peasant family. Of course, none of us children got any schooling.
>
> I lost my job as thousands did when the land went over to raising cattle instead of growing crops. My wife and I were living in a poor hut, and soon after that she died of typhoid—drinking polluted water. There was nothing else to do except 'emigrate' to the big city and hope that somewhere I could pick up work.

He arrived in Rio. He was lucky, finding a shack in an existing favela. Then, one day, the city decided to build a highway on the land on which the favela stood. The slum-dwellers had no choice but to move to a disused lot, a semi-swamp on which the Government was planning to build offices. It meant starting a new settlement from scratch.

Mine was the fourth house built in that shanty-town. We worked by day making up the sides of the hut out of packing cases and anything we could lay our hands on. Then when it was dark we would carry them over to the disused lot, put them together and have the family move in before the sun came up. I built three shacks that way. No building during the day, and scores of new houses appearing like mushrooms as the sun came up each morning.

You can imagine the condition of those shacks, built on swamp land, rushed up in a hurry, everyone fighting to get in a shack wherever he could find a bit of space. That is how the favelas of Rio grew up.

Trucks loaded with poor peasant 'immigrants' came down night after night from the north-east of Brazil, two weeks' journey away. Men, women and babies travelled in open trucks, sitting on planks lashed across the truck, with the family's possessions tied up in a blanket at their feet. They called them 'parrot perch' trucks. The trucks dumped the homeless families under the viaduct I can just see across from my house, and then set out north for another load. A day or so later there would be a few more shacks crowded into our already overcrowded favela.

This man was one of the first to trek to the cities in Brazil, which in its turn was one of the first countries to experience this great migration. Since he arrived in Rio, hundreds of millions of people all over the world have taken the same journey to cities; hundreds of millions have hastily thrown up their shanties; hundreds of millions have settled down to live in the stench, the disease, the violence and the insecurity of the proliferating slums. 'It can be argued', writes Barbara Ward, 'that those slums make up the most inhuman environments ever endured by man.' Yet the slums are home to at least one-third of the urban population in all developing countries, and they seem to be growing twice as fast as the towns and cities as a whole, so that soon they will have become the normal condition of urban life in the developing world. Even then much the greater part of the increase in the cities of the poor world has yet to come.

The increase is already putting enormous strains on totally inadequate facilities. The cities of the poor world were built to take a tiny fraction of the people who now live in them. Already nearly four out of every five of the citizens of Calcutta live with their families in one-room homes, and that does not count the hundreds of thousands who have to take what shelter they can find on the pavements and in the ditches. Across the subcontinent in Bombay, India's wealthiest city, conditions are little better—three-quarters of the families have only one room to live in, and many of them have to share that with another family.

Clean water is as important as shelter. The World Health Organisation estimated in 1970 that only half the people of the cities of the poor world had any access to regular water supplies, and half of those had to rely on public standpipes. Sewage disposal is usually either so scarce or so inadequate that human wastes carry their foulness and disease into the rivers, ditches, streams, and wells that have to serve for drinking water in the absence of public supplies. Indeed, in Calcutta sewage seeps even into public water supplies through vast cracks in both systems of pipes. The city's sewerage system, originally dug for a population of just over half a million, is silting up and rotting. It cannot reach many of the city's slums, which make do with earthen pits, occasionally emptied by the council. When the monsoons come the pits overflow, and the houses are flooded—one reason why the family wooden beds are constructed three feet above the ground. Yet at least Calcutta has some sort of underground sewage system, while some prosperous Third World cities have none at all. Lagos, for example, relies largely on open drains. Salvador, a growing industrial centre in Brazil, supplies less than eight thousand of its one and a half million people with main drainage. Dysentery is the main cause of death in the city, and half its infant deaths are caused by diarrhoea.

Of course, the slums get the worst conditions of all. Two-thirds of the shacks in slums in Cartagena, Colombia, are home to two or three families, at an average of more than six people to a room. Half of all the deaths in these slums are among children under four. One survey showed that only 5 per cent of the people living in them had been free of illness in the previous twelve months. Maurice Strong says that he expects a world epidemic to be bred in the slums of an overcrowded city within a decade. From there it could very quickly spread around the globe.

If conditions in the slums are so appalling, why do people in the countryside decide to migrate there? The trek to the cities is not a mindless, lemming-like rush. It is the result of shrewd decisions arising from a mixture of hope and despair. The migrants are pushed by the neglect in the countryside and pulled by the concentration of development, wealth, bright lights and excitement in the city. They are driven by the certainty that there is no opportunity for them in the country, and by the hope that things may be better in the city. Like Dick Whittington, or the migrants that continually flow to New York, they are looking for a springboard to a better life.

Indeed, bad as they are, the slums of the city may be better than conditions at home. Life in the Third World countryside is no rustic idyll. Half the city-dwellers may have access to public water—but only a tenth of the people in the countryside of the poor world ever get safe supplies. Sewage disposal may be bad enough in the urban areas, but 92 per cent of the rural people have no adequate means of getting rid of their wastes. Malnutrition may be appalling in both the slums and the villages, but of the two it is usually the people of the countryside who will starve. Wary governments, like the Romans before them, give priority to feeding the potentially threatening crowds of the cities. Income, little though it may be, is usually higher there than in the villages.

Physical conditions do not seem to be the most important reason. The element of hope seems much more important than the move from utter to modified degradation. Surveys among the slum-dwellers indicate that, above all, they come to the city because they believe it will give a better chance to their children. For that, it seems, they are even prepared to tolerate worse conditions than those they have left behind.

One old man in a Manila slum explained his reasons to the Filipino sociologist Dr Aprodicio Laquian:

> I am already old, with perhaps a few more years to live. But I decided to gamble and to leave my farm, living in this stinking community. I did not do it for myself. I was happy in the village. But my children, what would they become? I was a farmer. I owned three hectares [about $7\frac{1}{2}$ acres]. My father was a tenant, a *kasama*, and I was lucky to have owned land, when he died without ever achieving that. But my children—I have six of them. If I die, how will they divide three hectares between them? So I decided to try out my luck in Manila. Maybe they can get at least an education, a job. Who knows?

Who knows, indeed? A poor child in the poor world is lucky to get an education; lucky when he grows up to get a job.* But, the better the education he gets, the less likely he is to find employment. The parents may be ready to slog away for miserable returns at 'jobs' in the informal sector, but the better educated children will hardly want to follow in their footsteps.

The hopes of some of the migrants are realised. Small businesses do spring up in the informal sector even in the absence of government help. Some even get a chance to enter modern industry; some of those who get an education are lucky enough to land a coveted white-collar job. The news of such success triggers a fresh influx of people as word spreads among friends and relatives back in the village and underlines the promise of the city. But in most of the cities of the developing world today the vast majority of migrants are doomed to see their hopes frustrated.

The frustration is particularly bitter after the trek of hope has been made because there is usually nowhere else for the migrants to go. It is unlikely that they will be enticed back to the neglected villages, and the children of the migrants, who suffer the most, quickly become children of the city. Their frustration is given another twist by the poles of wealth in the city. Expensive cars flash past the *favelas* and *villas miserias*; fine houses can be seen from the shanties. Every day all the paraphernalia of conspicuous

*Chapter 6.

wealth is paraded before the poor by their own rich elites or by tourists from the Western World. Increasingly the wretched are learning at first hand that, in Barbara Ward's words, their conditions are 'not an Act of God but the choice of Man'.

She adds, 'The Angry Eighties lie ahead.'

Many share her fears. After all, elitist governments and orthodox revolutionaries will at least agree that the greatest danger to the established order lies in an urban proletariat. There have already been riots, and counter-violence, in poor world cities.

Jorge Hardoy, an Argentinian planner, believes that the increasing concentration of the poor in cities will awaken 'forces dormant for generations, made lethargic by hunger, repression and segregation'. And P. K. Sen, a former police chief of Calcutta, adds that the conditions of the city have 'given birth to a generation of cynical youth ready to resort to desperate measures to achieve their ends'. 'Unless conditions are improved for the vast majority', he goes on, 'agitation and violence will not end.' He put his finger on perhaps the greatest potential for violence—the frustration of the children of the city. The people of the cities of the poor world are overwhelmingly the young.

And yet there have been surprisingly few uprisings so far. The reservoir of hope in the new citizens is not yet exhausted, and there does still seem to be time for voluntary, bloodless change. Indeed there are some signs that solutions are in the making, and can be applied to the urban crisis.

Chapter 16

Hope from the Slums

'A city', says Dr Jorge Hardoy, 'reflects within its space the values and character of the society to which it belongs'. And by the same token answers to the urban crisis must be found through changes in the policies and priorities of nations as a whole. The signs of hope for Man's habitat and the prospect of solutions to its problems lie in such principles as rural development, the priority of tackling the needs of the poorest, and the importance of giving the ordinary man the chance to use his own resourcefulness. There must also be labour intensive processes, appropriate technology that enhances work and avoids pollution, energy conservation, a new economic order—and the new attitudes, political will and public pressure needed to bring such a programme about.

It is a long list, but the actions it represents would make all the difference to the escalating crisis of the cities. Indeed, these general principles need to be recognised when problems, which are particularly linked to the cities and to the other settlements of man, are being tackled. In the next three decades, for example, we are going to have to erect as many buildings as already exist; by the end of the century we may need 1,400 million new homes. Building those houses would be a daunting enough task even for rich countries, particularly considering the failure of nations like Britain, the U.S.A. and France to ensure that millions of their own citizens have adequate dwellings.* But by far the greatest need, of course,

*Sixteen million French people live in houses without a bathroom, shower or indoor lavatory. Four million homes in Britain are unfit for human habitation. A quarter of the population of the U.S.A. is said to live in nearly sixteen million slums or near slums.

is going to be in poor countries. In the next twenty years alone they will have to find the resources to put up as many buildings as the rich countries have achieved in the last two hundred years. And building a house is only part of the problem. They must also provide clean water, sewage disposal and power.

Brazil was one of the first third-world countries to experience the rush to the cities. In 1940 the country contained only about forty million people, and less than a third of them lived in towns and cities. By the end of this decade its population will have trebled, and two-thirds of the people—double the population of the whole country in 1940—will be crowded into its urban areas. In 1920 there was only one favela in Rio. By 1947 there were already more than a hundred, home to 138,000 people. By 1964 there were 1,370,000 slum-dwellers; one-third of the people of the city.

So far Rio's experience was much the same as that of most of the third-world cities today. But at this point the story changed. Today the city has grown still further, and is home to six million people. But the number of people in favelas has actually fallen—to about a million.

The reason usually given for this achievement is a vigorous housing policy instituted by the national government after the revolution of 1964. It established a National Housing Bank to finance the building of low-cost homes all over the country, ingeniously giving the Bank its economic muscle through the administration of a new fund for workers' insurance. All employers have to deposit 8 per cent of their pay-roll on behalf of their workers; the money earns interest (in fact, there was a three-year delay before interest was paid), and is indexed against inflation; it can be withdrawn on certain occasions—for example, if a worker is dismissed, dies, gets married or wants to buy a house. This compulsory savings fund is joined by a voluntary system of savings and loans.

The Bank finances housing for people across a wide spectrum of incomes, and the homes are sold on widely differing terms. The poorest people have twenty-five years to pay off the debt at only 1 per cent interest; the richest have only fifteen years, and have to pay 10 per cent.

'As this is basically a social bank our main goal is to supply poor people,' says Paulo Cesar, an adviser to the bank's president. Modern five-storey blocks of flats with all mod. cons. have sprung up all over Rio and the other main cities. Many favelas have disappeared. Once, at the foot of a hillside, was part of an old favela so oppressive that it was called 'the hot hole'. The favela is gone now, the hillside is a miniature forest of young bamboo and grass, and the people who once lived there proudly point out their new homes—modern apartments on the skyline across the valley.

Up to the end of 1975 the Bank had financed just over 600,000 units of what it calls 'social' housing. This, together with the houses built for wealthier people, provides a total of almost one and a quarter million units constructed in eleven years. The Bank reckons that the stimulus its work has given to the building industry has indirectly produced another two and a half million homes.

This programme has been one of the key elements in the Brazilian economic miracle. By the early 1970s the construction industry alone was creating half a million new jobs every year, and was enabling thousands of unskilled workers to learn a trade. Personal savings, which were virtually nil in 1964, have now grown to some 500 million dollars through the bank's system.

It seems almost too good to be true. At one stroke, almost, the government provides the basic social need of decent housing, increases jobs through a labour intensive industry, and mobilises the personal savings that are one of a country's greatest financial resources. What is more, building houses can stimulate any number of subsidiary industries from glass manufacturing to steel making, from doorknobs to furniture, from electrical goods to pots and pans. Singapore chose housing as a lead sector in its economic growth, building houses for 40 per cent of its people between 1960 and 1974. Mexico embarked on a programme similar to Brazil's. The answer, it appeared, had been found.

Unfortunately, as far as the really poor are concerned, it *is* too good to be true. Despite all its economic achievements, the Brazilian programme has failed in its basic objective of housing the *poorest* people. This is now openly acknowledged in the Brazilian National Housing Bank itself. Even the low-cost houses are too expensive for most of the poor people. Many of those who are already buying their own homes cannot keep up the payments; in 1975 nearly 80,000 of the Bank's home buyers were in arrears. There were no records for another 50,000, and the Bank admitted that they were not likely to be paying up either.

Meanwhile, most of the favelados cannot contemplate even attempting to buy a National Housing Bank home. This may seem strange when so many people have already been moved. But it is only puzzling if one assumes—as the Bank appears to have done too readily—that all Brazilian slum-dwellers are the same.

Obviously most people are in the slums because they are poor. But others—perhaps a third of the favelados of Rio—are relatively well off. Their homes may boast television sets, refrigerators, even air-conditioning. They are earning several times as much as their neighbours. The reason they are still in the slums is that too few houses have been built in the past. As the new estates are completed it is these people who have mainly benefited from the seemingly successful housing programme. The basic problem has remained unchanged, for the poor, the real favelados, have been left behind.

One night I was in one of the favelas perched high in the hills of Rio, talking to the leader of its people. He drew me to a window. We looked down, almost vertically it seemed, over the roofs of tightly packed shacks, built almost on top of one another, to new housing lit up far below.

'Here's the difference between us and those who live down there,' he said. 'They can buy a house and feed themselves, we cannot afford to buy a house *and* eat.'

So it is no surprise that in 1975 Brazil's National Housing Bank, which gives no subsidies, had up to half its housing blocks unoccupied in some areas of the country. Sixty per cent of the houses financed by the Bank are supposed, by law, to go to the poor, but recently only about a third of the Bank's homes have been bought by poor people. As Bank officials put it, the poor just do not provide the market demand.

Brazil's experience shows that public housing programmes and a concentration on the construction industry can be of great value in stimulating the economy—if there are enough people to afford the houses produced. But these are not the answer to the problems of the really poor. Evidence from all over the world underlines the lesson that the basic issue is not house-building but poverty. A World Bank study in Madras, Ahmedabad, Nairobi, Mexico City and Bogotá came to the conclusion that even the cheapest public housing being built was too costly for between half and two-thirds of the people; and this is optimistic, for the Bank based its calculations on generous estimates of the proportions of their income that the poor can afford to spend on shelter.

Many of the poor do not have the regular employment that provides the steady and secure income needed to buy or rent a house. Even when they do have a steady job it seems that people need to earn about four or five times a subsistence level wage to be able to buy any public housing. John F. C. Turner, one of the leading authorities in the field, reports that huge publicly-financed cheap housing programmes have been driven to the brink of bankruptcy because of the failure of the new householders to keep up their payments. It is unusual, he says, for agencies to receive more than half the money due to them. And a study in Mexico has shown that people who were able to live relatively well in a slum have slipped beneath the subsistence level when they moved to a government low-cost estate, partly because they simply could not afford the payments.

Governments could, and should, set out to build cheaper houses. They could experiment with new techniques and be much less insistent on building to international standards which put housing well out of reach of the poor. They could also institute subsidies. But none of these measures will get to the root of the problem. Even in relatively prosperous Venezuela, for example, nearly half the urban people who need houses cannot afford to pay *anything* towards buying or renting them. They would have to be given them outright. And most poor countries could not possibly afford to run any extensive scheme of subsidies whatsoever.

So what is the answer? There are clues in the favelas of Rio, after all; for where the pattern imposed by the State has failed, the resourcefulness of the slum-dwellers has produced success. It is the favelados themselves who are responsible for the disappearance of large areas of slums.

They started with nothing. Not only had they no water, sewage disposal, electricity, schools or rubbish collection, but the authorities were reluctant to install such services, for to do so would be to recognise the squatter's right to be there. And since their homes were built illegally, the favelados were considered to be outside the law.

One day in 1954, a young worker, Herondines Seraiva de Carvalho, went canvassing in the favela of Penha. 'I was standing for election as a local councillor,' he said. 'As I went round I met many people who supported me, but were illiterate. Because they could not write their own names the law did not allow them to vote. So I spent a lot of time in the favela and did not get anywhere. I lost that election. So I thought "At least I can do something about that; I can make sure that people learn to read and write!" '

In fact he was so shocked by the conditions he had seen that he went back to the favela, brought together some of the most enterprising people and set up a co-operative association. It was probably the first of its kind in Brazil, and one of the first ever to be formed in the slums of a third-world city. They levied a subscription of two cruzeiros a month (10p or 20c at present rates of exchange).

They bought a shack for 12 cruzeiros for use as a meeting hall at night and a school by day. They found two teachers to give classes to the children. And from the first day they began rebuilding the houses of the favela in bricks and mortar. Soon they were recruiting new members and campaigning for essential services; they chose clean water as their first priority. Herondines worked with them every weekend for the first few years, and then left them to run affairs entirely by themselves.

In the spring of 1976 I visited Penha with him. We swung into a broad tarmac street flanked with shops, the entrance to the old favela. 'That was a mud track in 1954,' I was told. We drove past solid two-storey brick houses and pulled up at the new meeting hall. There I met twenty men and women, among them the founders of the association and the people who run it today.

Penha has grown some five times over since 1954. Seven thousand families live there now. Yet, I was told, 80 per cent of the houses had been rebuilt in brick or concrete by the people themselves; they had been laid out in streets for proper access; every house has running water and electric light. Every home is linked to a main sewer—a remarkable achievement, because the favela was built on ground once designated as a cemetery, but abandoned because the ground was too rocky for graves.

All the work has been planned, financed and carried out by the people of the favela working through their co-operative. They say that the only help they have had from outside was one 1,000-cruzeiro cheque given by the state government in 1960. The co-operative carries out all maintenance on the services, and employs some fifty people to do the work. It even built and owns the police station; only the policemen are provided by the state.

The transformation of Penha, from a slum to a suburb, was only made possible by the enterprise and pride of the favelados themselves. As well as a tremendous physical achievement, it was a triumph of planning, persuasion and organisation. For example, about a third of the shacks had to be moved in order to change overcrowding into spaciousness, to turn winding dust paths into streets, to lay electricity, water and sewerage. Each displaced family was found land elsewhere in the favela and persuaded to move.

Other favelas have followed Penha's example. In 1960 the state government decided to tackle the growing slums for the first time. It made direct contact with the slum-dwellers, and set up a special commission, under Professor Jose Artur Rios of the city's Catholic University. The commission set out to find out what the favelados really wanted. They were encouraged to organise themselves into co-operatives, and for the first time a network of associations was set up. They were helped to 'urbanise' their slums—to use the favelados' word. Some rehousing in new projects began. Then came the revolution of 1964, and the new military government decided to spread the attack on bad housing to every state in the nation, and set up the National Housing Bank to consolidate and co-ordinate the programme. Unfortunately, of course, it developed in the wrong direction, but meanwhile the associations set up before the revolution went on working almost unnoticed.

Jonas Rodrigues da Silva, President of the Federation of Favela Associations for the state of Rio, says that 153 out of 376 favelas now have co-operatives. Three-quarters of them have managed to obtain clean running water. About a third have gone some way to rebuilding and replanning the whole favela.

Visiting the favelas makes those statistics live. Once a thousand people lived in the Scorpion's Nest—one of the most unpleasant of the city's slums, built on a swampy dip in the ground. They formed an association which drew up a map of their slum, counted heads and made new plans. Bit by bit they poured rubble into the dip, filling in the swamp and raising the land by six feet. When the whole slum was on a new level they shared out the land between families to a regular pattern, laid out streets and encouraged one another to build better houses. When it was done they thought that their home—now quite a pleasant suburb—needed a new name. They called it Happiness Park.

The São Joao favela association put concrete round huge boulders balanced precariously on the hillside above the shanties. The people of the Morro da Coroa quarried out part of their hill to make a public square. Before they get running water, the hill favelas often build concrete steps to replace slippery dirt tracks and ease the crippling job of carrying water from the bottom of the hill. Jacarezinho favela, the biggest in Rio, had its own solution to the water problem—it illicitly tapped a main, and defended its free supply for years. Many of the co-operatives set up schools and classes in literacy and skills to help their people find decent jobs.

All the time people are rebuilding their houses. If you go into a favela at a weekend or public holiday you are almost sure to see someone at work, some house evolving towards a sturdy, two-storey brick construction. All over the Third World poor people are building and improving in this way. The United Nations reckons that such 'spontaneous self-help' building accounts for more than half of all housing construction in poor countries. As soon as they can, poor people turn their shanties into solid homes, the wood or leaf walls into brick or concrete. Often the brick is built like a second skin around the outside of the existing walls. When self-help building is forbidden, some slum-dwellers change tactics. They build the brick home *inside* the shanty, demolish the old shell overnight and present the world with a fait accompli.

As a man's family or prosperity grows over the years, he may build on extra rooms. The house that eventually evolves is often extremely impressive. Oliver Cox, a British architect, reports that houses built in Jamaica by people with incomes barely above subsistence level are 'substantial in size—well above Parker Morris standards—well built and an object of pride'.

In some ways building the house is the simplest part of making a home, and not always the most important. Even rudimentary shelters can be adequate, particularly in warm climates, but no one can do without clean water or a safe form of sewage disposal. These and other services like education, health care, electricity, and roads cannot normally be provided by the slum-dweller in the same way as he can build his own house.

Obtaining these services has been the main point of the Rio co-operatives and their counterparts in both the town and the country in other parts of the world. Another approach is for the authorities to acknowledge that they cannot build houses cheap enough for poor people and leave the building to the home owner—but lay on the services instead. This can be done by improving existing slums or by laying out fresh land in plots complete with all that is needed. Faced with the failure of its conventional building programme, the Brazilian National Housing Bank has changed its policy to include both these ideas. It has initiated a crash programme called PROFILURB. The first new plots were sold in April 1976, and the plan was to provide sites and services for more than one and a quarter million homes by 1979. The World Bank is encouraging countries to go for 'sites and services' programmes, and in 1974 twelve nations already had projects under way.

The Brazilian change of policy is important, for Brazil has been the arch-exponent in the Third World both of national house building programmes and of the Trickle-down road to development. The change amounts to an admission that even its rates of economic growth will not meet the basic needs of the poorest, and a conversion to a housing policy which draws on new thinking in development strategy.

As the new approach to housing gains acceptance, controversy is already growing over how far the State should be involved. Professor Rios stresses the importance of doing things *with* people rather than *for* them, and believes that the PROFILURB programme still has many of the failings of the public housing schemes. He would prefer to see a programme that subsidised the basic materials but worked through the co-operatives and the people themselves; and one where Government emphasis was on employment so that people could better afford to make their own improvements. On the other hand, Dr Hardoy, who is equally enthusiastic about the potential of poor people and equally convinced that the primary emphasis must be on basic needs economic strategies, believes that, where possible, housing should be provided for poor people as of right, like education or health care. He is worried by the legitimising of injustice in an approach where poor people have to spend time that they can little afford in building their houses while those who are wealthier have the work done for them.

The co-operative approach is not only cheaper but also ensures much greater participation by the people, and gives them a considerable amount of self-government. Certainly government intervention can blunt the initiative of the squatter or swamp it with bureaucracy and regulation. The story is sometimes told of a drainage scheme in Guatemala. The Government decided to organise the squatters, and so destroyed their own informal groupings. It installed new drains, but inefficiently and at much greater expense than what the people had already begun to build for themselves.

There must, however, be some government involvement. Some communities will never manage to organise themselves, will be rent with personality clashes, or sunk in despair. They must not be neglected. Communities can do a great deal for themselves in education and health care, but this will have to be knit in to a wider system. Usually they are dependent on outside authorities for clean water supplies; indeed, however they are actually installed, making these available must be a government priority. It will be too easy for governments to use the formidable abilities of the slum-dwellers, and the growing fashion among development experts for 'self-help', as an excuse for continuing neglect.

Some government-inspired successes are emerging. Calcutta is surprisingly beginning to become a symbol of hope. Its Metropolitan Development Authority decided that the only practicable strategy was to improve slums, not destroy them. About half the city's slums have now been made habitable; water is being piped in, alleyways paved, electricity provided, and proper septic tanks—a more feasible option for most poor country cities than prohibitively expensive sewerage—are being installed to provide adequate sanitation. Caracas, capital of Venezuela, has begun to transform its slums with a particularly imaginative scheme that aims to provide small factories and workshops, and subsidised food stores along with more usual facilities.

The right balance between government and people will vary from situation to situation, but there are two things that governments should invariably do. They must institute basic needs economic policies. This is a prerequisite for any chance of solving the crisis of the cities, just as it is for balanced development in poor world countries as a whole. Providing such needs as water, health care, education and sewage disposal can merely be part of such a strategy. For it is only through new economic policies that the poor will have a chance to escape from desperate want, to realise their potential and, incidentally, to earn the money to invest in improving their surroundings. Second only to this in importance, governments must give squatter settlements security by handing them the right to their land.

This fundamental legal recognition is essential, and the slum-dwellers know it.* At present not one of the favelas of Rio, for example, owns the legal title to its land. The work done at a place like Penha could be destroyed overnight, with no compensation whatsoever, if—for example—the local authority decided to build a new highway through it. Settlements have been razed to the ground, almost as a matter of course, often simply to 'beautify' a city. And though the bulldozers may have become less busy as the potential of the slum-dwellers begins to be recognised, they are still at work. The UN Habitat Conference in 1976 loudly affirmed the self-help principle, but just as it was breaking up one of the internationally acclaimed models of what slum-dwellers could do for themselves, the Janata colony of Bombay, was being flattened because scientists at a nuclear research establishment wanted the land for a park, a recreation area and a swimming pool. Meanwhile, 600,000 people were dumped on the outskirts of Delhi after their homes had been demolished without notice in 'resettlement schemes', part of the Indira Gandhi regime's much-heralded campaign against poverty. As one of the victims told the Indian news magazine *Himmat*: 'Whether they remove poverty or not, they sure have removed the poor.'

By contrast the President of Colombia legalised all squatter

*One slum leader has even spoken to me of the 'right to pay rates', meaning that if the slum were legalised the people would have a legitimate call on government help in providing services, and would have the security of the rate-payers of the city.

settlements in 1972. Obviously the more secure the slum-dwellers are, the more they will do to improve their areas. The Caracas scheme ingeniously not only gives them titles to their land but encourages them to use these as collateral to borrow money at a special interest rate to improve their homes or build new ones.

Legalising squatter settlements is an important step towards recognising the dignity of the poor man, which in turn is essential if there is to be any hope of solving the human crisis. All over the world, in cities and in the countryside, in rich countries as well as developing ones, the poor man has a passionate desire to be treated as a person rather than a problem. All the favelados and favela leaders I met in Rio, for example, were unanimous that they did not want to be given anything free: they wanted to pay for, or work for, everything. And, if poor people are treated with respect, the work can increase their dignity. Hassan Fathy, an Egyptian architect, wrote after the construction of one village:

> The maturing of skill is an experience of considerable spiritual value to the craftsman, and a man who acquires the solid mastery of any skill grows in self-respect and moral stature. In fact the transformation brought about in the personalities of the peasants when they build their own village is of greater value than their material condition.

The growth of the skills can be economically valuable too. Just as the National Housing Bank programme played a key role in the Brazilian economic miracle, self-help housing and services can stimulate the beneficial spiral of growth of the basic needs strategy, creating jobs, teaching skills, mobilising savings, and increasing the capital stock of buildings. Small construction firms spring up when they have a chance. In Tanzania it has been found that such firms build houses very much faster and more cheaply than big ones. They use local materials, consume only a fraction of the precious energy swallowed up by 'modern' building techniques, and employ more people.

Most important of all, poor people must be given every chance to participate in the decisions that will mould their lives. That is not only a fundamental human right, but practical good sense. In city after city slumdwellers have come up with much more sophisticated solutions to urban problems than experts or statutory authorities. And it will not be possible to mobilise their energies to the full unless they believe in what they are doing. Indeed it is hard to imagine how a city of 30 million people, the size of Mexico City by the end of the century, can possibly be held together unless there is real participation by the masses in the way it is run.

To quote Barbara Ward again:

> If societies can find some way of seeing in these millions not a drag on the living standards of those who have already 'made it', but as a prime source for the energy, intelligence, dedication and work needed to build the new settlements, it will first be discovered that prodigies can be performed. And then it will be found that self-reliant and responsible citizens are being shaped. . . .

Indeed, it is that very responsibility that offers one of the greatest grounds for hope. The poor are rarely given credit for it. The slum-dwellers of the cities have been feared, the people of the countryside despised. This was one of the most frequent points made to me by the favelados of Rio. Like squatters all over the world, they were regarded as outlaws, a threat to life and property. 'This is a very great mistake,' I was told by Jose Almeida Neto, a favelado for thirty years and one of the foremost leaders of his people. 'Proof of this is the fact that when the favela associations were formed they always asked for four things: water, light, schools —and the police. They would not be asking for the police if it were not for the fact that most of them are law-abiding people.'* This suggests that the slum-dwellers will not easily turn to violence. As long as they are given a chance, as long as their hopes are not frustrated and their dignity not flouted, they at least are willing for peaceful change.

A strategy based on such principles as rural development, giving priority to the needs of the poorest, encouraging the small man,

*This is not to say that there is not violence in the favelas but to emphasise the wish of the majority to be protected from it. Shortly before I visited one favelado he had been sitting outside his house rocking to and fro. As he did so a shot rang out, and the bullet grazed his throat. Another favela leader denied that there was fighting in his slum. 'I do not fight,' he said, 'I kill.'

saving energy and protecting the environment does not guarantee workable cities in the poor world. But we do know that the old approach that takes no account of these principles produces unworkable giants.

If the old approach were to work anywhere it would be at São Paulo, one of the wealthiest of all third-world cities, whose people ask you to admire their skyscrapers, a sturdy crop of steel and concrete stalagmites stretching to a claustrophobic horizon. They boast 150 cinemas, 30 theatres, 18 radio stations and six television channels. There are nearly as many cars per head of population as in New York. And yet, partly because of these superficially impressive statistics, São Paulo is earning a world reputation as an urban disaster. It combines many of the problems of rich and poor world cities, a sort of twentieth-century Tokyo imposed on a nineteenth-century Manchester, or a blend of Los Angeles and Bombay. Cars jam up the city centre for hours on end. Their fumes blend with those from the 47 per cent of Brazil's industry that is crammed into the city, to build pollution up to crisis levels. As a result, emergency plans to close down industry and ban people and traffic from parts of the city may have to be implemented several times a year. Meanwhile three million people get their water from wells sunk into a water table heavily polluted with sewage. Partly because of this, partly because of poverty, the infant mortality rate has almost doubled in fifteen years. Nearly half the children who survive are undernourished. Between one and two million people live in slums and rotten housing. Yet attempts to rehouse the poor are made much more difficult by land speculation. In parts of São Paulo land prices have multiplied fifteen times over in two or three years. Much of the land that could be used for building remains unoccupied while its owners wait for its value to appreciate still further.

Four hundred million dollars are being spent in three years to try to supply fresh water. New schools are being built. There is a belated drive to improve public transport. But Erwin Fuhrmann, chief executive of the city, says that even São Paulo just does not have enough money to buy its way out of trouble.

Brazil accepts the trek to the cities as inevitable, indeed welcome, believing that it shows the modernity of the economy. Yet it means that every year about a quarter of a million people come to São

Paulo, drawn by the promise of its wealth. Paulo Nogueiro Neto, Brazil's Secretary for the Environment, says: 'Because of this increase nothing is sufficient for São Paulo. They are always putting in new water pipes and new sewage equipment. They think that in a few years the water supply will be sufficient. By then more people will be living badly than now.'

There is a good deal to be said for taking a look at São Paulo and deciding to do the opposite. Of course, the kind of rural development and regional city programme already discussed could not stop the trek to the cities altogether—population is growing too fast for that.* But the programme could slow the rush, and make the influx more manageable. It is the only hope.

The migration to Calcutta, for example, is guided by a fairly shrewd assessment of the relative advantages of life in the city and the countryside. If conditions were improved in the rural areas many people would prefer to stay at home. Indeed, Dr Laquain reports from the Philippines that even the bright lights and juke boxes brought to the countryside by electricity have helped to keep people down on the farm.

The priority given to the private car seems ludicrous enough in a city like Dallas or Los Angeles, where over half the city is given over to roads and parking space—or indeed in New York, where it still takes longer to cross Manhattan on four wheels than it did by horseback in 1911. It is crazy planning to have a third-world city clogged up with cars while there is no adequate transport to take people to work, and while the people in the countryside do not even have proper access to markets. Yet not only are there cities like this all over the developing world, but the trend towards the private car is expected to grow. São Paulo may have two million more cars by the end of the century.

The traditional answer to the inequity, pollution and paralysis so often brought on by the private car is to improve public transport. That this can be done even in the most difficult circumstances is shown by the example of New Delhi. Until recently the Delhi bus system was famous for its inefficiency and chaos. There seemed no solution; plans for an underground railway were impossibly

*Even if the flood continues at its projected rate, rural population is expected to grow by half as much again by the end of the century.

expensive. Then a young planner proposed reorganising the routes so that they ran like spokes of a wheel instead of snaking irregularly through the capital. When this was done the buses ran punctually and the number of passengers increased by 40 per cent over six months.

But improving public transport is not the full answer, because, however good the buses are, they may be too expensive to enable the poor man to get to work, particularly, as often happens, if his home has been moved, through slum clearance or public housing programmes, to the outskirts of the city far from sources of employment. The best solution will often be to reduce the need for transport as much as possible, by bringing jobs and facilities to the people. Singapore has set up eight clusters of housing, community facilities and industries surrounding the old city. Karachi is planning its growth around neighbourhoods of 40,000–50,000 people, based on self-help housing, and provided with water, sewers, schools, markets, health clinics and labour-intensive industry. Dodoma, the new Tanzanian capital city, has been planned entirely on these principles. Everyone will be no more than fifteen minutes' walk away from his work or community services. There will even be open spaces within this distance in which people can grow their own food. Only the administrative centres and noxious industries will be away from the neighbourhoods, and fast roads reserved exclusively for buses will connect them. Cars will have to take a circuitous route.

Enrique Penalosa, Secretary-General of the Habitat Conference, believes enough in the principle of self-contained neighbourhoods within cities to say that with them 'even a city of 75 million is still going to work'. You do not necessarily have to be as optimistic as he to see their potential. For their creation does more than relieve city congestion and provide access to necessities for the poor. It saves energy by reducing the need for transport. It also helps to create and sustain a feeling of community, the surest defence against alienation.

Of course, this applies just as strongly to rich world cities as to poor ones, for many of their problems are surprisingly similar. Indeed, solutions being found in the rich world can be adapted to meet the needs of developing countries, and vice-versa. The planners of Dodoma took the idea of the special busways direct from Runcorn, while Stevenage was one of the first places to apply the idea of neighbourhoods.

Similarly, some rich countries are pioneering ways of building up regional cities and towns so as to take the pressure off the capital and spread opportunity more evenly. Britain's policy of building new towns has become less fashionable following the discovery of the neglect of the inner cities, but its fall from favour does not reduce its potential, properly applied, elsewhere. France has particularly comprehensive urban plans; they include creating communities within the capital, encouraging people to move out of Paris to five new cities around it, and strengthening sixteen other cities around the country to counter-balance the capital. Meanwhile Rumania has managed to reduce the preponderance of its capital city in favour of smaller cities.

Equally, some solutions first studied in the poor world are also relevant to developed countries. The stimulation given to the Brazilian economy by the house building programme has led to calls for rich country governments to pay much more attention to their own housing industries. Promoting housing not only fulfils a social need but encourages the growth of dependent industries.

However, just as in developing countries, public housing schemes are not always the answer to the problems of the poor. Many of the houses pulled down for redevelopment are quite habitable, at least with improvement; 60 per cent of those demolished in London between 1967 and 1972 had been classified as in 'good or fair' condition. The land lies waste for years, and sometimes in the end less houses are built than were destroyed.* Worse still, the new houses can cost so much to build that the people who used to live in the area cannot afford them. Rehabilitating old houses is emerging as a preferred technique. And, just as in poor countries, the people who live in the houses show themselves only too ready to improve them if it is clear that they are in control of what they they are doing and are not being exploited. There have been several important self-help schemes in Britain, and the U.S., where remarkable improvements have been achieved, community spirit created and alienation, vandalism, despair and crime cut, and 136 self-help projects were counted in New York city alone in 1973.

*A study in Camden, London, found that during its redevelopment programme two people were 'dishoused' for every one housed.

Employment, of course, is at last being recognised to be more important than housing. As the authorities add up the jobs that have disappeared from British inner cities, they are discovering that a remarkably high proportion were in small workshops that employed no more than a few people. Politicians and planners are beginning to regret their mistake in demolishing them, and to say that small firms must be encouraged to start up again as soon as possible. We are therefore beginning to hear the same philosophy advanced for our inner cities as for the shantytowns of the Third World. At the end of 1976 the Chairman of the Greater London Council Planning Committee said, 'We are not going to get anything big like Fords back into London. To see a revival of industry in London we have got to start with the small man.' At the other end of England, Newcastle gained Parliamentary authority to waive old planning rules; 35 small firms employing 400 people were created, and the city was hailed as a pioneer. Indeed, one of Britain's leading 'urbanologists' has suggested that Commonwealth immigrants would prove the salvation of her inner cities because of their experience in improving housing, and their ability as small entrepreneurs. Above all in both poor and rich countries the root of the crisis of the cities is poverty, and the real issue is whether or not governments and societies are willing to tackle it properly.

The comparison cannot be stretched too far. Most of the measures that need to be taken in rich and poor cities are widely different. Furthermore, while developed countries need turn their attention to their inner cities, developing ones must place their main priority on rural development. But there is enough similarity to lead us to hope that the crises of the cities may bring a more vivid understanding that we do, after all, live in a global village.

Most of the world's cities have grown up haphazardly, and two-thirds of the world's urban population live in areas that have no plans for comprehensive development, and no adequate planning and development authority. In many countries planning is still seen as an unwarranted interference with the property rights of the individual. However, if there are to be solutions to the crisis of the cities there must be some control of land use and speculation.

Nevertheless, in all but the most technical sense of the word, 'planning' for cities, towns and villages must mean more than deciding and influencing the use of land. It must mean working out how to meet the basic needs of man, both physical and spiritual.

One set of figures may put the proposition in perspective. World Bank studies suggest that the basic needs of the majority of the world's people could be met through an annual investment from the rich of $12\frac{1}{2}$ billion dollars (at 1974 prices) over ten years—125 billion in all. It sounds a great deal of money, and may well be an underestimate; but the figure is dwarfed by two expenditures that we take for granted. Every year the world spends 350 billion on arms, so over the ten-year period in question we can expect to spend 3,500 billion. And every year people in the rich world spend eight times the World Bank figure on alcohol. An interesting view of our choice of priorities.

A change in the system to meet the needs of man will also produce changes in the political relationships of the world. After all, a transfer of money usually means a transfer of power. Such changes would surely be for the better; but it is asking a lot of those who already have the money and power—both the people of the rich world and the rich of poor countries—voluntarily to forgo them, even if it is in their long-term interest to do so. More specifically, it is asking for a change of attitude, not just among governments, but on a mass scale in society at large. To put it in the words of Enrique Penalosa: 'We are experiencing the most important and dramatic change in the history of mankind. We have a choice between a new philosophy or chaos and anarchy.'

Chapter 17

Changing Philosophies

'To give food to countries just because people are starving is a pretty weak reason', declared the National Security Council's representative at interdepartmental U.S. Government meetings on food aid at about the time that the Council was given final control over the nation's food surpluses.

That ungainly statement was one of the more worrying manifestations of a new morality advocated by some people in rich countries. This 'lifeboat ethic', as it is sometimes called, has been advanced by the biologist Professor Garrett Hardin of the University of California. The rich nations, as he sees it, are in a crowded lifeboat. The rest of the world is drowning in a sea of starvation. If the people in the lifeboat show compassion by letting others climb aboard the boat will sink; so we must repel boarders.*

A bill was put before Congress in the spring of 1975 to phase out food aid for countries that fail to keep down their populations. It was supported by Professor Hardin and by Earl Butz, then US Secretary of Agriculture. The idea has been given a dubious theological blessing by Dr Joseph Fletcher, the author of *Situation Ethics*, a book which suggests that any action, however criminal, can be 'the choice of love' if the situation demands it.

*Sometimes a somewhat similar case is made out for 'triage'—named after a practice in the First World War. When the numbers of wounded were so great that they could not all receive medical attention, the casualties were separated into three groups; those who would die no matter what was done; those who required immediate help to prevent them from dying; and those who could safely wait until later. Help was given first to the middle group. The suggestion now is that the same principles could be applied in a starving world.

In another part of the world, Sir Philip Baxter, a former Chairman of the Australian Atomic Energy Commission, has urged his country to provide itself with bacteriological, chemical or nuclear weapons or 'anything else which will enable one man to hold off a hundred' in order to stop the homeless and starving refugees of world disaster climbing aboard the lifeboat of Australia.

Less has been heard of the lifeboat in Britain, but that does not mean that the same philosophy is not canvassed. 'Of course the poverty of the Third World is terrible,' we are told. 'But we have our own problems and can do nothing to help. Charity begins at home.'

In poor countries, too, there are rich people who claim that the most humane thing to do is to let people starve. And among the poor there are self-styled revolutionaries who plan to kill the rich after taking power, so as to benefit their own class.

Most people, surely, will find the lifeboat theory morally repulsive. It is also out of touch with the real situation in the world. There is no absolute shortage of food, nor need there ever be one. The immediate problem is one of distribution; the long-term need is to develop the enormous potential to produce more in the poor world. Both solutions depend on making it possible for the poor to acquire the food that can be grown. When people in the rich countries consume five times as much grain as those in the poor world; when we import protein from poor countries so that our animals can consume more than all the people of India and China; when our prosperity has been gained and the rest of the world's poverty maintained partly as a result of unfair trade relationships; when development is possible, and when population control in the poor world depends on greater prosperity, not less; where is the logic or morality behind the lifeboat theory? Against such a background it sounds like a desperate attempt to maintain inequality and indulgence at the cost of other peoples' lives. The name for that is genocide. It is the ethic not of the lifeboat but of the gas chamber.

If, however, we do agree, in face of the evidence, that there are too many people on the planet, that there is too little food, and that therefore some people must die, why should we assume that we, the rich, are not the superfluous ones? Since we use the resources of the world so wastefully perhaps it is we, not the citizens of the poor world, who constitute an intolerable burden.

And if, by some tragedy, the rich nations of the world were to act upon the lifeboat theory? 'Can we imagine', asks Robert MacNamara, 'any human order surviving so gross a mass of human misery piling up at the base?' Our precious lifeboats could be overturned by the hands clutching at them from the water. Big holes could be blown in them by the nuclear bombs likely to be in the hands of third-world countries and terrorist groups. The engines might stop because they were no longer supplied with oil, or the greed of the people in the lifeboat might lead to fights which would imperil the whole enterprise.

It is easy to react against the callousness of the lifeboat theory, but it would be wrong to see the people who propose it as out of tune with the mood of Western society. What they are suggesting is that we deliberately extend something that we already do, through indifference and ignorance. By putting our own greeds before other people's needs, both now and in the past, we are largely responsible for the deaths of more than fifteen million children a year. There is a great deal of genuine, sympathetic concern about the plight of the poor world; there is also little awareness that we are responsible for that plight and that it would not be a very hard task to end it. Eventually, when we realise that we are to blame, the state of the poor will be seen for what it is, an historic injustice as foul as the slave trade, the Irish famine or the exploitation of children in the mines and sweat shops of the last century.*

*Interestingly, many of the arguments used for maintaining these evils were similar to those used against those who would reform the world system today, and many of the same prophecies of economic collapse if ethics entered politics are trundled out today as they were in the nineteenth century. During the Great Hunger in Ireland, Charles Trevelyan, the civil servant responsible for famine policy, refused to allow the procurement of British cereals for relief because it would 'disturb the market'. His argument was echoed by Earl Butz at the World Food Conference when he announced a US refusal to provide another million tons of food aid, and in our own obsession with the price of food.

'The whole fabric of society would go to pieces if the wedge of abstract right were once entered into any part of it, Lord St Vincent declared at the time of the battle over the slave trade.

Dundas, who long fought Wilberforce, eventually suggested a 'moderate' approach—regulations to see that more slaves were born in the West Indies rather than imported. Fox replied: 'We cannot modify injustice. The question is to what period of time we should prolong it.'

The fate of the starving is the most dramatic of the issues that face the world, but others are equally vital to the future of human civilisation. Our present political philosophies have allowed these crises to develop, have failed to answer them, and have failed even adequately to realise that they exist. My own view is that this is because our great political, industrial and even social debates are a century out of date. They are fought by the two great economic philosophies of the nineteenth century, socialism and capitalism. They are sometimes fought over the issues of the nineteenth century. But, above all, they are fought by both sides with implicit faith in one great assumption of the nineteenth century—that the material progress of the rich world has no limits, and should be allowed to have none. Both sides agree that growth should be maximised, the debate is merely over which classes of the rich should get which shares.

In this Tweedledum and Tweedledee encounter the heat of the battle has absorbed almost all our political energies. The socialist seems not to have noticed that the principal claim on his deep concern for economic justice comes from the three-quarters of the world outside his immediate vision. The Marxist, as he proclaims his doctrine of class war, has apparently not noticed that he has become, by any global standard of measurement, one of the upper class fighting for relatively marginal improvement in his lot, like a nobleman at a Renaissance court or a big investor on the stock exchange. Equally, the Conservative does not appear to grasp that his 'enlightened self-interest' logically demands the economic enfranchisement of three-quarters of humanity. None of them seem to realise that the world has changed, that the continued long-term expansion of economic growth in the tradition of the past hundred years may not be possible or even desirable.

Such wide generalisations should not hide the fact that there are people of all parties and philosophies who care passionately that the real global priorities are recognised, and who work hard to try to bring them to the attention of their colleagues. Nor should they be shrugged off as a condemnation of politicians. For in a democracy political activity can only take place within guidelines laid down, or at least accepted, by the public as a whole. Those guidelines are dictated largely by our prevailing philosophy, which —whether we owe allegiance to Left, Right or Middle—is predominantly one of materialism. In the rich countries of the communist block, too, materialism is the dominant ideology.

Materialism, however, should not be the common philosophy, but the common enemy. To say this is not to argue for no growth. The argument over whether we should have growth or not is fought on the wrong ground. The question is not one of growth or no growth but one of greed or no greed; one of the distribution rather than the desirability of growth.

Some degree of growth is not only essential for poor countries, it is also vital for rich ones. To end growth abruptly would bring about an economic collapse which would help nobody; but we ought to be willing to moderate our growth so that the poor countries can accelerate theirs, to see growth in terms of *all* mankind, not just a section of it. There is enough food and other resources to meet everyone's need, but the present economic system will always serve the greed of the rich before the need of the poor; while both development and population control depend on greater sharing and economic justice. The widening gap between rich and poor may lead to economic or nuclear anarchy. Rich countries are called upon to sacrifice only a part of their future growth, and that sacrifice may turn out to be beneficial. Indeed, continued waste and rapidly increasing consumption of energy in the rich world *cannot* continue, and a philosophy of growth at all costs carries a heavy price in pollution.

Materialism is eventually self-defeating because its demands are never satisfied. The drive of greed and envy does not slacken when the standard of living goes up. There is no sign of any falling off in the demand for wealth within rich countries. Advertising seems to present an almost millionaire standard of living as a normal goal, and luxuries become necessities with breathtaking speed. But while materialism carries no limiting mechanism within it, the world in which it has to be applied does. To demand a doubling in our use of energy every fourteen years, when we have not the means of supplying it, is a recipe for inflation and, ultimately, for economic disaster.

Dr E. F. Schumacher wrote:

If human vices such as greed and envy are systematically cultivated, the inevitable result is nothing less than a collapse of intelligence. A man driven by greed and envy loses the power of seeing things as they really are, of seeing things in their roundness and wholeness, and his very successes become failures. If whole societies become infected by those vices, they may indeed achieve astonishing things but they become increasingly incapable of solving the most elementary problems of everyday existence. The Gross National Product may rise rapidly; as measured by statisticians but not as experienced by actual people, who find themselves oppressed by increasing frustration, alienation, insecurity and so forth. After a while, even the Gross National Product refuses to rise any further, not because of scientific or technological failure, but because of a creeping paralysis of non-cooperation, as expressed in various types of escapism on the part, not only of the oppressed and exploited, but even of highly privileged groups.

One can go on for a long time deploring the irrationality and stupidity of men in high places or low—'if only people would realise where their true interests lie!' But why do they not realise this? Either because their intelligence has been dimmed by greed and envy, or because in their heart of hearts they understand that their real interests lie somewhere quite different. There is a revolutionary saying that 'Man shall not live by bread alone but by every word of God'.

Nothing can be 'proved'. But does it still look probable or plausible that the grave social diseases infecting many rich societies today are merely passing phenomena which an able government could eradicate by simply making faster use of science and technology or a more radical use of the penal system?

C. Gordon Tether, when writing the Lombard column in the *Financial Times*, said:

There can be little doubt that a visitor from another planet dropping into our world today would take a very jaudiced view indeed of man's claim to be regarded as homo sapiens. Where is the wisdom in a species that has destroyed its own sense of well being and put its entire economic, financial and social structure in mortal peril by insisting on abusing a simple device that it had invented to facilitate exchanges of goods and services—money?

That was at the beginning of 1975. At the end of the year his view had not changed. 'What makes the past year's experience of special significance is that it has shown that our present system cannot even be relied upon to serve the best interests of the mass of the people in the regions which it has traditionally pampered.' The need, he says, is for a 'new world order', and that depends on our recognising 'that moral considerations rather than economic ones ought to be our guide'.

Until we can free ourselves from the worship of economic growth for its own sake we shall find it hard to make sensible choices about the kind of growth that we really need. Our present preoccupation with growth has produced economic rules which fail to take enough account of the effects of pollution, of resource depletion, and of costs to society. Nor does it respond properly to such obvious needs for future growth as those in housing, in the relief of poverty and depressed areas, in a transport system that becomes more, not less, accessible to all the public, and in pollution control and the recycling of waste.

Maurice Strong suggests that economic growth in countries, like physical growth in people, is natural and healthy up to a certain point. After that it can become cancerous, or as self-indulgent as an expanding waistband. From that stage we should regard real growth as intellectual, moral and social.

It may be objected that such talk is an indulgence of the rich. Even if we accept that greed and envy should no longer be the forces on which rich countries base their own economies, surely the powerful drive of selfishness is needed in countries which still have to build up their economies? This idea is contradicted by some of the most respected of the leaders of poor nations. Mahatma Gandhi's philosophy was the antithesis to the cultivation of greed and envy. Chairman Mao, whose philosophy was materialist in so far as it accepted no God, spoke of the need for spiritual values in building China. Men should 'neither seek fame nor gain, nor fear hardship and death, but toil body and soul for the people.'*

Julius Nyerere, who is building a promising new order in

*Massive indoctrination from early childhood is designed to breed out bourgeois values. Promotion goes only to those who seem to have absorbed it. The Chinese claim that this will change human nature within two decades. The rest of us may be more doubtful.

Tanzania, agrees. 'Can you really say "People are selfish" and then base society on selfishness?', he asks. 'Can you really argue this as a basis for development? Of course selfishness can be dynamic, but I think we have to fight it precisely because it is so dynamic.'

Nyerere's own experience is that it is unrealistic just to promote systems that require an unselfish or farsighted approach in the hope that people will rise to the challenge.

His vision of 'ujamaa', whereby Tanzanians should live together in villages, jointly own the means of production and share equally the fruits of their labour, has been set back. The idea was that it would arise from the people themselves, as, with government encouragement and education, they would choose to live that way. Some did, but on the whole the 'ujamaa' spirit has not emerged. Villagers frequently failed to turn up on the days they themselves had allocated for collective work on communal land, while it proved difficult to persuade some of their leaders to condescend to do manual work. There was mismanagement and misappropriation of collective funds, and villages became increasingly dependent on the state bureaucracy. Moreover, many people did not want to live and work together at all. The government eventually decided to bring people into villages at all costs, by force if need be; and they dropped the more socialistic parts of the programme, placing much more emphasis on the private ownership of land. It is still hoped that the co-operative spirit will emerge in time, but the resort to coercion—slight though it may have been in comparison to that exerted in many countries—will in itself have made this more unlikely.

Meanwhile Nyerere was also setting up a remarkable rural health network to tackle the widespread disease which debilitates the people and provides a major obstacle to development. But many of the health workers, having received their government training, go off to the towns where they can earn more by working for doctors in the private dispensaries which cater for the wealthy.

Such setbacks do not prove that Nyerere's policies have been wrong or should be written off. On the contrary, they are regarded as an example to the rest of the Third World, have already produced considerable achievements, and may yet come to full fruition.

Leaders of the favelas in Rio de Janeiro have a similar preoccupation. In theory co-operatives may be ideal for their poor communities; but in practice they can institutionalise hatred, jealousy and factionalism and end by destroying such spirit and informal co-operation as there was in the first place. The leaders emphasise the importance of working together. And it is a fact that several of the most effective pioneers only became active after achieving a personal victory over selfishness.

Corruption undermines development.* Few third-world countries are free of its permanent drag on their economies and on efficient administration. And few are free of the unscrupulous enrichment of tribal and economic elites, which, even when within the law, is directly against the national interest.

Unless the importance of these moral factors is appreciated, one views development with political, social or economic tunnel-vision. Just as a scientific solution proves to be no solution unless social factors are taken into account, so the mere change of a system solves little by itself. New and better solutions than those provided by the Trickle-down theory are being found, but they cannot be proof against the evil side of human nature. Perfect men are not going to be available in either the rich world or the poor, but there is every reason, as Nyerere sees, to join the struggle for the right moral climate.

The facts being as they are, it is not surprising that the need for change of attitude is now common ground between most of the international experts grappling with the human predicament. It is generally agreed that the basic crisis is a spiritual one, and that the ethics taught by wise men and the great religions can no longer be thought desirable only so that people may lead 'good' lives. On the one hand they are the condition of survival. On the other, they are the missing factor in freeing the world from hunger and poverty. As Barbara Ward has put it: 'In this age of ultimate scientific discovery our facts and our morals have come together to tell us how we must live.'

*Corruption in the Third World undermines sympathy in the West, and is often used as an excuse for doing little to help poor countries. In return it can of course be argued that the whole economic system that binds poor countries to rich ones is corrupt. The stories of poor country officials who steal food aid are paralleled by the United States investigations into fraud by grain companies, the indigenous corruption by the bribes, and worse, brought in by some multinational companies.

In Maurice Strong's view: 'It will take a moral and spiritual revolution which goes far enough to alter our life-styles and penetrate our political and industrial systems'—a statement which makes it clear that the revolution will have to change both individual lives and national and international conditions.

The two are inseparable. It is beguiling to hope that doing only half the job will be enough. Whole generations have fallen into that trap in the past. Sometimes it has been fashionable to think that all that needs to be done is to change the system, and then people will automatically change their attitudes and live to their highest potential. At others it has been thought that change in personal life is all that matters, and that social conditions and unjust systems will automatically fade away.

Both these false alternatives are common today. The first is often associated with communism, although the rigid capitalist, who believes that everything will be solved if the State takes its hands off the economy, is entrenched just as firmly in the same fallacy. Its inadequacy is recognised even in the Soviet Union. The 22nd Congress of the Soviet Communist Party resolved at its meeting in 1961: 'The Party considers the creation of the new man as the most difficult part of the communist transformation of society. Unless we can root out bourgeois morality and educate people in communist morality, renewing them morally and spiritually, it is not possible to build a communist society.' Others might point to Soviet society as evidence enough. For the change of system failed to change motives either among leaders or led, so that the eventual result has been a system not far different from the one that was overturned in the first place.

The second fallacy is often associated with religion. There have been, and are, religious movements and moods which are concerned with personal life in a vacuum. Yet the great religions are, in reality, shot through with a social message. Christianity is a revolutionary challenge to unjust systems, and has been regarded as such from ancient Rome to modern Russia. Certainly those of us who are Christians could provide more of a challenge to the injustices of the 'free' world. The Archbishop of Canterbury, following his call to Britain in 1975, emphasised that 'the right approach is from both ends, that is both trying to make better people and trying to make better structures in society'. A force like Moral Re-Armament provides contemporary examples of important social, national and even international changes stemming from radical change in individuals. And Sir John Lawrence, in his book *Take Hold of Change*, writes:

> We make our problems insoluble if we try to separate those two aspects; if we treat material problems as if their solution did not depend on the quality of human life, or if we speak of moral and spiritual standards as if they existed in a vacuum, apart from the material conditions of society.

During the course of this book I have tried to indicate changes that will be needed in our economic and social systems. They provide some guidelines, but no blueprint, because our knowledge is not nearly great enough to provide one: nor would any blueprint be universally applicable.

There are wider questions, too. How, for example, do you ensure long-term thinking in governments? How, if the thinking is done, do you see that the long-term perspectives are not immediately blotted out by the short-term crises? Short-term advantages are always easier to see; short-term pressures always the greater. Both the oil crisis and the food crisis are testament enough to the need for long-term perspective. Both were predictable. Group after group, expert after expert, warned governments of what was likely to happen. Their advice was not heeded.

Indeed, it is worth asking whether we are right in placing our trust in the nation state as the predominant unit of government and decision-making. On the one hand, it often seems too big. As it attracts more and more powers to itself, people become more and more remote from decision-making. This breeds alienation in the rich countries; it often directly hinders rural development and the meeting of basic needs in poor ones. Several authorities commend the principle of 'subsidiarity'. This holds that jobs that can be carried on effectively at a local level should remain decentralised and not be usurped by a bigger body. Only when the interests are too big and wide for a local body should they be handled by a higher authority.*

*The British civil service is said to have a maxim that to get what you need you should go to 'the lowest effective person'. In practice when the citizen visits officialdom he may discover it hard to find one!

On the other hand, the nation state may often be too small. None of the issues covered in this book can be dealt with by nations working in isolation. A relatively small issue such as how to deal with pollution that crosses frontiers might be tackled effectively by several nations working together. But the big issues can only be resolved by action representing virtually the whole of humanity.

The United Nations, which is the one available forum where all nations can meet, discuss, and even decide to act on the global issues, has many faults, but it is also much maligned. Considerable progress has been made in getting to grips with global issues; all the more remarkable considering the possibilities for deadlock in a system where the poor countries control most of the votes, while the rich provide more than 80 per cent of the budget.

Within the United Nations there is obviously great need for reform. For example, there are too many autonomous agencies, many of them doing much the same jobs; the assembly structure is geared to debate more than to decision-making; resolutions are passed and then promptly ignored by many of the states at the meeting; the bureaucracy proliferates and generally works at a snail's-pace.* Some reforms are now being worked out. Evan Luard, one of the members of a high-level committee set up by the Secretary-General to propose changes, says 'What is being discussed is essentially how the United Nations can be made better-equipped for serious negotiation instead of for ill-focused argument and diffuse declaration.' The world has greatly changed since the United Nations came into existence. The great global issues have emerged. The experts have proposed plans to co-ordinate and merge agencies and to set up a new procedure where small negotiating groups of representative countries could hammer out practical agreements on issues which the main assemblies had decided to tackle in principle. Unfortunately the failure of the Paris negotiations on the new international economic order, which were carried out between a relatively small, representative, group of countries, has made developing nations more suspicious of the idea. Until the rich world shows more readiness to change the economic

*Anyone who has visited a UN agency for a while has a quiver full of horror stories. I know of officials who have gone without pay for months while the bureaucracy sorted its way through the formalities; and one occasion when it took more than a day to authorise visiting journalists to have a cup of coffee.

system, they say, they prefer to keep negotiations within the main UN bodies where they have an overwhelming majority.

The actions of the United Nations ultimately depend on individual governments, and the actions of governments depend on the assent (or absence of powerful enough dissent) of their peoples. Structures and systems are made by people, and therefore can be changed by people. But first people have to realise the need for change, and this may mean that their own attitudes have to alter.

Although the people at 'the top' who create the structures and determine the system have most of the power, the rest of us have a good deal more of it than we realise. This power is not confined to elections. Outside elections, political pressure can be brought on a good representative, and even on a bad one in a marginal or insecure seat. He will pay attention to the points raised by rational constituents, and if enough individuals express themselves strongly about an issue, the programme of his party may shift so as to attract the votes. If the pressure is strong enough no party will feel able to leave that particular issue out of its programme, and that may be the best solution of all. In the Netherlands both the Socialist and the right-wing Liberal parties promote world development, while a change of government in Sweden after forty years brought no departure from her progressive policies on the new economic order; in both countries there is great popular support for a better deal for the Third World.

Outside politics, there is the power of the individual as a consumer. Anyone who doubts that need only scrutinise the amount of money companies are prepared to spend in advertising to sway his mind. Consumer power is the strongest economic power of all in an economy where choice is maintained. The decrease in meat eating during the winter of 1974–5 played a part in easing the worst of the food crisis, although it was brought on more by the economic depression than by an appreciation of world needs. An aerosol manufacturer replaced fluorocarbons as propellants in the United States long before bans were announced; but did not do so in Britain—concern over the ozone layer had led to a marked falling-off in the sales of aerosols in the U.S.A. Willingness to pay more for a third-world product can make even a tariff barrier impotent. Refusal to use electricity for heating can save vast amounts of fuel, and force governments into more rational energy policies. One could cite many other examples.

Then there is the power of association, the power of communication, the freedom to spread views; ordinary people can greatly increase the power they already have by joining pressure groups and political parties, by becoming active in their trade unions or professional groups, and by informed use of their votes, their pens and their purses.

There must be structural changes to provide people with more power. Many increasingly important issues, like most of those discussed in this book, have normally been regarded as technical ones; the province of experts. There have therefore been no institutional channels for finding out what ordinary people feel about them, and for making sure that their opinions serve as a guide to policy making. Some countries, including Sweden and Austria, have begun to experiment with public participation over forming energy strategy, but serious work in this area has scarcely begun. Similarly, more needs to be done to improve the power of people to initiate. The State of Washington undertook one promising exercise; first making a systematic attempt to find out what developments its people would like to see by the year 2000, and then translating some of their goals into legislation. The enabling of a large number of people to force a referendum on important issues is worth considering where this right does not already exist. There is also great need to examine how much power elected representatives have to ensure that the laws they enact are implemented as they intended, and how free they are to initiate action.* And the media, besides discussing all these issues, should also seek out ways of increasing free communication. The correspondence columns of newspapers have always provided one outlet; it is encouraging that some newspapers and television networks provide 'Open Door' space, and that broadcasters find 'phone-in' programmes worthwhile; the growth of small, 'alternative', newspapers and magazines should also be welcomed on principle.

*In Britain the answer to that question seems to be 'surprisingly little'. The top civil servant has much more chance to initiate legislation (through a proposal to his minister) than most MPs; and once legislation is passed, the administration proceeds (often almost entirely unexamined) into civil service hands.

In a democracy a change of attitude usually has to precede a change of conditions, and a change of conditions cannot lag far behind the demand caused by a widespread change in attitude. Here lies hope, because attitudes can change remarkably fast. The growth of a change of attitude is exponential; like the growth of population and food demands, but faster.*

Of course, bringing about a widespread change in attitude is an enormous task; because a society that has been moving in one direction for decades acquires its own momentum. The force of inertia is very strong, and history provides plenty of examples of peoples who have refused to change until it is too late. But history also provides examples where attitudes have been radically transformed, by Wilberforce and his colleagues and successors in early nineteenth century Britain, for example, or by the Christians in ancient Rome. Changes may need to be more rapid now, but modern communications offer infinitely greater possibilities. The media increasingly confront citizens of the rich world with at least some information of what is happening around the globe, the basis for any change of mind. What is more, there are signs which could mean that we are entering the first phase of such a revolution of opinion.

In the main, people are much more sensible, intelligent and well-intentioned than seems to be believed by politicians, administrators, or the press. They both can and do fundamentally change their attitudes when faced with the basic facts needed for a decision. I draw a good deal of my relative optimism from my personal experience. My own attitudes changed radically when I first began to learn about the issues in this book. Then, when working on the *Yorkshire Post*, I found that we were overwhelmingly backed by our readership when we took a stand on environment and development issues and campaigned upon them. Northern, conservative and not predominantly youthful, our readers might not seem to be the most likely to have done so. They are not lightly persuaded, do

*You can make ridiculous extrapolations for population growth, which nevertheless illustrate a point, and you can do precisely the same here. If one person goes out with an idea one day and convinces one other, if the next day the two convince two more and the process continues at the same rate it would only take thirty-one days—in theory—to convince the whole world.

not have much time for passing fashions and are tenacious in their views once they have formed them.

Our first major campaign on the environment was about the state of Yorkshire's rivers, which are among the most polluted in Europe and which were continuing to deteriorate while rivers in the rest of Britain were improving. We named twenty-five firms and local authorities as polluters, and found too that the Yorkshire River Authority itself was failing to do vital work on river pollution because of a shoe-string budget. The Authority rarely used its powers of prosecution, and when it did generally prosecuted farmers rather than the companies and local authority sewage works that were the major polluters. Our investigation caught our readers' imaginations, and immediately took off into a campaign. The response soon came back to us through public pressure and action taken by MPs and local authorities. Within three weeks the River Authority decided to increase its pollution prevention department by 250 per cent, to give them new offices and a more effective laboratory, and to draw up a master plan for dealing with pollution. Within a year all those we named as polluters had taken action to clean up. The River Authority set 1980 as its target for clean rivers, and in the two years following our first articles there were more than thirty-five prosecutions, compared to eight in the previous three years. Many firms and local authorities were among them.

During our investigations we had come up against secrecy clauses in British pollution legislation, which laid down that people who identified polluters could be imprisoned for three months, while even the most dangerous discharger could not be troubled for more than a fine. One of our next campaigns was directed against these clauses, and again we had similar public support. We found, for example, that a consultative document on one bill was proposing two years' imprisonment for journalists or officials who published details about air pollution from buildings or about conditions inside them. After an eleven-day campaign and an outcry in public and in Parliament, we were told that these proposals were to be scrapped. The campaign gathered particular momentum when we published a detailed exposé of the asbestos tragedy at Hebden Bridge, for a similar secrecy clause forbade factory inspectors to warn workers of any danger they faced. Eventually a new law was enacted which not only removed the secrecy clause but put a statutory duty on managements in all industries to inform their workers, and the general public, about any dangers they might face as a result of their companies' work. For the first time in British statute law it was laid down that people have a right to know when their health is threatened by pollution.

The Minister responsible for the new Act, Mr Harold Walker, said: 'The section in the Act which compels employers to inform staff and the general public about any dangers connected with their work was included largely as a result of the *Yorkshire Post* pressing for this information to be made public.' This generous tribute was, in a sense, an oversimplification. The change came because of the public pressure for which we had been the catalyst. The pressure, channelled particularly by Mr Max Madden, the MP for the Hebden Bridge area, also led to an investigation by the Ombudsman into the tragedy which in turn sparked off a Government inquiry into the safety of asbestos and a review of the British Standard.

Ours was not an isolated experience. Early in 1975 the *Observer* colour supplement published a long article summarising 'seven enemies' facing mankind; the population explosion, food shortage, scarcity of resources, environmental degradation, nuclear proliferation and terrorism, technology beyond human control, and the moral blindness and inertia of man and his institutions. It concluded with an offer to provide a list of organisations working in the field, and of suggested reading for those who wanted to pursue the issues further. Nine thousand requests for this list and eight thousand requests for reprints of the article, and more than one thousand letters of comment came in. Ronald Higgins, who had written a pessimistic, if challenging, article, said later: 'As I further explore the threats they appear even more ominous and more pressing. Yet the brave and unselfish concern of so many who wrote and telephoned is another truth—one which helped hold me back from total despair.'

Sweden's experiment in involving the public in energy policy attracted more than 70,000 participants, more than five times as many as expected; American experiments similar to the one in Washington state have shown that people are eager to participate if they feel it will have an effect, and that when they do they surprise the planners with the sense of their ideas.

Meanwhile American public opinion polls provide other straws in the wind, one showed that 61 per cent of the people it questioned thought it was 'immoral' that the United States, with only 6 per cent of the world's population, should consume 40 per cent of the world's energy and raw materials. Another found that 79 per cent thought it more important to 'teach people how to live more with basic essentials' than to 'reach higher standards of living'. Indeed a business intelligence report from the Stanford Research Institute has estimated that by 1985 over 35 million Americans will adopt a less-consumptive way of life, 'voluntary simplicity'. Meanwhile a Norwegian poll reports that 76 per cent of the people consider the country's standard of living is too high.

One of the most hopeful signs of all is the proliferation of prophets. Not many years ago it was rare to find people who raised in public the fundamental issues of resources, world development and environmental degradation. It was rarer still to find people who seriously questioned the materialist thrust in society or our conceptions of growth and progress. Now it is becoming hard to avoid them. The questions are being asked not only by churchmen, whose role it should be to do so, but by scientists, politicians, newspapers, television, and businessmen.

Scientists have shifted from a mere preoccupation with knowledge to concern about the uses to which it is put. Perhaps the change began with the atomic bomb, but it has certainly accelerated recently. Scientists were the first to warn about the environmental consequences of the scientific revolution, and there is every sign that their concern has grown. Its strength can be seen reflected in the success of magazines, like *New Scientist* in Britain, which spend much of their space on the *social* concerns of the scientist.

Sir Bernard Lovell, President of the British Association for the Advancement of Science in 1975, said in his presidential address that he had changed his mind about the responsibility of the scientist, and that he no longer believed that science 'is neutral in its impact'. 'The simple belief in automatic material progress by means of scientific discovery is a tragic myth of our age,' he said.

'The vital question is whether the framework of society in which science is pursued can develop the ethical basis and moral purpose necessary to ensure that in our future progress we overcome the forces leading to decay and destruction.'

There have already been shifts in attitudes to policy, at least in theory. The discrediting of the Trickle-down theory and the new consenus on population are two examples.

In most countries too there are leading politicians who have campaigned, sometimes with considerable effect, over issues of environment, resources and world development. A surprising number of ministers in office seem to wish to go further than their government's policies allow, cutting loose in speeches which demand radical changes in attitude. David Ennals, when Minister of State at the British Foreign Office at the beginning of 1976, spoke of the challenges posed by the population explosion, the food crisis, resource depletion and environmental depredation. 'So far I am by no means convinced that either the world's leaders or their people are genuinely facing the challenges. We know what needs to be done to avoid catastrophe; above all, we know that the solutions must be global ones. But are we prepared to do it?'

He added: 'I am personally convinced that growth and more growth as a target to be pursued for all time is an illusion and a dangerous one. In the end it will kill us all.' He suggested that Britain could show the way to the West in coming to an orderly standstill in the growth of living standards.

Perhaps we are victims of a breakdown of communication. On the one hand there are many ordinary people who think that things should be changed but remain quiet because they believe that no one will pay any attention; on the other there are politicians who know that such changes are necessary but do not think that the public would support them. This may be an oversimplification but it is not without foundation.

In discussing the change of attitude which is needed, Barbara Ward says that there is only one way of finding out whether it will take place: 'That is to ask whether in fact we are witnessing changes in our imagination radical enough to suggest a period of profound intellectual and moral upheaval. If these changes are taking place, a new epoch is unavoidable'.

The change in imagination and attitude is only a starting point. It has to be followed by action. 'In the end,' says Dr Mostafa Tolba, Executive Director of UNEP, 'solutions come from individual people doing something different.' Development and environmental groups are proliferating now, and there is a widespread search for new lifestyles more in harmony with what is needed in the planet.

One of the most interesting movements has taken place in Scandinavia. It began when a Norwegian advertising executive, Erik Damman, wrote a book, *The Future in Our Hands*, in which he concentrated on how solutions depended on people individually deciding to change their values and work out new ways of living. Within a few months 20,000 copies had been sold—in a comparatively sparsely populated part of the world—and his morning post came in sackfuls. He announced a meeting, advertising it in a small way, and sceptics expected just a few cranks to turn up. The 2,000-seat hall was crowded out, and hundreds had to be turned away. The movement started growing at the rate of a thousand people a month.

Much of its appeal is that it asks people to begin with themselves. 'Never forget,' Erik Damman told that first meeting, 'that the new and humane course we are pursuing will remain a beautiful dream right until each one of us is prepared to change the course of his or her own life.' This idea is not new, of course, it lies at the heart of Christianity, and has been practised, sometimes more, sometimes less, throughout the ages, but nowhere nearly enough. It is still true, as G. K. Chesterton put it, that the Christian ideal has not been tried and found wanting, but found *difficult* and left untried. The basic truth remains that as I am, so is my nation, and so is the world.

E. F. Schumacher wrote in *Small is Beautiful*:

> Wisdom can be read about in numerous publications, but it can be found only inside oneself. To be able to find it, one first has to liberate oneself from such masters as greed and envy. The stillness following liberation—even if only momentary—produces the insights of wisdom that are obtained in no other way.
>
> They enable us to see the hollowness and fundamental unsatisfactoriness of a life devoted primarily to the pursuit of material ends, to the neglect of the spiritual. Such a life necessarily sets man against man and nation against nation, because man's needs are infinite and infinitude can be achieved only in the spiritual realm, never in the material . . .

> How could we even begin to disarm greed and envy? Perhaps by being much less greedy and envious ourselves. An ounce of practice is generally worth more than a ton of theory.
>
> It will need many ounces, however, to lay the economic foundations of peace. Where can one find the strength to go on working against such appalling odds? What is more: where can one find the strength to overcome the violence of greed, envy, hate and lust within oneself?
>
> I believe Gandhi has given the answer: 'There must be a recognition of the existence of the soul apart from the body, and of its permanent nature, and this recognition must amount to a living faith in God.'

I have great respect for the atheist who sets out to change his life and motives in his own strength; but I know that, for myself, a greater power is needed. Such knowledge and experience as I have leads me to a conviction that sure grounds for faith can be found by those who honestly try to put their lives into the hands of God, in the testing nature, if you like, of a scientific experiment. My experience is only faltering and at its earliest stages, but I have seen the results in much greater strength in others.

Be that as it may, it is clear that, without a moral and spiritual revolution, we will neither build the new world that is technically possible, nor overcome the impending crises threatening our present one. And I am sure that people will know themselves what is the right course of action for them to take. Each person should have the right to choose it for himself, rather than be told what it is or be commanded to do it.

Gandhi used to say, 'I acknowledge no dictator but the still small voice of God.' In his philosophy that voice, conscience, should be the final judge of the rightness of every deed and thought. In Barbara Ward's words: 'From the beginning of time people have heard this "still, small voice" of obligation and brotherhood. When they have listened, society has worked. When they have refused to listen, society has broken up.'

APPENDICES

1. A Note on Sources and Further Reading
2. Select Bibliography
3. Index of Main Subjects

A Note on Sources and Further Reading

The object of this book has been to distill an enormous amount of widely scattered information into a concise and comprehensive view of the issues. This means that it has drawn on a very large number of disparate sources, not on relatively few main texts. Indeed, I find that I have listed more than two thousand sources which have directly provided me with information.

For these reasons it would be misleading to select a few reports, books and specialist articles and present them as the principal sources I have used, even on a chapter by chapter basis. By and large I have needed to use different works for each of the five hundred and more topics covered in this book, even though some have been of more general value. Unfortunately, when I prepared even a modified system of references it proved to be far too unwieldy for inclusion. However, should anyone wish for this information, either as a starting point for research into any of the topics or for verification of any of the facts, I shall be delighted to provide it, if written to care of the publishers.

Wherever possible, when I have stated facts in the text I have verified them from at least two sources, and I have placed particular importance on using works of acknowledged reliability and on avoiding reliance on people, groups, or organisations with a known bias. Where there has been a conflict that I have found irresolvable I have either given both versions in the text or given a median or conservative one. Many of the global statistics used in the book have been taken from a wide variety of UN sources, for, whatever its failings in other fields, the United Nations' specialist agencies are particularly valuable collectors of statistics. However since these statistics sometimes rely on rather dubious information from certain governments I have by no means always used them, sometimes choosing other figures in preference and sometimes giving a range of estimates. Further information on conflicting evidence can again be provided on application.

In order to give some guide to the kind of material I have used, however, and to provide anyone who wishes to study the issues in more depth with some entry points into the literature, I have heavily cut back my list of sources to a Select Bibliography, where I have limited myself to exactly two hundred books, reports and presentations which I believe will prove useful to others. I have not included specialist articles, though these make up a large proportion of my sources; by and large these were used for specific short passages in the book, often of only a few sentences. I have therefore restricted myself to naming some twenty of the periodicals that I have used most frequently (instancing some special issues that are particularly helpful) and have included these in my list of two hundred sources.

Yet if this book has done its job, many readers who have no desire to tackle even a relatively limited bibliography will be interested in a few books which take individual subjects further. I have therefore extracted a few titles, and am listing them separately before the main list, adding brief comments. In general, they have been chosen for their readability and availability as well as for their coverage of particular fields. They are grouped roughly in the order in which their principal subject comes in my book.

Jonathon Power and Anne-Marie Holenstein, World of Hunger, A Strategy for Survival, (Temple Smith, 1976). A concise and persuasive treatment of the world food crisis which places particular weight on the potential of the small farmer, and considers patterns of development in poor countries and the population issue.

Reshaping the International Order, A report to the Club of Rome; Jan Tinbergen, Co-ordinator, (Hutchinson, 1977). Not the most digestible of these books for the general reader, but a distinguished group of experts do provide a great deal of basic factual information and while concentrating on the new international economic order, put forward plenty of suggestions on how most of the crises covered in my book should be tackled. Not all these suggestions are convincing, but they are thought-provoking.

John Cole, The Poor of the Earth, (MacMillan, 1976). Valuable for an excellent exposition of the employment crisis and the case for 'basic needs' strategies and redeployment of industry. Gives detailed case histories, and a more general review of trade issues.

Dom Moraes, A Matter of People, (André Deutsch, 1974). The human side of the population issue. An anecdotal and entertaining account of the author's experiences investigating the question on four continents for the UN Fund for Population Activities.

Mason Willrich and Theodore B. Taylor, Nuclear Theft; Risks and Safeguards. A Report to the Energy Policy Project of the Ford Foundation, (Ballinger, 1974). The classic work on the dangers of nuclear terrorism and illicit bomb-making. For an extremely gripping, more popular, book that covers the same ground through the author accompanying Theodore Taylor on investigations, questioning him on the issue, and telling his life story, see *John McPhee's The Curve of Binding Energy (Farrar, Straus and Giroux, 1974).*

Royal Commission on Environmental Pollution, Sixth Report, Nuclear Power and The Environment, (HMSO, 1976). My highest recommendation for reading on nuclear power. Remarkably readable, it gives a sane and comprehensive view of the controversy.

Walter C. Patterson, Nuclear Power, (Penguin, 1976). Another excellent book on the subject. After a clear explanation of the technical side of nuclear power it describes its development, treating the controversy historically.

Gerald Foley, with Charlotte Nassim, The Energy Question, (Penguin, 1976). A concise view of the whole energy scene and a strong plea for conservation with much useful information and many good points, but, in my view, an overpessimistic verdict on many energy sources. On the whole I prefer *Wilson Clark's Energy for Survival, (Anchor Books, 1975).*

Nuclear Crisis, A Question of Breeding, Edited by Hugh Montefiore and David Gosling, an account of the submissions and cross-examination of many of Britain's leading energy experts at hearings arranged by the British Council of Churches, also provides a useful discussion of the energy issue, but it probably requires some previous knowledge.

Amory B. Lovins, Soft Energy Paths, (Penguin, 1977). A controversial and stimulating case for transition to a steady use of energy based on renewable sources which is already attracting a wide popular following.

Barbara Ward and René Dubos, Only One Earth, (Penguin, 1972). The famous book commissioned for the Stockholm Environment Conference. Some of the facts are, naturally enough, a little out of date now and if it were rewritten some parts of it might well be changed, but it is still the main inspirational, and most eloquent book of the environmental movement.

Barbara Ward, The Home of Man, (Penguin, 1976). A compelling book, which goes well beyond the crisis of the cities to consider the whole human predicament. Probably the first of these recommended books to read for anyone interested in the whole field.

E. F. Schumacher, Small is Beautiful, (Abacus, 1973). Another brilliant book, which demolishes the cult of materialism and other sacred cows, explains Intermediate Technology, ranges over many other issues, and has become one of the formative influences in the thinking of our time.

A number of magazines can do more to keep one up-to-date with these subjects than almost anything else. *New Scientist* is usually the best for the science-related issues, especially energy, pollution, food, and the nuclear proliferation. Its coverage of development issues is growing but the main magazine for these is the *New Internationalist*, particularly since it has been concentrating each issue in depth on a different topic.

There are three other periodicals especially worth watching for particular reasons. *Development Forum*, which covers the field fully, is sent out free by CESI/OPI, United Nations, Palais des Nations, CH–1211, Geneva 10, Switzerland.

Scientific American occasionally produces special issues on such topics as food, population or energy. And for energy/nuclear proliferation and terrorism questions it is useful to subscribe to *The Bulletin of the Atomic Scientists*, 1020–24 E 58th Street, Chicago, Ill., 60637, USA.

Select Bibliography

Advisory Council on Research and Development for Fuel and Power, *Energy R and D in the United Kingdom*, 1976.

Ambio, published by Royal Swedish Academy of Sciences/Universitetsforlaget, Vols IV–VII 1975–1977, particularly special 'water' issue Vol VI no 1, special 'hazards at work' issue, Vol IV no 1.

Armstrong, G., 'Coal and the Energy Crisis', speech to the British Association for the Advancement of Science, 12 August 1974.

Armstrong, G., *World Coal Resources and their Future Potential*, Royal Society, 1973.

Arvill, Robert, *Man and Environment*, Penguin, 1974.

Ashby, Eric, 'A Second Look at Doom', Fawley Foundation Lecture, 1975.

Atomic Energy Authority Special Constables Act, HMSO, 1976 and Houses of Commons and Lords debates on the Bill reported Hansard during February to May 1976.

Bairoch, Paul, *The Economic Development of the Third World Since 1900*, Methuen, 1975.

Blair, Thomas L., *The International Urban Crisis*, Hart-Davis MacGibbon, 1974.

Blanchard, Francis, 'Employment, Growth and Basic Needs, A One-World Problem', Report to the Tripartite World Conference on Employment, Income Distribution and Social Progress, and the International Division of Labour, ILO, Geneva, 1976.

British Occupational Health Society, *Hygiene Standard for Chrysotile Asbestos Dust*, Pergamon Press, 1968.

Brodeur, Paul, *Asbestos and Enzymes*, Ballantine Books, 1972.

Brookes, L. G., *The Plain Man's Case for Nuclear Energy*, United Kingdom Atomic Energy Authority, 1976.

Brown, Lester, *The Politics and Responsibility of the North American Breadbasket*, Worldwatch Institute, 1975.

Brown, Lester, *World Population Trends: Signs of Hope, Signs of Stress*, Worldwatch Institute, 1976.

Brown, Lester and Erik P. Eckholm, *By Bread Alone*, Praeger for the Overseas Development Corporation, 1974.

Brown, Lester, Patricia L. McGrath, and Bruce Stokes, *Twenty-two Dimensions of the Population Problem*, Worldwatch Institute, 1975.

Bulletin of the Atomic Scientists, 1975–7.

Calder, Nigel, (ed.) *Nature in the Round*, Weidenfeld and Nicolson, 1973.

Carson, Rachel, *Silent Spring*, Hamish Hamilton, 1963.

Carter, Jimmy, speech to the United Nations Conference on Nuclear Energy and World Order, New York, 13 May, 1976.

Ceres, 1974–1977.

Chapman, Peter, Fuel's Paradise, Penguin, 1975.

Cole, H. S. D., Christopher Freeman, Marie Jahoda and K. L. R. Pavitt, editing for the Science Policy Research Unit of Sussex University, *Thinking About the Future, A Critique of The Limits to Growth*, Chatto and Windus for the Sussex University Press, 1973.

Connelly, Philip, and Robert Perlman, *The Politics of Scarcity, Resource Conflicts in International Relations*, published for the Royal Institute of International Affairs by Oxford University Press, 1975.

Costa, Rubens Vaz da, 'Demographic Growth and Environmental Pollution', Statement before the Special Parliamentary Commission for the Problem of Environmental Pollution of the Legislative Assembly of the State of Rio Grande do Sul, 13 September, 1972.

Dawson, Keith, *Alternative Energy Sources for the United Kingdom*, Energy Technology Support Unit, Harwell, 1975.

Department of the Environment, Inner Area Studies, HMSO, 1977.

Department of Health and Social Security Standing Medical Advisory Committee, Standing Sub-committee on Cancer, 'Control of the Cancer Hazard Due to Asbestos to the General Public', Document SAC (M) SSC (680).

Development Forum, Vols I–V 1972–1977.

Division of International Security Affairs, 'Nuclear Power Prospects 1975–1990; Commercial, Economic and Social Implications', Report for the US Energy Research and Development Administration, 1975.

Doll, Sir Richard, Sir Ernest Kennaway Lecture, Royal Institution, 11 November, 1976.

Dolphin, G. W., 'A Comparison of the Observed and Expected Cancers of the Haematopoietic and Lymphatic Systems Among Workers at Windscale', National Radiological Protection Board, 1976.

Dubos, Rene, *So Human an Animal*, Rupert Hart-Davis, 1970.

Dunham, Sir Kingsley, 'Natural Resources, the Engineer and the Environment', 19th Graham Clark Lecture, Council of Engineering Institutions, 1974.

Earthscan, Energy for the Third World, 1977.

Eckholm, Erik P., *Losing Ground*, W. W. Norton for Worldwatch Institute, 1976.

Eckholm, Erik P. and Frank Record, *Two Faces of Malnutrition*, Worldwatch Institute, 1976.

Ehrlich, Paul and Anne, *Population, Resources, Environment: Issues in Human Ecology*, W. H. Freeman and Company, 1972.

Energy Research Group, Cavendish Laboratory, Cambridge, Energy Prospects, prepared for Advisory Council on Energy Conservation, 1976.

Environmental Conservation, Vols 1–3, 1974–1976.

Flood, Michael, and Robin Grove-White, 'Nuclear Prospects, A Comment on the Individual, the State and Nuclear Power', Friends of the Earth

Ltd., in association with The Council for the Protection of Rural England, and the National Council for Civil Liberties, 1976.

Food and Agriculture Organisation, 'Assessment of the World Food Situation Present and Future', World Food Conference, 1974, document E. Conf. 65/3.

Food and Agriculture Organisation, 'The World Food Problem, Proposals for National and International Action', World Food Conference, 1974, document E. Conf. 65/4.

Foreign Affairs, 1975–1977.

Francis, John, and Paul Albrecht (eds), *Facing Up to Nuclear Power*, St Andrew's Press, 1976.

Franklin, N. L., speech to the British Nuclear Energy Society, 19 May, 1977.

Freeman, S. David, *Energy, the New Era*, Vintage Books, 1974.

Gandhi, M. K., *The Village Reconstruction*, Pocket Gandhi Series No 14, edited and published by Anand T. Hingorani, Bharatiya Vidya Bhavan.

Gandhi, M. K., *An Autobiography*, Navajivan Press, 1927.

George, Susan, *How the Other Half Dies: The Real Reasons for World Hunger*, Penguin, 1976.

Gilson, J. C., Michael Williams Lecture, 10 February, 1972.

Gofman, John, Mike Gravel and Wilson Clark, 'The Case for a Nuclear Moratorium', Environmental Action Foundation, Washington DC, 1974.

Graham, Frank jnr., *Since Silent Spring*, Hamish Hamilton, 1970.

Greenwood, Ted, George W. Rathjens, and Jack Ruina, 'Nuclear Power and Weapons Proliferation', Adelphi Paper No 130, International Institute for Strategic Studies, 1977.

Grimwood, P. D., and G. A. M. Webb, 'Assessment of the Radiological Protection Aspects of Disposal of High-Level Wastes on the Ocean Floor', National Radiological Protection Board, 1977.

Harboe, Henrik, *The Importance of Coal for Heat and Power Generation*, Stal-Laval, 1974.

Hart, Judith, 'New Perspectives in North–South Relations, A Radical View of World Poverty and Development', Address to the Institute for Policy Studies and Johns Hopkins School for Advanced International Studies, April 1977, published as Overseas Development Paper No 7, HMSO, 1977.

Harwell Bulletin, 1974 and 1975.

Hayes, Denis, *Energy, The Case for Conservation*, Worldwatch Institute, 1976.

Hayes, Denis, *Energy, the Solar Prospect*, Worldwatch Institute, 1977.

Hayes, Denis, *Nuclear Power, The Fifth Horseman*, Worldwatch Institute 1976.

Health and Safety Executive, 'Some Aspects of the Safety of Nuclear Installations in Great Britain, Replies to Questions Submitted by the Secretary of State for Energy to the Nuclear Installations Inspectorate', January 1977.

Health and Safety Executive, Selected Written Evidence Submitted to the Advisory Committee on Asbestos 1976–77, HMSO, 1977.

Higgins, Ronald, 'The Seventh Enemy', pamphlet published by the Observer, 1975.

Hill, Sir John, 'Note to Mr Anthony Wedgwood Benn, Minister for Energy', Department of Energy 1976.

Hill, Sir John, 'Nuclear Power Comes of Age', 4th Cockcroft Memorial Lecture, 6 November, 1975.

Hill, Sir John, 'The Abuse of Nuclear Power', Lecture to the *Financial Times* Conference on Nuclear Power and the Public Interest, 9 July, 1976.

Hirsch, Fred, *Social Limits of Growth*, Routledge and Kegan Paul, 1977.

House of Commons Select Committee on Overseas Development, 'The Forthcoming UNCTAD Negotiations', Second Report of the 1976–7 Session, HMSO, 1977.

House of Commons Select Committee on Science and Technology, First Report of 1974–5 Session, Energy Conservation, HMSO, 1975.

Hubbert, M. King, 'Energy Resources', in 'Resources and Man', National Academy of Sciences/National Research Council, 1969, see also an article in Scientific American, September 1971, which updates this.

Hunter, Donald, *The Diseases of Occupations*, English Universities Press, 1969.

International Labour Organisation, 'Time for Transition, A Mid-Term Review of the Second Development Decade', 1975.

Ion, D. C., *Availability of World Energy Resources*, Graham and Trotman, 1976.

Johnson, Anita, and Sidney Wolfe, 'Cancer Prevention and the Delaney Clause', Health Research Group, Washington D.C.

Johnson, Brian, *Whose Power to Choose? International Institutions and the Control of Nuclear Energy*, International Institute for Environment and Development, 1977.

Kahn, Hermann, William Brown and Leon Martel, *The Next Two Hundred Years, a Scenario for America and the World*, Morrow, 1976.

Kinnersley, Patrick, *The Hazards of Work*, Pluto Press, 1973.

Kostuik, John, 'Key Issues Facing the Future Development of the Uranium Industry', International Symposium on Uranium Supply and Demand, London 15–17 June, 1976.

Langoni, Carlos Geraldo, *Distribucão da Renda e Disenvolvimento Economico do Brasil, Expressao e Cultura*, Rio de Janeiro, 1973 (English version available from National Housing Bank, Rio).

Lappé, Frances Moore and Joe Collins, *Food First*, Houghton Mifflin, 1977.

Leach, Gerald, 'Energy and Food Production', International Institute for Environment and Development, 1976.

Leach, Gerald, 'Conservation of Energy, Alternative Energy Sources and their Implication for Environmental Conservation and Future Ways of Life', International Institute for Environment and Development, 1975.

Leach, Gerald, Written Evidence to the Windscale Inquiry on Behalf of Friends of the Earth Ltd., 1977.

Lean, Garth, and Sidney Cook, *The Black and White Book*, Blandford, 1972.

Leontief, Wassily, and others, 'The Future of the World Economy', Centre for Development Planning, Projections and Policies of the Department of Economic and Social Affairs of the UN Secretariat and the Government of the Netherlands, 1976, documents E.76 II A.6 and E/A.C/54/L. 76.

Llewllyn-Jones, Derek, *People Populating*, Faber and Faber, 1975.

Lima Declaration, issued after Second General Conference of United Nations Industrial Development Organisation, 1975.

Lipton, Michael, *Why Poor People Stay Poor*, Temple Smith, 1977.

Lockheed Corporation, The High Potential of Wind as an Energy Source, report for the US Energy Research and Development Administration, 1976.

Lovell, Sir Bernard, 'In the Centre of the Immensities', Presidential Address to the 137th Annual Meeting of the British Association for the Advancement of Science, 29 August 1975.

Lovins, Amory B., *Nuclear Energy, Technical Bases for Ethical Concern*, Friends of the Earth, 1974.

Lovins, Amory B., *World Energy Strategies: Facts, Issues and Options*, Friends of the Earth, 1975.

Luard, Evan, *The Control of the Seabed, A New International Issue*, Heinemann, 1974.

McNamara, Robert S., 'Address to the Board of Governors', World Bank Group, 1975.

Maddox, John, *Beyond the Energy Crisis*, Macmillan, 1974.

Maddox, John, 'Prospects for Nuclear Proliferation', Adelphi Paper no 113, International Institute for Strategic Studies, 1975.

Maddox, John, *The Doomsday Syndrome*, Macmillan, 1972.

Makhijani, Arjun, 'Energy Policy for the Third World', International Institute for Environment and Development, 1976.

Mark, James (ed.), 'Britain and the New International Economic Order', Commentary by the United Kingdom Chapter of the Society for International Development, 1976.

Martin, Angus, *The Last Generation, The End of Survival*, Fontana, 1975.

Mason, T. J., F. W. MacKay, R. Hoover, W. J. Blot, T. F. Fraumeni, Atlas of Cancer Mortality for US Counties 1950–1969, NIH 75–780, Department of Health, Education and Welfare, 1976.

Massachusetts Institute of Technology, 'Man's Impact on the Global Environment, Assessment and Recommendations for Action', Report of the Study of Critical Environmental Problems, MIT, 1971.

Meadows, Donella H. and Dennis L., Jorgen Randers, and William W. Behrens III, *The Limits to Growth*, Potomac Associates, 1972.

Merewether, E. R. A., and C. W. Price, 'Report on the Effects of Asbestos Dust on the Lungs and Dust Suppression in the Asbestos Industry', HMSO, 1930.

Mesavoric, Mihajlo, and Eduard Pestel, *Mankind at the Turning Point, The Second Report to the Club of Rome*, Hutchinson, 1975.

Mhlanga, Liberty, 'Africa; Case for Environmental Development', Adlai Stevenson Institute Working Paper 11, 1974.

Mitre Corporation for the Ford Foundation, 'Nuclear Power, Issues and Choices', 1977.

Montague, Katherine and Peter, *Mercury*, Sierra Club, 1971.

Morton, Kathryn and Peter Tulloch, *Trade and Developing Countries*, Croom Helm in Association with the Overseas Development Institute, 1977.

Mwaluko, E. Paul, 'Address to the 24th Congress of L'Union Internationale de la Propriété Foncière Bâtie', Florence, 1976.

National Academy of Sciences, 'Halocarbons, Environmental Effects, Chlorofluoromethane Release', NAS, 1976.

National Academy of Sciences/National Research Council, Division of Medical Sciences, 'The Effects on Population of Exposure to Low Levels of Ionizing Radiation', Report of the Advisory Committee on the Biological Effects of Ionising Radiations, 1972.

National Radiological Protection Board, 'Evidence to the Royal Commission on Environmental Pollution 1974–6', NRPB, 1976.

Nature, Vols 250–267, 1974–1977.

New Internationalist Nos 15–55, 1974–7, particularly special issues 15 and 52 on 'population', 32 on 'the new international economic order', 38 on world trade, 39 on employment, 42 and 43 on basic needs.

New Scientist, Vols 63–76, 1974–1977.

O'Neill, Helen, 'A Common Interest in A Common Fund', Proposals for New Structures in International Commodity Markets, UN, 1977.

Organisation of Economic Cooperation and Development, 'Development Cooperation Reviews' for 1975, 1976 and 1977.

Organisation of Economic Cooperation and Development, 'Energy Conservation in the International Energy Agency', 1976 Review.

Organisation of Economic Cooperation and Development, 'Energy R and D, Problems and Perspectives', 1975.

Organisation of Economic Cooperation and Development, Nuclear Energy Agency/International Atomic Energy Agency, 'Uranium, Resources Production and Demand', 1975.

Owen, Wilfrid, 'Transportation, Energy and Community Design', International Institute for Environment and Development, 1974.

Page, J. K., 'Solar Energy Prospects and Their Significance for Electrical Engineering', paper to the Institution of Electrical Engineers, 8 April, 1976.

Parliamentary Commissioner for Administration, 'Report to Max Madden M.P. of the Results of His Investigation into a Complaint made by Mr J. P. Birch', 1976 C253/V.

Patel, I. G., 'Address to 44th Couchiching Conference', Geneva Park, Ontario, Canada, 1975.

Patterson, Walter C., *The Fissile Society*, Earth Resources Research, 1977.

Peccei, Aurelio, *The Human Quality*, Pergamon, 1977.

Pirie, N. W., *Food Resources, Conventional and Novel*, Penguin 1969.

Pirages, Dennis C., and Paul R. Ehrlich, *Ark II, Social Responses to Environmental Imperatives*, W. H. Freeman and Co., 1974.

Populi, Vols III and IV, 1976 and 1977.

Power, Anne, 'Housing Policies in France, Holland, Belgium and Germany', International Institute for Environment and Development, 1975.

Pugwash Council, 'Statement Following 26th Pugwash Conference on Science and World Affairs', August 1976.

Ranger Uranium Environmental Inquiry, Australian Government Publishing Service, 1976 and 1977.

Rasmussen, S. *et al.*, 'Reactor Safety Study', WASH 1400 or NUREG 75/01, 1975.

Rattray Taylor, Gordon, *Rethink*, Secker and Warburg, 1972.

Righter, Rosemary, 'Save our Cities', Calouste Gulbenkian Foundation, 1977.

Robbins, Christopher and Javed Ansari, 'Profits of Doom: An Investigation into the World Food Crisis', War on Want, 1976.

Robertson, Colin, 'The Energy Crisis and British Coal', Hobart Paper 58, Institute of Economic Affairs, 1974.

Rogers, Paul, *Future Resources and World Development*, Plenum Press, 1976.

Rogers, Paul and Bob Dickson, 'Producer Power: The Third World Hits Back', World Development Movement, 1975.

Rotblat, J. (ed.), 'Nuclear Reactors; To Breed or Not to Breed', Proceedings of a Pugwash Debate at the Royal Society, Taylor and Francis, 1977.

Science, 1976–1977.

Scientific American, 1975–1977, see also special 'energy' issue, September 1971; special 'population' issue, September 1974; special 'food' issue, September 1976.

Schumacher, E. F., 'People's Power', National Council for Social Service, 1975.

Selikoff, Irving J., 'Presentation at the American Industrial Hygiene Conference', 21 May, 1973.

Skinner, Reinhard, 'Villa El Salvador, An Experiment in Worker's Participation in Peru', speech to the 1976 Annual Meeting of the British Association for the Advancement of Science.

Sharp, Robin, 'Whose Right to Work?', Oxfam Public Affairs Unit, 1976.

Smith, Eugene and Aileen, *Minamata*, Chatto and Windus, 1975.

Solokov, E. J., N. M. Singer, V. I. Savin, and M. M. Pik, 'The Role of District Heating in Increasing the Efficiency of Fuel Combustion and Decreasing Air Pollution in Large Populated Areas', World Energy Conference 1974, Detroit, 6.2–1.

Stein, Jane, 'Energy and Architecture, Implications for Human Settlements', International Institute for Environment and Development, 1975.

Stewart, Alice, 'Evidence to the Windscale Inquiry on behalf of the Town and Country Planning Association', September 1977.

Stockholm International Peace Research Institute, 'Armaments and Disarmament in a Nuclear Age', 1976.

Stockholm International Peace Research Institute, 'Yearbooks on World Armaments', 1975 and 1976.

Strong, Maurice, 'State of the World Environment' Report, 1974, to United Nations Environment Programme Governing Council, UNEP GC 14, Add. 1.

Swift, Jeremy, *The Other Eden*, J. M. Dent and Sons, 1974.

The Ecologist, *A Blueprint for Survival*, Penguin, 1972.

Tinbergen, Jan (Coordinator), *Reshaping the International Order; A Report to the Club of Rome*, Hutchinson, 1977.

Toffler, Alvin, *Future Shock*, The Bodley Head, 1971.

Tolba, Mostafa Kamal, 'State of the World Environment', Reports for 1976 and 1977 to the United Nations Environment Programme Governing Council meetings.

Tucker, Anthony, *The Toxic Metals*, Pan Ballantine, 1972

Turner, John F. C., *Housing By People, Towards Autonomy in Building Environments*, Marion Boyars, 1976.

United Kingdom Atomic Energy Authority, 'Atom', 1974–1977.

United Kingdom Atomic Energy Authority, 'Evidence Submitted 1974–5 to the Royal Commission on Environmental Pollution'.

United Kingdom Section of the International Solar Energy Society, 'Solar Energy: A UK Assessment', 1976.

United Nations Centre for Development, Planning, Projections and Policies, Document E/C 9/L.7 and Adds 1 and 2 and Corr. 1, 1975.

United Nations Centre for Housing, Building and Planning of the Department of Economic and Social Affairs, 'World Housing Survey', 1974, Document E. 75. IV. 8.

United Nations Charter of Economic Rights and Duties of States, General Assembly Resolution 3281, 12 December, 1974.

United Nations Children's Fund, UNICEF News, 1974–1977.

United Nations Children's Fund/World Health Organisation, 'Alternative Approaches to Meeting Basic Health Needs in Developing Countries', 1976.

United Nations Committee for Development Planning, 'Report of Ninth Session of Expert Group', 1973.

United Nations Committee for Development Planning, 'Report of the Twelfth Session' Document E. 5793, June 1976.

United Nations Committee on Natural Resources, 'Meeting on the State of World Mining', Report by OPI/CESI 17 March, 1975.

United Nations Compendium of Housing Statistics 1972–4, 1976, no. E/F. 75. XVII. 12.

United Nations Development Programme, Action UNDP, 1974–1977.

United Nations Economic and Social Commission for Asia and the Pacific, 'Economic and Social Survey of Asia and the Pacific', 1974, Document E/CN 11/L, 412.

United Nations Economic and Social Council, 'Current Trends in Innovation in the Energy Sector', Sc/Tech R.9, 1973.

United Nations Environment Programme, 'Establishment of an International Fund or Financial Institution for Human Settlements', document published 19 January 1974 for 29th Session of the General Assembly, Document, no. A/9575.

United Nations Environment Programme/United Nations Conference on Trade and Development, 'Symposium on Patterns of Resource Use, Environment, and Development Strategies', The Cocoyoc Declaration, 1974.

United Nations Institute for Training and Research/International Institute for Applied Systems Analysis, 'Proceedings of Conference on the World's Future Supplies of Petroleum and Natural Gas', 1976.

United Nations Population Division, 'Provisional City Projections', 1950–2000, February 1975.

United Nations, Preparing for UNCTAD IV, 1975.

United Nations, 'Report on the World Social Situation', 1974, see study number E/CN. 5/512/Add 14.

United Nations Statistical Yearbooks, 1973, 1974, 1975, documents no. E/F 74 XVII 1, E/F 75 XVII 1 and E/F 76 XVII 1.

United Nations, 'World Energy Supplies, 1969–1972', Document E. 74 XVII 7.

United Nations, 'World Energy Supplies, 1950–1973', Document E. 75 XVII 13.

Voluntary Committee for Overseas Aid and Development, 'Action for Development', 1976–7.

Ward, Barbara, 'A New Creation, Reflections on the Environmental Issues', Pontifical Commission for Justice and Peace, 1972.

Ward, Barbara, 'Human Settlements, Crisis and Opportunity, official report from a meeting of experts preparing for Habitat, in Ottawa', Information Canada, 1974.

Warman, H. R., 'The Future Availability of Oil', speech at Financial Times World Energy Supplies Conference, September 1973.

Wilhelmsen, Jens J., *Man and Structures*, Grosvenor Books, 1977.

Wilsher, Peter, and Rosemary Righter, *Exploding Cities*, André Deutsch, 1975.

Wilson, Thomas W. Jnr., 'World Food, The Political Dimension', Aspen Institute for Humanistic Studies, 1974.

Wohlstetter, Albert *et al.*, 'Moving Towards Life in a Nuclear Armed Crowd', Pan Heuristics Division of Science Applications Limited, for the US Arms Control and Disarmament Agency, 1976.

World Bank, Annual Reports 1974–1976.

World Bank, 'Rural Development', Sector Policy Paper, 1975.

World Development Movement, 'A New Deal for the Poor; What a New Economic Order Could Mean for Britain and the World', World Development Movement, 1976.

World Metereological Organisation, 'Statement on Climatic Change adopted by the Executive Committee', June, 1976, available as appendix to the organisation's report to the 63rd session of the UN Economic and Social Council, Document E/5955.

Index of Main Subjects